D0765582

Child Perspectives and Children's Perspectives
in Theory and Practice

International Perspectives on Early Childhood Education and Development

Volume 2

Series Editors

Professor Marilyn Fleer, *Monash University, Australia*
Professor Ingrid Pramling-Samuelsson, *Gothenburg University, Sweden*

Editorial Board

Early childhood education in many countries has been built upon a strong tradition of a materially rich and active play-based pedagogy and environment. Yet what has become visible within the profession, is essentially a Western view of childhood preschool education and school education.
It is timely that a series of books be published which present a broader view of early childhood education. This series, seeks to provide an international perspective on early childhood education. In particular, the books published in this series will:

- Examine how learning is organized across a range of cultures, particularly Indigenous communities
- Make visible a range of ways in which early childhood pedagogy is framed and enacted across countries, including the majority poor countries
- Critique how particular forms of knowledge are constructed in curriculum within and across countries
- Explore policy imperatives which shape and have shaped how early childhood education is enacted across countries
- Examine how early childhood education is researched locally and globally
- Examine the theoretical informants driving pedagogy and practice, and seek to find alternative perspectives from those that dominate many Western heritage countries
- Critique assessment practices and consider a broader set of ways of measuring children's learning
- Examine concept formation from within the context of country-specific pedagogy and learning outcomes

The series will cover theoretical works, evidence-based pedagogical research, and international research studies. The series will also cover a broad range of countries, including poor majority countries. Classical areas of interest, such as play, the images of childhood, and family studies will also be examined. However the focus will be critical and international (not Western-centric).

Dion Sommer · Ingrid Pramling Samuelsson ·
Karsten Hundeide

Child Perspectives and
Children's Perspectives
in Theory and Practice

Foreword by Kathy Sylva

 Springer

Prof. Dion Sommer
University of Aarhus
Dept. Psychology
Nobelparken, Jens Chr.
Schons Vej 4
8000 Aarhus
Denmark
dion@psy.au.dk

Prof. Karsten Hundeide
University of Oslo
Fac. Social Sciences
Dept. Psychology
0317 Oslo
Blindern
Norway
karsten.hundeide@psykologi.uio.no

Prof. Ingrid Pramling Samuelsson
Göteborg University
Dept. Education
SE-405 30 Göteborg
Sweden
ingrid.pramling@ped.gu.se

ISBN 978-90-481-3315-4   e-ISBN 978-90-481-3316-1
DOI 10.1007/978-90-481-3316-1
Springer Dordrecht Heidelberg London New York

Library of Congress Control Number: 2009939616

Printed on acid-free paper

Springer is part of Springer Science+Business Media (www.springer.com)

Foreword

During the last decade, the Scandinavian countries have been the scene of exciting research and new practices in the field of Early childhood education. The authors of this book are leaders in a new, Scandinavian Early Childhood pedagogy. They seek an understanding of what it is for adults to have a "child perspective", and how that might differ from the perspectives held by the children themselves, what they call "children's perspectives". The authors are key members of a group of researchers and practitioners who have worked together for many years in the Scandinavian countries to move beyond what used to be called "child centred" research and practice. They share an interest in applying theories about the development of children within society to practices in Early Childhood contexts, both inside and outside the home. This book brings together for the first time a detailed description of the new theories about child/children's perspectives and sets them firmly within Early Childhood practices. In fact, the authors aim to create a new space that lies between theory and practice, a space inhabited by those who go beyond the "new child paradigm" in sociology or contextual psychology. In doing this, they have created something fresh and useful.

When speaking about education, Jerome Bruner tells us that "there is nothing so practical as a good theory". This deeply theoretical book has much practical advice to offer to those working in childcare settings. This is because the new theory has been forged by a multi-professional team consisting of those who work in universities and others who work in childcare settings. The book takes as its main topic "children's perspectives", including what it is to be a child (as the child experiences it), how adults and children can live together in a "negotiated" way, and the creative role of children in democratic societies. The book is ambitious in its aims, far reaching in its theoretical content, and open-minded in its conclusions. But perhaps it is wrong to speak of them as "conclusions"; what the authors seek with this book is a dialogue on emerging theoretical and practical frameworks for guiding Early Childhood practices. They put forward their ideas to stimulate discussion and to receive feedback, i.e. to engage with others in a collegial way.

Child or Children's Perspective?

The term "child perspective" is used in many different ways and refers to different literatures that study and/or explain scientific or practical notions with the perspective of individual children in mind. This is different from a "children's perspective", which authors refer to as the perspectives of the children themselves. Although the two may sound similar at first, a "child perspective" is something that practitioners and scholars try to study using methods from the "outside in", often including sociology or contextual psychology. The children's perspective is the view or stance of the child from the "inside out"; in other words, a children's perspective is always expressed in the children's own words, thoughts, and images. More specifically –

Child perspectives *direct adult's attention towards an understanding of children's perceptions, experiences, and actions in the world.*

Thus, child perspectives are created by adults who are seeking, deliberately and as realistically as possible, to reconstruct children's perspectives, for example through scientific concepts concerning children's understanding of their world and their actions in it. This excludes all the theories on children and childhood that do not help adults understand the world from a child's point of view. But even though child-centred, they will always represent adults' objectification of children.

Children's perspectives *represent children's experiences, perceptions, and understanding in their life-world.*

In contrast to the child perspectives, the focus here is on the child as subject in his or her own world, the child's own phenomenology. This is what adults attempt to understand through their child perspective, for example in attempts at child-focused interpretations of children's intentional acts and statements.

The Scandinavian Model of Democracy and Welfare

The book speaks eloquently of the Scandinavian welfare model which has its roots in a social acceptance of a shared responsibility between society and individual families in the tasks of caring for and protecting the next generation. The book argues that the new "children's perspectives" are embedded in Scandinavia's Early Childhood curricula and also in their notions of "good practice". The distinction between "child perspectives" and "children's perspectives" is a golden theme holding the book together, a theme rooted in the Swedish notion of democracy and of "welfare" for all.

An intriguing chapter looks at changes in the developmental ecology of infants and young children in Scandinavian countries. It shows the very rapid change of employment patterns for women, a change that took women out of the home and into the employment sphere while, at the same time, setting up an innovative childcare system for the care of children while their parents worked. A strong argument is made about the "importance of the humanisation and individualisation processes" in Scandinavian countries, including the acceptance of children in these countries as citizens with certain rights, living in a society that is child-centred and values children as important members of a democratic society. The welfare state is described in some detail, with its emphasis on welfare directed towards preventative and educative purposes rather than the "rescue" of individuals or groups. Although children are not considered equal to adults in terms of capability nor power, they're certainly considered equal to adults as members of society whose voices are just as important as adults.

A New Research Paradigm

The authors report on a "reconstruction method" of research in which children are invited to solve intellectual tasks, similar to those of Piaget. However, after "the experiment" is over, children retell, demonstrate, and dramatize their experiences of what happened during the experiment itself. In this novel approach, an interview is carried out after the formal experiment is finished, and this is more important than the experimental task itself. The child's experience of what happened during the formal experiment is reconstructed in three ways: first, through telling about what he or she did; secondly, through demonstrating what was done; and finally, through role playing, often with the child taking the role of the experimenter/interviewer. This very novel experimental method builds on the original Piagetian paradigm and goes far beyond it. In this sense, children are truly "co-experimenters" in the study. Using research methods such as these will lead to co-constructed knowledge about children's development that will be a firm foundation for pedagogy in the future.

Learning Based on "Noticing Differences"

Through much of the book, the act of learning is defined as "proceeding, seeing or experiencing". The teacher has a central role "making it possible for children to experience the values, abilities and knowledge she and society, through curricular and social discourses, want children to develop". The authors have a special interest in the role of adults in fostering children's development. However, they conceive of the adult's role in radically different ways from other theories calling themselves child-centred. One way they do this is to have children discuss with one another how they have tackled personal dilemmas or real-world problems. In the discussion amongst children, they will "notice differences" amongst the views of peers, and these differences soon become the basis for new learning in children, either on their own or guided by the adults.

Developmental Pedagogy

"Developmental pedagogy" is described as a research-based approach that has been used in early childhood education by applying "phenomenography". The aim of phenomenography is to discover the subjective world of the participants in research and to discover new ways to develop children's understanding of the world around them. Phenomenography was developed by Ference Marton in Sweden, with close links to phenomenological approaches in European philosophy. Developmental pedagogy depends on the teacher's attitude: It is a way for adults to relate to children that is permissive and open-minded, but it still maintains an intention to enhance the children's development through "active teaching". The role of the child is not to produce the "right answers" as defined by the adult but to reflect themselves on what they have learned. Through reflecting alongside an adult (not under the direction of the adult), children will "see" their own understanding and perspectives.

In this book, the concept of play has a new meaning. Play can lead to discoveries, sometimes scientific, as well as exceeding boundaries. The authors believe that play and learning are different, but they are inter-connected through sharing common features. In fact, they refer to "the playing, learning child" in one breath, so to speak. In play, children create meanings related to their own perspectives, with or without the guidance of the adult. It is the unfolding of play that is important, not whether in partnership with an adult or not.

In short, this book invites the reader on a long journey with theoretical twists and many practical signposts. The journey begins with the Swedish welfare framework, continues with a serious consideration of the child as viewed by sociologists and contextual psychologists, before moving on to deliberations on what it means to be a caring, empathetic adult. Finally, the reader reaches the heart of the book, which is a fascinating description of "Developmental Pedagogy" – a new way for adults to nurture children's development by listening to their voices while still taking *an active role* to understand and extend their thinking. This is based on participation as partners in children's learning. The adults learn too. The book closes with some proposals for transforming early childhood education through democratic and participatory practice that is always closely aligned with research.

Oxford   Kathy Sylva
June 2009

Preface

Peter (five years old) and his father are walking together to daycare. The sunshine is reflected in an oil spot on the road. "Look dad!" Peter yells: "a dead rainbow!"

Children are remarkable people that interpret what they hear, see, feel, and smell and they experience situations in ways that not necessary will be compatible to the ways adults construe their world. On the other hand, the adult's perception of the child can be more or less realistically attuned to the child's meaning making. Perhaps forgetting how to be a child, and experiencing being a child, is one of the great losses of growing up. But adults are potentially capable, emotionally and cognitively, of "taking the perspective of the other", thus having the awareness and understanding of the other partner as a person with his or her idiosyncratic ways of construing the world. Let us start, then, by designating the adult's realistic effort and success in understanding a child's world from a "child perspective", and children's own experiences and utterances for "children's perspectives".

Recently there has been a growing interest in child perspectives and children's perspectives in Scandinavia and many other parts of the world. These concepts have become essential in relation to legislation on children's rights, in research, and in child-related professions. This interest is reflected in an increasing number of publications: In Scandinavia, *Norway* was early to embark on this trend, and Per Olav Tiller deserves credit as a pioneer (Tiller, 1984, 1989, 1991). In 1991, No. 1 of the journal *Barn* [Child] was a theme issue on child perspectives; other important Norwegian sources include Åm (1989), Telhaug (1991), Kjørholt (1991, 2001), and Eide and Winge (2003). In *Sweden* Ingrid Pramling published her doctoral thesis in 1983, *The Child's Conception of Learning* (Pramling, 1983), where the aim was to understand what learning looked like from children's points of view. Two years later *To Understand Children's Thinking – Methods for Interviewing Children* was published (Doverborg & Pramling Samuelsson, 1985/2000). This book was translated into Norwegian and Danish and has been widely read by early childhood teachers. Some years later the journal *Pedagogisk Forskning i Sverige* (*Educational Research in Sweden*) (2003) came out with a theme issue directly entitled *Barns perspektiv och barnperspektiv* (*Children's Perspectives and Child Perspectives*) edited by Eva Johansson and Ingrid Pramling Samuelsson, where researchers from various social disciplines take stock of the field. Child perspectives have also been addressed in

Denmark in various research projects as well as in professional practice (Reimer et al., 2000; Kampmann, 2000; Gulløv & Højlund, 2003; Andersen & Ottesen, 2002; Andersen & Kjærulff, 2003; Andersen, 2001; Carstensen, 2005; Sommer, 2005b; Kousholt, 2006; Espersen, et al., 2006; Fotel, 2007; Andersen & Højlund, 2007; Warming, 2005a, 2005b, 2007).

In the anthology *Researching children's perspectives*, Lewis and Lindsay (2000) address the topic in an English-language context, where there are numerous publications, particularly with respect to children's rights. This may give the impression that theory, methods, and concepts concerning child perspectives are well established by now, but this is far from the case. Upon closer inspection, the child perspective concept appears to be steeped in ideological, ethical, and moral values, and it is far from being a neat and tidy package with a common conceptual understanding of child perspectives or children's perspectives. Additionally a given child perspective "theory" (as shall be documented in this book) can be "imported" from other theories – for example using Foucaulian sociology, or a feministic approach that hardly, if at all, deals with children.

Furthermore, the terms are enmeshed in popular contemporary "child-friendly" humanist declarations that do not hold the same standards for conceptual clarity as scientific research. Indeed, Halldén's (2003) analysis of child perspectives concludes that the concept is exceedingly ambiguous. It is applied both as an ideological concept with considerable rhetorical capacity (Qvarsell, 2003) and in a scientific context as both a theoretical and a methodological term (Dockrell, Lewis, & Lindsay, 2000). To this comes that theoretical positions within the so-called new child paradigm in very generalized ways. These are adopted as identical to a child perspective with a very loose definition as a consequence. If a core concept is made synonymous with a subject field it becomes meaningless. So, one searches in vain for *specific theories* on child perspectives and children's perspectives. A review of the literature shows that the theoretical and empirical treatments of child perspectives and children's perspectives have been very diverse and often idiosyncratic, and the standard reference work has yet to be written. This book represents a search, a presentation, and a discussion of child perspectives and children's perspectives that are manifestly or latently occurring in various theoretical positions within childhood sociology, selected parts of recent developmental psychologies, and pedagocy. We intend to develop a genuine professional paradigm built on recent child research. Furthermore, we will present in depth child-oriented understandings that have relevance for practice as well.

This book will pursue a search for a child perspective and children's perspective in various theories and empirical research in general, but it is rooted in a Scandinavian and Westernized context as well. Behind our theories lie complex fundamental culture-specific values of historical origin, for example, concerning the way children, the family, male/female roles, developmental and education philosophies are constructed (Greenfield, Suzuki, & Rothstein-Fisch, 2006). Furthermore, cultures and societies in a modern global world differ considerably when it comes to how childhood is constructed with different consequences for children's actual experiences. Scandinavia forms part of a Western and a global world and shares fundamental values with many other countries, but important differences are emphasized as well. This book aims to highlight important underlying factors manifesting or latently contributing to the growing interest in a child perspective and children's perspectives when it comes to the Scandinavian context. But it is much broader in scope as we will also address the global context, focusing on cultural differences and on panhuman similarities as well.

This book is organized in distinct parts, where the authors' understandings of child perspective and children's perspective are presented, defined, scrutinized, and discussed. The authors do not agree always on all matters, but share the research-based fundamental professional beliefs and paradigms that are laid down in the Introduction of the book. Several common conceptualizations will be used and elaborated in each of the various parts of the book.

Dion Sommer and Ingrid Pramling Samuelson are the authors of *Introduction: Child Perspectives and Children's Perspective – The Scandinavian Context.* This introductory part describes a selected number of consequences of relatively rapid changes in the developmental ecology of children, mainly when it comes to the revolution in maternal employment and the daycare-for-all situation. Furthermore, it gives a brief presentation of the Scandinavian welfare model, which has its roots in a fundamental acceptance of a shared society–family responsibility as to the caring and protection of the next generation. This leads to a discussion of the importance of the humanization- and individualization processes in contemporary society, the acceptance of children as equal citizens, and distinct ideologies and values of child-centredness, important factors that manifestly or latently contribute to the growing interest in child perspectives and children's perspectives. Moreover, it is demonstrated and argued how child perspectives are embedded in Scandinavian curricula of early childhood education. The final part of the Introduction offers specific definitions of the interrelated, but conceptual difference regarding child perspectives and children's perspectives. The definitions both guide and will be elaborated in depth in the following parts of the book.

Dion Sommer has written Part I: *In Search of Child Perspectives and Children's Perspectives in Childhood Sociology and Developmental Psychology.* The sociology of childhood and recent parts of developmental psychology have frequently been used as being synonymous with a child perspective, and an "eye-opener" to children's perspectives, but with surprisingly little critical argumentation. Child perspectives and children's perspectives are searched from within the so-called new view/perspective of children or "the new child paradigm" occurring from the separate fields of childhood sociology and contextual-relational developmental psychology. These four questions will be answered:

(1) Are child perspectives apparent in certain aspects of childhood sociology? If yes, How are children conceptualized in ways that enhance adults' recognition and awareness of children's perceptions and life experiences?
(2) Are child perspectives apparent in certain aspects of contextual-relational developmental psychology? If yes, How are children conceptualized in ways that

enhance adults' recognition and awareness of children's perceptions of life experiences?

(3) Do children's own perspectives take a central position within these bodies of theories? If yes, How do these disciplines show and present children's own perceptions and life experiences?

(4) Are common conceptual platforms for a future integration identifiable? Which concepts are particularly imperative to an interdisciplinary integration of concepts from childhood sociology and contextual-relational developmental psychology?

Karsten Hundeide has written Part II: *A Child Perspective to the Care for Children in Practice.* In this part a child perspective approach to human childcare will be explicated, a position that is strongly influenced by a humanistic, cultural-dialogical, and interpretative theoretical orientation. First, a brief presentation of selected core professional features and beliefs about the child will be put forward. Second, the conditions that facilitate empathic care and identification with the child on the one hand and those that obstruct this care on the other will be explicated. Then the concept of a "zone of intimacy" into which a child can be included and cared for through empathic identification and sensitive availability of the caregiver to the child's needs will be introduced. But it is explained, too, how a child also can be expelled from the zone of intimacy with subsequent blockage of empathic identification, affective withdrawal leading to neglect and possibly abuse. After this a model sums up the positive versus negative developmental pathways that may emerge in the caregiver–child relationship. Then Part II turns to the interpretive approach as a child perspective orientation. The basic principles are described and the approach is discussed in relation to a critical examination of testing and diagnostic approaches. Then a method is introduced how to reconstruct how a child interprets his or her situation illustrated with examples from preschool communication and everyday practice. After that, situations are described how misunderstandings between an adult (teacher, researcher) end up being a deficit in the child. Part II ends with a description of how the intersubjective space in school classrooms implicitly and subtly regulates the communication between teacher and children. A final conclusion is reached by presenting a summary-model showing the markedly different consequences of using an interpretive, child perspective versus a normative competence/diagnostic-oriented approach.

Ingrid Pramling Samuelsson has written Part III: *In Search of Child Perspectives and Children's Perspectives in Early Childhood Education.* This part begins with a short review of the essence and history of ECE and how child perspectives always have been a feature separating early learning from school learning. The next step in this part is in trying to answer the question: What can we learn about child perspectives and children's perspectives from empirical research studies, specifically from the Nordic countries? The history and empirical research will then lead into a research-based pedagogy for ECE labelled, developmental pedagogy. But this part will also exemplify what it means to act in practice based on children's perspectives, that is, their meaning making. Part III ends will a theoretical discussion about the preconditions for an early schooling built on children's perspectives.

Ingrid Pramling Samuelsson and Dion Sommer are the main authors of Part IV: *Child Perspectives and Children's Perspectives in Theory and Practice – Summary, Discussion, and Conclusion.* It contains a critical discussion about the relevance of a child perspective and children's perspectives for a broader context than Western and Scandinavian cultures. First we summarize the Introduction and each of the book's parts. Then the question is discussed, whether a Scandinavian welfare value approach to children have a meaningful voice in a global context. After that the present and future status of the ECE is evaluated. Next some major problems and dilemmas in the globalization of a child perspective are discussed, especially in relation to cultural differences and panhuman similarities. The book is closed with a final conclusion addressing a global, everyday and educational theme.

Aarhus   Dion Sommer

Contents

Introduction: Child Perspectives and Children's Perspectives – The Scandinavian Context

Introduction

The search for child perspectives and children's perspectives takes its starting point in the UN Convention of the Right of the Child, as well as in the Scandinavian context. In Scandinavia there has been a long tradition of family policy where the ideology has been a universal model for all children. Welfare services are based on equality and equity, children's health and mother care, and also on early childhood education and care for all children as a right. A children's ombudsman, law against violence towards children, but also curricula stating children's participation and influence, and research showing a culture of negotiation, are some factors putting Scandinavia as a trendsetter towards child perspectives and children's perspectives. But also research based on and showing children's perspective has developed in this context and by this constitutes the foundation for the analysis of child perspectives and children's perspectives in theory and practice. Realizing that the terms child perspectives and children's perspectives are widely used although surprisingly hazily defined, the two interrelated but clearly distinct concepts are specified and defined.

Changes in the Developmental Ecology of Infants and Young Children

Despite increasing global competition from various countries and regions such as China and eastern Europe, the Scandinavian welfare societies have not only maintained but also increased their international trade, and since the mid-1990s, their economic growth has been well above the average for western Europe. The Nordic countries, including Scandinavia, also have lower unemployment rates and GNP standards of living that are well above the general level in western Europe and, indeed, most countries in the world (Nyt fra Danmarks Statistik, 2006). Thus, Scandinavian children are growing up in societies that must be characterized as highly affluent. Socio-economic differences do exist but are relatively modest seen in a global perspective.

D. Sommer et al., *Child Perspectives and Children's Perspectives in Theory and Practice*, International Perspectives on Early Childhood Education and Development 2, DOI 10.1007/978-90-481-3316-1_1, © Springer Science+Business Media B.V. 2010

Scandinavian Mothers in Employment

After World War II, particularly since the early 1960s, the lives of families and children in Scandinavia changed considerably. A main source of these changes was the strong economic growth in the post-war years. In the 1940s, few Scandinavian women had joined the work force, and this situation lasted through most of the 1960s.

In terms of overall employment rates, Denmark, Netherlands, and Sweden top the list of the 27 EU countries.

Figure 1 illustrates that employment rates are under the EU average in 11 countries ranging from France slightly under the average to Italy, Hungary, Malta, and Poland in the bottom. Denmark has had the highest employment rates for women in the EU since 2004, closely followed by Sweden, while in 2006 this goes as well for Danish men (Statistical Yearbook, 2008). Relating this to children's families, growing up with an employed mother and father is the typical situation for the Nordic child today.

Women are relatively modestly employed in southern and eastern European countries in comparison with the Nordic countries, where Denmark, Sweden, and Finland top the list (Statistisk Årbog, 2007, p. 114). Thus, the change in women's role in society has happened considerably faster and been much more pronounced and pervasive in the Nordic countries than in most other nations in Europe or, for that matter, around the world. Such a striking change in such a short amount of time cannot be explained only by reference to increasing demands for labour. This demand existed in other European countries too, but only caused rather modest changes in the traditional definition of roles within the family and to a relatively smaller growth in affluence. The Nordic countries, however, which were already somewhat egalitarian, saw a complex and rapid change in thinking and practice concerning traditional gender roles within the family.[1] The Nordic countries quite

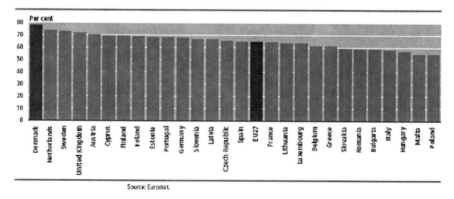

Fig. 1 Total employment rates in the EU countries, 2006
(*Source:* Statistical Yearbook, 2008)

---

[1] This demand for change put the distribution of roles within the family under pressure. As one dramatic consequence, this doubled the Danish divorce rate in a matter of only 5 years. Nevertheless, most children in Scandinavia still grow up in intact nuclear families (Sommer, 2008).

quickly became established welfare models that enabled families to function after the women had joined the workforce. In most of southern Europe and some eastern European countries, women have not entered the job market in equally large numbers, and many countries do not offer widespread public daycare services, as the Nordic countries do. Sommer (2008b) summarizes the temporal changes in women's employment patterns as follows:

- *In the 1950s*: Few mothers worked outside the home. They ran the home and looked after the children. The fathers were the sole providers – thus, at the time, the typical pattern was "dad provides for the family".
- *In the 1960s*: The women began to work outside the home but typically took a break while the children were young.
- *In the 1970s and 1980s*: More and more mothers worked away from home but usually part-time. With the fathers still working full time, many families had now become one-and-a-half-income families.
- *In the 1990s and into the twenty-first century*: More and more mothers work full time, even while the children are young. Today, typical Scandinavian families have two incomes.

So, in today's Scandinavia the housewife, i.e. a woman whose principal occupation is to look after household, husband, and children, has largely left the private family arena. This is reflected not only in statistics (only 1% of the women in Denmark are housewives) but also in daily language use. The term housewife is now almost exclusively used rhetorically in reference to a historical phenomenon, for example the natural role for women in the role-dichotomized nuclear family as it appeared before the major changes took place in the 1960s. Today, the term is rarely used in the social sciences, since it marks a phenomenon that has no widespread empirical basis in contemporary Scandinavia.

Conclusion: Although maternal employment is not an isolated Scandinavian phenomenon, Scandinavian mothers do have the highest employment rates in the world. Not only are mothers of school-age children heavily involved in the workforce, the same goes for mothers with infants and preschool children. Additionally, the majority of these women are in growing numbers employed on a full-time basis. That raises the question: Who looks after the infants and young children while mom and dad are at work?

School-for-All: A Growing Global Phenomenon – Daycare-for-All: A Scandinavian Welfare Right

Although the family has ceased to be the only developmental context for children growing up in Scandinavia, it is still crucially important, but other arenas have heavily affected its role in development and socialization. The two most important public arenas fundamentally affecting children and childhood are school and daycare.

A fact structuring childhood is that children past the toddler stage spend many hours every day away from their family in secondary socializing and educational public facilities – so-called early childhood education[2] (Qvortrup, 1999). Although, for example, Danish law specifies only mandatory education, not mandatory schooling, practically all children spend many hours a day in the institutional setting of a school. In elementary school, this is true of 97.5% of the boys and 98.4% of the girls, and this has been the situation for many decades in many countries all over the world (UNICEF, Education Statistics: Denmark, February 2007b, http://childinfo.org).

This schoolification has become a pervasive part of childhood in general to such a degree that developmental psychologists refer to a certain age span as school age, which is evidence of the crucial influence of schooling in human lifespan (Berk, 2006). Social psychology coined the phrase secondary socialization, which plays out in the years from 6 or 7 when children start school. This term underscores the very different character of children's socialization and learning here, compared with so-called primary socialization, which as a given thing was supposed to take place in the family. The historical transition from classical child labour and the practical learning that it entailed (for example in farm labouring) to formalized education revolutionized the mid and late childhood periods in human lifespan. Mandatory education was, for example, in Denmark introduced by law in 1814 (Qvortrup, 1999). Over time, there have been tremendous changes in educational philosophy, the perception of children's learning, and the content that is taught in elementary schools. But the presence and status of the school itself as a public arena for socialization and learning in childhood is not a recent feature, historically.

Daycare for preschoolers, however, is neither a global nor, historically, a widespread phenomenon. Substantial differences still exist among the European countries in terms of the existence and availability of qualified daycare. But massive preschool attendance as an instrument for early education and care is not solely a Scandinavian phenomenon. For example, children between 3 and 5 years of age in publicly supported care are now reaching 90–100% in France, Belgium, and Italy, with Denmark and Sweden at the top, too (Lamb & Ahnert, 2006). This is not the case in various southern and eastern European countries, the UK and the USA. The NICHD Study of Early Child Care and Youth Development documents the present situation in the USA. In a section called "The call-to-action findings" these two major findings are highlighted:

1: "...the fact is that child care in the United States is highly fragmented and erratic".
2: "...the vast majority of child care is of unacceptably low quality and in the first 3 years of life does not meet even minimal recommended guidelines" (The NICHD Early Child Care Research Group, 2005, p. 432).

---

[2] This is not the place for a presentation of the existing vast amount of school research; instead, we merely wish to point out the huge impact of schoolification on the structure of childhood. The same goes for the discussion on preschool, daycare, where we will not be discussing educational approaches here and philosophies. This will be done in Part III, where a specific approach on early childhood education will be presented and evaluated in relation to child perspectives and children's perspectives.

This situation is far from the case in Scandinavian societies, but even a comparison between two very close northern European countries, such as Denmark and Germany, reveals big differences. In a critical report on the conditions in Germany, Bertram (2006) concludes that a strong and pervasive ideology regarding the mothers' natural obligations to her family and young children blocks any real change.

The Nordic countries embraced the view that it was in the best interest of society to provide qualified and widely available daycare to support working families. The family is no longer an exclusive, private arena for the child's primary socialization (Dencik, Jørgensen, & Sommer, 2008). This can be illustrated with Denmark as a case in point. So, what changes have there been in external family care attendance between 1983 and 2006?

During a relatively brief historical period there has been a dramatic increase in the number of children in daycare to around 80% today (see Fig. 2). The remaining 20% includes the youngest infants who are at home with their mother during her maternity leave. The slightly older preschoolers now spend as much time in public facilities as the school children: In 2006, 96% of children aged 3–5 years attended kindergarten or some other daycare facility. The average Danish preschooler is in daycare from 8:00 a.m. until 3:30 p.m., a total of 7.5 h a day (Danmarks Statistik, 2007). Such a fundamental re-structuring of daily life includes the partition of young children's lives into family time and daycare time. It also dramatically expands the range of people close to the child in the early years and fundamentally alters his or her experiences. This revolution was not from the beginning primarily driven by some public goals of educating or socializing children at an even younger age. What made daycare a growing and widespread phenomenon was the Scandinavian societies' response to this simple necessity: In

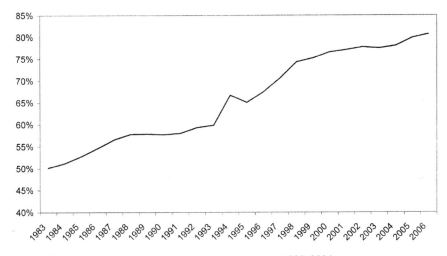

Fig. 2 *Share of 0–6-year-olds in external care arrangements 1983–2006*
(*Source:* Danmarks Statistik [Denmark Statistical], 2007)

the mid-1960s an urgent need arose for the placement of hundreds of thousands of young children whose mothers left the home in order to work. This necessity aspect is, for example, reflected in the Danish term for early non-domestic care fremmedpasning (alien care), which was the typical phrase at the time. The word signals the underlying ideological view that placing young children outside the family was an unnatural thing to do. In time, this connotative term was replaced by the neutral term daycare.

We will characterize the restructuring of early childhood taking place in the Scandinavian countries from the 1960s until today as the biggest revolution in childhood developmental ecology in recent history. Just as researchers involved in middle childhood had to construct a school age, early childhood researchers have had to invent new terms in order to grasp and interpret this new and developmentally unusual situation. The challenge of interpreting young children's changing developmental ecology is tremendous and has rendered a vast amount of conceptual and empirical understanding out of context and far behind contemporary reality. So much research is needed, but even high international standard textbooks, mostly American such as *Child Psychology* by Berk (2006a), do not capture the full consequences of this situation, despite a brief Introduction to daycare research and a growing acceptance of the importance of context. In Scandinavia there is a tendency to split research on infants and young children into either family or daycare research. Then it is overlooked that a typical young child is experiencing *both* developmental and socializing arenas. As a start a Nordic research project on early childhood has suggested the term *dual socialization* to replace the classical, but outdated term primary socialization (Sommer, 2005b, Chapter 2). This concept has been an attempt to grasp the relatively complex situation that the typical Scandinavian infant and young child was not solely growing up in his or her family, but in a dual context interacting with a host of developmental partners. But the concept of dual socialization is merely a structural approach that does not capture the phenomenological nature of the changed context. A child perspective and children's perspectives are not possible to derive from such type of construction. During the 1970s and the 1980s various developmental and educational discourses have been in action, many not specifically related to a child perspective or children's perspectives. But Halldén (2007) argues that, especially since the 1990s, more educational work has growingly been aimed at understanding children on their own terms and at including their voice in educational research and practice. In other words, the child perspective has, with time, become a key feature in the educational discourse about children.

To understand the "Scandinavian revolution" it has been necessary to examine the existing data on the widespread use of daycare in early childhood in Scandinavia. In this book, we use the rather neutral term daycare[3] because this is the term used in everyday speech, research, and statistics, for example concerning the number of preschoolers who are looked after by someone other than their parents during

---

[3] Except when we talk about the pedagogy in Early Childhood Education.

the day. Despite such a relatively neutral term it implies a fundamentally different everyday life for the current generation of Scandinavian children in comparison with earlier generations of preschoolers. As we shall demonstrate later, this change went hand in hand with the development of distinctly humanist child-oriented views, reflected in national curricula as well as educational theory and practice.

The increase in women's participation in the labour force is not an isolated Scandinavian phenomenon, but the public strategies in how to handle the consequences for children varies considerably in various countries. The large number of women who joined the workforce has placed great pressures on societies to provide "alternative arrangements". In the USA and the UK, for example, this situation has led to heavy conflicts and problems with securing qualified and widespread care for preschoolers while both parents are at work. Even today, this is ideologically considered a "private matter", solely the family's responsibility (Clarke-Stewart & Allhusen, 2005). In the Scandinavian welfare approach this is considered a "shared responsibility" between the state, local government, and family.

Conclusion: Changes in Developmental Ecology

Over the course of a generation, dramatic changes have occurred in the care of developmental ecology of infants and young children to such a degree that the upward trend will have to level out soon, as it has in some Scandinavian countries approached a maximum level. A possible reversal of this situation would have to come from a future dramatic drop in employment rates for mothers and/or fathers of young children or a dramatic expansion of maternity and parental leave. Neither of these options seems realistic in an age of globalization with a growing demand for labour, coupled with today's men and women's desire to engage in a work life outside the family. These Conclusions can be drawn:

- Scandinavian mothers of infants and young children have one of the highest employment rates in the world. Even infants' mothers are increasingly working on a full-time basis. For example, in Denmark today only 1% is living the traditional family life solely as housewives.
- The schoolification of childhood has become a global phenomenon. Public daycare for nearly every young child, however, is a more local feature given as welfare rights in the Scandinavian societies. Thus, socialization and development in early childhood must be interpreted in a qualitatively different way in this context than in other contexts where daycare is not prominent.
- Statistically, it is now the norm in Scandinavia that infants and young children are cared for outside home. Today it is the exception for a child to spend the early years only at home, which was the typical developmental context 40 years ago.
- This reality poses a tremendous challenge developing a new contextual sensitive scientific understanding of early childhood and development in Scandinavia of today.

The Welfare Model and Values Facilitating a Child Perspective

In this part of the Introduction first we will present in brief the basic features of the so-called Scandinavian welfare model. This model is rooted in a fundamental public acceptance of societies' and families' shared responsibility for supporting, protecting, caring, and enhancing the life conditions for the next generation. Aspects of the welfare model that has specific relevance for the topic of this book will be dealt with (for a more extensive presentation, see *Children's Welfare in an Ageing Europe*, www.svt.ntnu.no/noseb/costa19/nytt/welfare/book.php; see also Kristjansson, 2006). This leads us to a discussion of the importance of the humanization and individualization processes in Scandinavian societies, the acceptance of children as citizens with certain rights, societal values of child-centredness, and child perspectives as possible ideologies. After that it is demonstrated in which ways child perspectives are embedded in Scandinavian curricula of early childhood.

The Scandinavian Welfare Model – A Brief Introduction

The term "welfare state" is commonly used in order to localize those societies in which the public sector has acquired extensive responsibilities for securing the welfare of its citizens. An influential definition of the key features of welfare came from the Finnish sociologist Allardt (1975, 1998). He specified welfare by identifying three basic needs to be fulfilled of the individual in society "to have", "to be", and "to love". The Scandinavian welfare model is a so-called universal one, compared to the continental European model based upon employment-based models and the Anglo Saxon model (e.g. England and the USA) that is regulated by market forces. Danish Ministry of Science, Technology and Innovation spells out the fundamental principles behind the Scandinavian welfare model:

> The principle behind "the Scandinavian welfare model" is that all citizens have access to social benefits regardless of their social or ethnic background. Citizens enjoy extensive financial security. They are supported in time of sickness, unemployment and old age. Supplementary services include help with rent payment and with expenses on children. Furthermore, citizens are offered extensive advanced services such as day-care centers, healthcare and home care. Contrary to most other EU member states, social benefits in Denmark only depend on employer contributions and direct contributions to a very limited degree, and people's rights to benefits depends only to a limited extent on their former activity on the labour market. (www.workindenmark.dk/Welfare)

This type of model is portrayed as a "caring state" that in principle gives every citizen a universal right to receive various benefits. To provide for the vital needs of every person who of various reasons are incapable to work or care for himself and herself are not seen solely as a problem on the individual level, but as a collective societal problem as well. A central tenet of the Scandinavian welfare model is the government-protected minimum standards of income, nutrition, health, housing, and education, assured to every citizen as a *political right, not charity*. So, the model is not only encompassing poor parents or children with special needs, welfare is directed towards more general preventive and educative purposes too.

An important underlying widely shared belief, however, is that every citizen is expected actively to monitor and be responsible for his or her own life and not to be a passive recipient of benefits. In fact this is what the vast majority does.[4] If not, the whole system will brake down, because welfare is financed by and based on a redistribution system channelled through the tax system. The more basic intentions and purposes behind the state sponsored welfare may be said to have been twofold: first, to soften the mass destitution resulting from an uncontrolled global marked economy; second, to reduce social conflict and unrest stemming from poverty by the softening of big differences in income and wealth. Related to that a notable characteristic of the Scandinavian welfare model is the combination of a strong economy, high standards of living for most people, and a relatively equal distribution of income.

The Scandinavian welfare model is not only characterized by grandiose visions of humanistic belief systems (i.e. undeniable civil and egalitarian rights, humanizations, care and protection of the underprivileged and fragile) it is strongly implemented by legislation as a "policy regime" (Esping-Andersen, 1990). For example, from infancy to old age it is free of charge to be treated in any hospital that goes for education through primary school and university as well. Of specific relevance for children's welfare are the following universal right to benefits (see more in Dencik, Jørgensen, & Sommer, 2008):

- Child family benefits
- Preventive health care
- Maternal and paternal leave
- Day-care-for-all
- Support and benefits for children and families in special need

Family policy – with child allowance, paid parental leave, and extended preschool or daycare settings – has given substantial support for family life quality in our century (Björnberg, 2002; Pramling Samuelsson, Mauritzen, & Izuni, manuscript). Early childhood education (ECE) from the early years is an important contribution to children's everyday life in contemporary Scandinavia. With a massive number of children enrolled in daycare the professional demands of teachers have become stronger, as seen in national curriculum in all Scandinavian countries (see a forthcoming section Curricula of Early Childhood Education and Child Perspectives (page 29) in this Introduction).

---

[4] For example, a very small number of women and men, enrolled in the workforce, live on unemployment benefits in Scandinavia compared to other European countries that have even poorer unemployment benefits.

Individual persons and institutions have fought for children's right, which can be a question of taking a child perspective and implicitly can be a question of taking the children's perspectives (see, e.g., Korczak, 1998). Norway, however, was in 1979 the first country in the world, legally forbidding parents to spank their children. One year later Sweden took the same step, and in 1997 Denmark entered the Scandinavian group. Furthermore, most Scandinavian countries have an *ombudsmand* for children, whose work is commissioner with statutory rights and duties to promote and protect the rights and interests of children and young people at a national level.[5]

Children's Health and Well-Being in the Scandinavian Welfare States

The USA is an example that success in the global marketplace, national wealth, a comprehensive healthcare system, high expenditures to cure sickness, and free market mechanisms do not in themselves protect children. The tradition in the Nordic countries is to use tax policies and welfare measures in a systematic effort to soften extreme differences in the citizens' access to health care by making high-quality health care available and free of cost to everyone. Is this also reflected in the general distribution of children's health and well-being?

There are only a few international comparative studies of children's health and well-being. However, UNICEF's (2007a) report "An Overview of child well being in rich countries" is the most comprehensive assessment to date, and it provides insight into the well-being of children and adolescents in various industrialized nations. The report provides a thorough analysis of the following main categories: material well-being, health and safety, educational well-being, family and peer relationships, behaviours and risks, and subjective well-being. Each category is assessed on the basis of at least three different indicators. The study looks at a total of 40 indicators of children's well-being. It is not possible to cover all the findings here, but we will briefly address a few important points pertaining to the well-being of Nordic and Scandinavian children[6]:

- *Material well-being:* Nordic and Scandinavian children top the chart.
- *Health:* Nordic children's health condition ranks among the best in the world. Among the wealthy nations, American children have the lowest health rating. For example, the USA has more obese children than any other of the rich countries.
- *Well-being:* Nordic and Scandinavian children are far above average, while children in the USA and the UK are found to have the poorest well-being of all selected nations.

---

[5] In Denmark there's not an ombudsmand, but a "children's council" (børneråd).

[6] We refer interested readers to the UNICEF report, which also describes the many indicators and clarifies how well-being is measured in the specific categories. It also specifies how "good" and "bad" well-being are measured and assessed.

- *Subjective well-being:* Here, too, Scandinavian children have a high ranking, with, for example, 85% Danish children reporting a high level of well-being.

When the findings for all the main categories are pooled, children in some European countries are ranked high. The Netherlands, Sweden, and Denmark are top scorers for child well-being among the many rich countries in the world included in the study, while the UK is the lowest ranking in Europe. The UNICEF study provides very clear documentation: Some countries that have benefited from globalization to become relatively rich societies fail to turn this affluence into well-being and welfare for the coming generation. The UK and the USA are examples of this. The Nordic and Scandinavian countries, on the other hand, exemplify that it is possible to combine affluence with well-being for the general population, including the children, in a society characterized by a universal welfare model.

The Ethos of Humanization

Studies are showing that child-centredness and children's rights are stronger and more pervasive in Scandinavia than in many other countries (Therborn, 1993). With that follows an interest in understanding children's worlds, i.e. taking a child perspective and children's perspectives. So, why have child perspectives and children's perspectives become such buzzwords in Scandinavia? The reasons for this are historical, societal, political, and cultural – and thus, also value-based. Let us take a look at some of these values.

The humanized philosophy of man goes relatively far back in European history, while the growing emphasis on emotions and empathy that has fostered a child-friendly view seems to be a relatively recent historical phenomenon. For example, just before World War II the general view of children was radically different. This was a period of the non-empathic adult perspective, where strict discipline was a normal element in childrearing. In education and childrearing, corporal punishment was recommended as the responsible course of action towards misbehaving children. In 1930s an expert of the time professor Monrad recommended heavy-handed discipline for children under 1 year of age (Monrad, 1936) – a nearly unthinkable recommendation from a modern-day child expert. In the course of just a few generations, fundamental changes have occurred in the common view of adult–child interactions. A key source of these changes has been social and cultural, including changes in philosophy, psychology, and education. Most prominently, after World War II, the authoritarian model has been replaced in the Scandinavian democracies with what has been termed a *negotiation culture* (Sommer, 2005a). Innovation-driven societies of late modernity ask for the development of certain interpersonal competencies, where the ability to cooperate and negotiate has become crucial in a world where pre-set moral imperatives are crumbling. Authoritarian management styles have been replaced by a negotiation culture where success is achieved through the exchange of opinions, argumentation, and attempts to understand the perspective of the other. Not to say that authority has collapsed in contemporary Scandinavian societies, but the *ideal* for constructive interpersonal relationships is no longer a system based on indisputable sovereignty stemming from tradition, gender, position, rank, or role. Instead, the more or less implicit goal is to build mutual relationships with other people. Hence, contemporary parent and educators can no longer solely rely on externally imposed rules, as in professor Monrad's day, but are expected instead to be able to engage in empathic adult–child interactions to create a shared *interpersonal* world (Stern, 2004). Thus, there is an underlying cultural understanding that a contemporary adult should be able to understand and empathize with children's perspectives. Parents, educators, social workers, and researchers all operate under the current *ethos of humanization*, which requires acceptance of others as equals in their own right and respect for the individual (Sommer, 2007).

As a minority group in society, children are included in these humanization efforts. It is no coincidence that the United Nations' *Declaration of the Rights of the Child* was possible only after World War II. Only in a humanist era does such an ambitious declaration of children's right to be "heard", "seen", and "included" make any sense. The UN's *Declaration of the Rights of the Child* has been influential for the growing adoption of the child perspective and for maintaining respect for children's perspectives of their world. This historic change in the view of children has not occurred everywhere in the world, however, and the child perspective is absent from the grand narratives in many non-Western societies. This reflects the impact of culture and values on basic views of life and humanity. Regard, care for and protection for the weaker groups in society is, however, an essential aspect of the Scandinavian welfare model. This humane view is also concerned with the minority groups' perceptions of their own reality.

To explore the rise of the child perspective, however, it is not enough to simply view children as victims requiring protection or as an inarticulate minority group that should be "given a voice". One may apply a dual perspective: While childhood may be viewed as an age and minority category in a society organized by adults (Qvortrup, 1999), children are, simultaneously, increasingly acquiring the role as independent individuals (Sommer, 2005a). This is manifest, for example, in contemporary Scandinavian individualized parenting, which emphasizes respect for the child's unique character (Sommer, 2001). The negotiation culture that characterizes contemporary families and society is unfeasible unless the parties basically acknowledge each other as separate minds – individuals each holding personal perceptions and opinions that form the very basis for conversations and negotiations. This respect for the child as an individual participant is also evident in the type of legislation stating the overriding goal of securing the *best interests of the child*. Children are legal persons with rights; they are essentially unique and thus in principle separate from the interests of society and the family. Modern legislation protects children as a minority group – and it does so on *the individual's terms*. This is clearly in line with the growing individuation trend described by researchers (Beck, 1997; Dencik & Jørgensen, 1999; Giddens, 1994; Jørgensen, Dencik, & Sommer, 2008). Perhaps the strong individuation perspective on the child is one of the most remarkable and persistent child-view of late modern Scandinavian cultures, as a part of Western culture. The perception of self is coined as highly *independent* compared to the collectivized child-views of *interdependence* inherent in Asian cultures (Shweder, et al., 2006; Greenfield, Suzuki, Rothstein-Fisch, 2006), for example coins *amae* – a Japanese word for the child's ideal relationship with others – the young child's total dependency on his or her mother. Indeed, specific research on Scandinavian parenting values and practice in late modernity confirms that children are required to develop independence, and they are given the opportunity both to be "seen" and to be "heard" very early in life (Sommer, 2005a). A view that is seen reflected in parenting practice too. This may, but does not necessarily, lead to the upbringing of a generation of selfish children. Scandinavian parents, on the other hand, as well as educators, highly value the development of interpersonal sensitivity too (Sommer, 2001). But in comparison to the so-called Asian perspective, this relatively high complementary socialization pressure – i.e. the enhancement of early self-expression together with interpersonal competence – shapes a culture-specific developmental pathway of "generative tension" (Rothbaum, Pott, Azuma, Miyake, & Weiss, 2000).

Children as Citizens and Child-Centredness as a Vital Societal Value

The humanization and individualization processes paved the road for the understanding of children as citizens. The notion of children as citizens springs from the sociological term *citizenship*. Regardless of voting rights, all citizens are equal members of society – inequality stemming from ethnicity, sex, social group, or age is unacceptable to a humanistic perspective. In this view, although young children do not match adults in terms of competence or experience they are still considered their *equals*. Humanist societies espouse an ideology with special considerations and accommodations for minority groups. In relation to a child perspective, the principle of child citizenship should be adjusted and adapted to take children's perceptions into account. Incorporating children's points of view may help adults acknowledge them as equal citizens. But this (emerging) acknowledgement of children's perspectives is also the consequence of a *Zeitgeist* that endorses the notion of universal citizenship. In other words, children are in focus in the sense that their thoughts, feelings, opinions, and perceptions are the object of interest. More specifically, the UN's *Declaration of the Rights of the Child* explicitly mentions children's position in society. The convention gives the child *citizen status*. In a democracy, this gives an individual certain social, political, and civil rights (Rasmussen, 2002). In this view, the child perspective is an aspect of the strengthened democratic status of the child: an appreciation of the child as an *inviolable person* whose thoughts and opinions matter and whose interests must be protected.

The consideration of children's perspectives is not just emphasized in treaties and legislation and in the daily interactions between (some) adults and children. In research, children's status has also changed as a consequence of their citizen status (Andersen & Ottesen, 2002). Children's own world-views have become the object of serious research. Andersen and Kjærulff (2003) put forth the following rationale in their report about research involving children "*Hvad kan børn svare på?*" (What questions are children capable of answering?):

> During recent decades, there has been a distinct shift in the view of children and in the way that research addresses children, a shift that springs in particular from a growing desire to make children visible as independent individuals, both in a broad societal context and, more specifically, in social and cultural research. (p. 23)

Research is often portrayed as objective and value-neutral. Now that children as citizens and the child perspective have become key terms in social research, one may expect these concepts to be relatively free of any ideological charge. This is far from the case, however, and there is an ongoing struggle to define and patent what constitutes "good", "proper" childhood. One should bear in mind, therefore, that the interest in the child perspective is part of this struggle for hegemony and the power to define "the best interests of the child" (Kampmann, 2003).

Child Perspectives Without Ideology?

So, vital concepts regarding children might be constructed, narrated, and loaded with underlying ideology and fundamental values. Hence philosophies celebrating a child perspective enter into a discourse that is ideologically charged beforehand. This is rather difficult to avoid in a democracy and in scientific and professional cultures with many different views and opinions.

Children embody the future, and in Scandinavia in recent years, growing qualification requirements in response to global competition have deepened the gap between the notions of *children as our key future resource* versus *children and childhood in their own right*.[7] In this debate, the child perspective belongs to the latter position. It is therefore unwise to think that an interest in the child perspective and children's perspectives can remain neutral, detached from ongoing controversies about the values that should govern the constructs of "childhood" and "children". *Anti-humanist values* have seen a comeback, for example in Denmark, due to a combination of neo-conservatism, Christian dogma, xenophobia, and an underlying fear of globalization. For example, Krarup (2001) has stated that the principles of human inviolability and universal human rights are merely a sign of untimely human pride and vanity. According to this view, it would be nonsense to claim that

---

[7] Two examples of today's opposed learning ideologies in Scandinavia: 1. Concern for competition in the global knowledge economy causes a growing pressure towards early-formalized education. The PISA surveys compare and rate academic performances in various countries. In Denmark (and Norway), this has led to demands for mandatory tests and increased government control of schools, which would have been inconceivable only a decade ago. The effect is strengthened by neo-conservative political trends. 2. A contrasting trend is the growing interest in education methods that accommodate "mulTiple intelligences", based on Howard Gardner's theories (Gardner, 1993). This approach rests on values that are worlds apart from methods based on findings from the PISA surveys. The struggle between these contrasting value sets has become more intense in recent years.

children as part of mankind have any claim to universal (human) rights.[8] According to anti-humanism, this view dates back to the Age of Enlightenment and its abstract secularized ideal of man, detached from religion and tradition, at the centre of the world.[9] Professor of Law Andersen (2005) has criticized the "excessive use of human rights" in the EU in general, and at the Institute for Human Rights in particular. It is unclear whether Andersen's criticism is based on anti-humanism or not, but it does signal a new tone in a Scandinavian country, where the previously nearly untouchable idea of Human Rights has been challenged. Despite this trend, and in contrast to it, Scandinavian societies still represent very strong humanist features, with the notion of the child perspective as a specific example.

Curricula of Early Childhood Education and Child Perspectives

Whether caring for children in daycare is beneficial or not is to some degree ideologically loaded, and some may argue that the child's daycare socialization may be out of tune with the best interest of the child. Wagner (2006) argues that children in the Nordic countries are part of a democracy also in early ages. When Wagner compares childhoods in Nordic countries with the USA, she says,

> A key difference is that American preschools and schools are not conceptualized as democracies, but, rather, as places where students learn about democracy. It is often said that the purpose of education in America is to prepare children to participate in a democracy and to teach them to use freedom when they are adults. In contrast, Nordic people expect that children should experience democracy directly from their early days. This means, then, that Nordic children have rights and attendant freedom that American children are only preparing to experience later in life. (Wagner, op. cit., p. 294)

Let us in the following give a brief glimpse of the national curricula ECE guidelines in Denmark, Norway, and Sweden in relation to the child perspective and the children's perspectives. The *Danish curriculum* was introduced in 2006 and is the most minor of them all, with a law on only 1½ pages. This reflects a strong Danish tradition of not being controlled in details by the state, but having considerable freedom to manage and decide on local levels. There are six major content areas of focus in the Danish curriculum. Children should become acquainted with and develop knowledge about nature and phenomena related to it, themselves as a person, social competences, language and communication skills, body and movement, and cultural ways of expressions and values (Schjøtt Rohweder, 2006). In the law it says,

> The professional staff shall support, lead and challenge children's learning, which the children are co-producers of, or support situations that give the children possibilities for

---

[8] This also explains why anti-humanists oppose the European Union. The European project is essentially based on the Declaration of Human Rights, which in turn has its roots in eighteenth-century Enlightenment.

[9] This view originated in western Europe and led to the individuation process mentioned above. Without the emphasis on the individual, there would be no subsequent interest in a child perspective.

renewal, preoccupation, change and experience (Ministry for Family and Consumer Affairs, www.minff.dk)

What is special with the Danish curriculum is that it particularly focuses on preventions of problems and possibilities to be an independent and self-containing person. It states, "...this law aims to promote each individual's possibilities to take care of themselves or to facilitate every day life and to improve life quality" (p. 1). Focus on children's perspective is specifically formulated in the Dagtilbudsloven (2007) (Law of daycare offer) concerning the so-called children's environmental evaluation:

> Children's environments shall be evaluated in accordance with a child perspective, and children's experiences of their child-environment shall be involved according to the children's age and maturity. (Paragraph 12, part 2, p. 4, www.minff/1/familieomradet/)

A basic idea behind this legislation is to challenge "educational adultocism" by making clear that taking a child perspective is crucial when it comes to the evaluation of, for example, daycare environmental quality. As a consequence measures and evaluations solely based on adult's opinions and experience are not valued as good professional practice. Children's own voices shall be heard in order to promote their experience of the milieu. In the section specifying the central national goals for the daycare is a statement of "participatory democracy": "Daycare shall secure children's rights to participation, joint responsibility and enhance the understanding of democracy" (Paragraph 7, part 4, p. 3). Not being directly taught what democracy is, but by own daily experience and practice together with equals. An example of how a children's rights perspective is of crucial educational importance from early in life.

The *Swedish curriculum* from Ministry of Education and Sciences was introduced in 1998. It has 14 pages and states what the commissions of the preschool is, a perspective of learning and knowledge formation and 27 goals to strive for, of which 3 are about children's participation.

The preschool should try to ensure that children

- develop the ability to express their thoughts and views and thus have the opportunity of influencing their own situation,
- develop their ability to accept responsibility for their own actions and for the environment of the preschool, and
- develop the ability to understand and act in accordance with democratic principles by participating in different kinds of cooperation and decision making (op. cit., p. 12).

Children's participation presupposes that children's perspectives are taken into account. The whole idea is to become an active democratic person. The goals as a wholeness focus on norms and values, development and learning, influence of the child and cooperation between home and preschool as well as cooperation with preschool class, the school and leisure-time centre. There are no methodological directions besides interaction, communication, and play as key notions.

The *Norwegian guidelines* for ECE are called a framework plan and is the most extended of the three. It was first published in 1996, but is now revised in 2006. The revision is by the commission of the preschool group, which is responsible for the content of the work. The content areas are close to the school subjects like communication, language, and text; body, movement, and health; art, culture, and creativity; nature, environment, and technique; ethics, religion, and philosophy; local environment and society, number, space, and shape. But here is also a section about children's participation. It says,

> Children in preschool should have their rights to express their views on every day life in preschool. Children should also continuously get possibilities to actively participate in planning and evaluation of every day activities. Point of views of children should be taken into consideration in relation to age and maturity. (Kunnskapsdepartementet, 2006, p. 13)

In all three national curricula the children's own active participation is strong although the way it is talked about differs to some extent. Participation is related to value questions and democracy. Here we can see that although the Danish law states that cultural expressions and values are important, it does not specify those values. The Swedish curriculum uses democracy as a frame for the whole value base, while Norway uses Christian humanistic values as a basis (see further Alvestad & Pramling Samuelsson, 2001). Further, we can see that the Danish perspective is that the child who may get problems later in life, and whose problems are supposed to be prevented in a high-quality preschool, where the child could learn to be independent. But the learning of democracy during participation is also focused upon. In Norway we can sense the UN convention and the child's right to be listened to, but also democracy in practice by letting children take part in planning, according to their ages. It seems that democracy is not possible when children are not sufficiently mature. The most clearly expressed goals are in the Swedish curriculum, where children should develop the ability to express themselves and to influence life in preschool. But the curriculum also points at basic democratic values like responsibility for themselves and the environment and learn about and live democratically. It appears that Denmark and Norway have more of a child perspective, helping children to be independent citizens or helping the child to be able to participate with adults adapting activities to each child's age. In Sweden it is taken for granted that all children independent of age can express themselves and have to be listened to.

In a Swedish study different professionals were asked to critically scrutinize children's perspectives in the curriculum 2006 (Pramling Samuelsson, manuscript). One of the questions 10 professionals from other fields than education were given was, In what ways are children's perspectives visible in the curriculum, and is it possible to make them even more visible?[10] Most of the participants in the study emphasize and

---

[10] The definition the participants got was *Children's perspectives*. In research there is a clear difference between children's perspectives and a child perspective. A child perspective is seen as a perspective which adults with great knowledge about children and their lives can take up by asking themselves; what is best for children if I take my own knowledge about children into consideration? When researchers speak about children's perspectives it is not something an adult can take up without children being present, children act and express themselves and adults interpret what

exemplify how children's perspectives are expressed in many places and in many different ways in the curriculum. An example of this:

> According to the given definition that children's perspective is present only when children are actively involved and when children act and/or express themselves and adults interpret, it is possible to read in the value foundation and the commission of preschool, under the heading understanding and brotherly feeling. Children's needs to, in different ways, reflect upon and share their thoughts about life questions with others must be supported. This could also be found in the first chapter under objectivity and versatility. Each child should be given opportunities to form their own opinions and make choices based on their own circumstances. Further, under the commission of preschool: Children's curiosity, initiative and interests should be encouraged and their willingness and desire to learn should be stimulated. //...// Preschool should offer a safe environment to the children, an environment that at the same time is challenging and enticing children's play and activities. The children should be inspired to explore the surrounding world. In preschool children should meet adults who see each child's possibilities and engage themselves in the interplay, both with the single child and the whole group of children //...// Children should be given opportunities to develop their abilities to observe and reflect. The last sentence could be seen as an example that quite clearly points at children's perspective in accordance with the stated definition. The child should also have possibilities to make deeper studies and search for answers and solutions for personal reasons. In the creative and moulding play, children can be given possibilities to express and work on adventures, emotions and experiences. The practice should start out from the children's world of experience, interests, driving forces and motivations to search for knowledge. (Stina, 46 years)

Above we can see how a person has analysed the texts of the curriculum and emphasized a number of examples on how children's perspectives are expressed through the consideration shown for children, the impact children's own actions and reflections have for the learning and knowledge formation, but also how children's world of experience is seen as very important for what children do and how they create meaning. Also, in the next statement a relation has been highlighted, the goals and the practical work with children, but here is something that, with necessity, must be different. Here it also becomes obvious that those who work with the children need to work with the interpretations of the text in the curriculum. By that you could say that the curriculum exists in the mind of the observer.

> The curriculum should contain goals for the practice and not describe the professional implementation in preschool. As a teacher you should scrutinize the curriculum with your knowledge about children as a point of departure. What is best for the children when taking these goals as a point of departure? Teachers are professional in how to engage the children, make it good for them and make the curriculum visible through the preschool practice. You have to understand children's perspectives in order to carry through the intentions of the curriculum in a qualified way. The curriculum gives the impression that children should be able to think abstractly to a much greater extent than they actually can. This creates an over-confidence in children's abilities. Good role models both in preschool and in the goals of the curriculum are important. (Eva, 33 years)

---

children express as their meaning and their voices. It is the latter perspective we see as important to use in scrutinizing the curriculum.

Also in the above statement we can see a certain worry about aiming too highly in the curriculum, that is, the goals could be interpreted as that the children have a higher ability than they actually possess, and because of that the demands on the children could become too high. The relation between adults and children's perspectives becomes obvious in the following quotation too:

> Public steering documents, with necessity means that it is the "adults' perspectives" that have been formulated. //. . .// I believe it is more or less impossible to write a curriculum with "children's perspectives". There are many good child perspective formulations in the curriculum text. But, "children's perspectives" can and should be provided on the pedagogical shop-floor where children and adults meet each other. This dilemma ought to become more explicit in the curriculum.

The above statement points at the problems of letting children's voices be heard in a curriculum, when the aim of the curriculum is just only to make the intentions of the society accessible to those who work with the children in practice. Children cannot express the intentions of society. However, this person means that the actual relation between the intentions of the society and children's participation and perspective could be problematized in the curriculum. Summarizing, there is an intention in the curricula in Scandinavia to see children as active participants with rights to influence their every daily lives in ECE.

Child Perspectives and Children's Perspectives: Distinctions and Definitions

In this section we will present and discuss various conceptual and theoretical views on how child perspective and children's perspectives may be understood in order to reach a final Conclusion. In doing this we will start with the broad, everyday, commonsense use of the word and end up with a much narrower scientific and professional satisfactory definition.

The term "child perspective" is used with a wide variety of meanings in sociology, anthropology, and educational studies as well as in various child-related professions. Often, the term is used loosely as a self-explanatory concept, which leaves anyone free to read into it his or her own idiosyncratic perceptions. This makes the term quite versatile but also renders it vague and unsuitable for meaningful conceptualization. It would seem appropriate, therefore, to establish the nominal definition of "child perspective" from the outset. Let us begin with the last segment of the term: what does "perspective" mean? The word stems from the Latin "perspectus", which means to look at, look through, examine. As a compound noun, then, "child perspective" essentially would mean "a particular view of children", "a way of looking at children". This defines the everyday, mundane use of the term. It does not claim to be a scientific definition or particular to any one discipline, and indeed, it makes the term too broad for both research and professional use. In this sense, any view of children can be considered a child perspective, as in "Children thrive with thrice-daily thrashings" – a child perspective in accordance with the basic, mundane definition. Furthermore, any sociological, psychological, or educational statement may be considered a child perspective as long as it concerns children. This extreme versatility renders the term meaningless. Thus, a definition of "child perspective" based on everyday language is of little use in a scientific discourse about children. We need to narrow down the definition.

Despite these difficulties, or perhaps because of them, researchers from many disciplines are attempting to gain insights into children's perceptions and experiences. They approach this endeavour in various ways, for example with the use of *scientific constructions and concepts*. Here, we are approaching an understanding of the term that may include adult attempts at gaining insight into children's experiences and perceptions and clarifying and systematizing adult perceptions of children's perceptions. The developmental psychologist Stern (1985) points to the basic problem that adults face when trying to understand children's perspectives. In his groundbreaking and still highly relevant book *The Interpersonal World of the Infant*, he points to the infant as an excellent example[11] :

> Since we can never crawl inside an infant's mind, it may seem pointless to imagine what an infant may experience. Yet that is at the heart of what we really want and need to know. (...) These notions make up our working hypotheses about infancy. (p. 4)

Adults may be barred from entering a child's world, but by observing and interpreting children's coordinated acts in interactions, and through sound empathic imagination, we may begin to develop an understanding of the child's perceptions of the world. In practice, this actually *works*: In daily interactions with their baby, parents assume that "what you display to mom and dad reflects your actual feelings." Thus, when an infant pulls up both corners of his or her mouth we call it a "smile". We further venture to conclude that the "smile" means that the baby is "happy" – i.e. that the smile expresses a positive internal experiential quality. When instead the baby frowns and cries, we are convinced that he or she is "unhappy". We intuitively assume that the baby is experiencing an internal emotional quality, which is related to the baby's external expression in a systematic and ordered fashion. This presupposes a *correspondence between the child's internal experiential world and the child's external behavioural expressions*. However, we can never be quite sure whether the infant's mimicry (e.g. facial expressions) in fact corresponds with internal states. According to Stern (1985), we simply cannot know whether infants actually feel what their faces, voices, and bodies express so strongly, but it is difficult for anyone witnessing these expressions to reach any other Conclusion. As children grow up, our access to their subjective world becomes both easier and more difficult. It helps when they begin to talk about their experiences, but the development of language also complicates matters, as children gradually learn to hide their internal states and even to lie about them.

To approach children's perspective of their world essentially requires a child perspective based on everyday experiences and/or professional insights, i.e. insights

---

[11] The infant example is useful to clarify the epistemological distinction between "child perspectives" and "children's perspectives".

that represent adults' realistic perceptions of children's perceptions and experiences. For example, Stern (2000) claims that even 2-month-old pre-verbal infants have a "sense of a core self". This concept of *mental organization* is very different from any given child's actual self-perception. Instead it represents the researcher's construction of the child's experiential world, based on an inferential interpretation of what the child's actions mean. This invention of Stern's and its inherent child perspective may be replaced or supplemented by other ways of understanding the subjective life of the 2-month-old infant. But it brings us one small step closer to determining some necessary elements of a child perspective. Stern proposes a construct concerning mental organization, but this construct works in aiding (if indirectly) our understanding of children's subjective life.

However, the precise definition of a child perspective remains elusive. Extensive reading leaves the following impression: the term is used loosely and self-referentially in many contexts, with few attempts at an actual definition. Halldén (2003) also appears to have found the task difficult and chooses not to narrow down the term:

> A child perspective may mean to pursue what is in the best interest of the child, but this is not the only possible meaning. In this context, I am not going to propose any final definition of the term child perspective. The concept is unavoidably ambiguous. (p. 13)

"Pursuing what is in the best interest of the child" is clearly not a precise definition; it rather seems to suggest a children's rights ideology. However, Halldén does specify that the distinction between child perspectives and children's perspectives may be similar to the distinction between "child culture" and "children's culture": Who is shaping the perspective or the culture? Is it the child or someone *representing* the child? The argument would be that a child perspective may be based on children's perspectives, but always as it is interpreted by an adult, for example a parent, a researcher, or a practitioner. This view receives support from articulate sceptics: The ethnographers Gulløv and Højlund (2003) do not believe that it is possible to apply a child perspective independent of adult constructs:

> ... a child perspective is not an empirical entity that emerges from the study of children's statements and actions alone but rather an analytical construct, related to one's theoretical considerations. (p. 29)

However, it is important to consider how close the analytical constructs and theoretical considerations are to children's own perceptions of their lives. One should constantly ask oneself: How insightful are my perceptions – not about children as such but about their perceptions, knowledge, and experiences?

A more precise distinction – between, on the one hand, analytical constructs/theoretical considerations about children and, on the other hand, types of constructs that enhance our understanding of children's unique perceptions of their own lives – would help us distinguish a specific child perspective from all other types of knowledge about children.

Uri Bronfenbrenner (1979) was one of the first within developmental psychology to offer a specific and reasonably precise definition of a child perspective: a perspective that represents adults' relatively successful attempts at understanding children's thoughts about and perceptions of their own lives. This helps us narrow down the concept and resonates well with Stern's ideas. In other words, adults' constructs about children only make up an actual child perspective insofar as they facilitate adults' understanding of children's thoughts about and perceptions of their own lives. One consequence of this is that the general perceptions of the child in grand developmental theories are rejected as a potential child perspective. Descriptions of children's current living conditions also do not qualify as child perspectives. A child perspective only exists when these living conditions are related to and anchored in adults' perceptions of and constructs concerning children's perceptions and experiences of living with and under these conditions. Thus, a child perspective is not about any given society, culture, or childhood as such, although such knowledge is indispensable to the social sciences. Instead, a child perspective revolves more specifically around the "metabolism" between society and actively engaged, perceiving children – albeit interpreted and put into perspective by adult observers.

Definitions of the term "child perspective" in specialized dictionaries and reference books are rare. In the latest edition of the Danish *Pædagogisk-psykologisk Opslagsbog* (2006) (*Educational and Psychological Handbook*) a child perspective is defined as

> . . .seeing, understanding and empathizing with a child's needs, motives, intentions, actions, etc., i.e. the ability to interpret from a child's perspective, to seek to understand and empathize with the child's world and the way it is perceived from the child's point of view. (p. 25)

This definition resonates well with our discussion so far. It emphasizes that the key criterion is (adults') understanding of and empathy with children's view of their world. This means that a vast amount of knowledge about children and childhood should be considered external to the child perspective – regardless of how relevant this knowledge is in other contexts. We are now able to establish the key criterion of a specific definition of the term child perspective:

- **Child perspectives** *direct adult's attention towards an understanding of children's perceptions, experiences, and actions in the world.* Thus, child perspectives are created by adults who are seeking, deliberately and as realistically as possible, to reconstruct children's perspectives, for example through scientific concepts concerning children's understanding of their world and their actions in it. This excludes all the theories on children and childhood that do not help adults understand the world from a child's point of view. But even though child perspectives attempt to get as close as possible to children's experiential world they will always represent adults' objectification of children.

By contrast, *children's perspectives* refer to the perceptions of the non-adult subjects themselves. From the outset, children "are" in their world, as they perceive it. At an amazingly early stage in life, children develop experiential knowledge about their physical and social environment (Legerstee, 1992; Karmiloff-Smith, 1995). Over time, they develop a growing ability to reflect on their experiences. Hence, children's perspectives are not fixed entities; they undergo qualitative changes throughout life. According to Pramling Samuelsson and Sheridan (2003) children's perspectives concern his or her own "own contribution", their expression and presentation of their perceptions, experiences, and feelings. The key criterion for the definition of children's perspectives will be this:

- **Children's perspectives** *represent children's experiences, perceptions, and understanding in their life world.* In contrast to the child perspective, the focus here is on the child as subject in his or her own world, the child's own phenomenology. This is what adults attempt to understand through their child perspective, for example in attempts at child-focused interpretations of children's intentional acts and statements.

This book, guided by the definitions of child perspectives and children's perspectives, will search for child perspectives and children's perspectives in selected theoretical and empirical approaches. In Part I we scrutinize the so-called new childhood sociology paradigm as well as key aspects of contemporary developmental psychology.

Part I
In Search of Child Perspectives and Children's Perspectives in Childhood Sociology and Developmental Psychology

Introduction

In the late 1980s, a Norwegian book with the thought-provoking title *På jakt etter barneperspektivet* (In search of the child perspective) was published (Åm, 1989). Åm claimed to have found a child perspective in selected theories interpreting the meaning of children's social play – i.e. general approaches to the functions of play constructed by adults on behalf of children. The precise content of the child perspective in general and children's perspectives in particular remained vague, however. We will not search for a child perspective within the relatively narrow realm of play theories, however. Instead, the ambition of Part I is to scrutinize a child perspective and children's perspectives within selected and potential promising parts of the so-called new child perspective of both childhood sociology and recent contextual-relational developmental psychology.

The primary intention is to explore whether recent childhood sociology and contextual-relational developmental psychology may improve our essential understanding of children's perspectives on their own live-worlds. This may not be an easy task, because theories that were originally developed to address completely different and adult relevant topics have been used as if they represent a genuine child perspective. For Example, Alanen (1988) and Alanen and Mayall (2001) apply feminist theory as a perspective on children, with the rationale that children are suppressed in society, as well as women. Another Example is James, Jenks, and Prout's (1998) use of a general Foucaulian analysis of power, time-regulation, and school discipline, in order to study "real children" and even the "experience of being a child". Such types of theory, however, are "imported", i.e. the approaches are not originally constructed with the main purpose of developing a unique child perspective theory.

This search may prove to be in vain, but the process may uncover interesting views and conceptual understandings inherent in very influential contemporary theories on children and childhood.[1] Childhood sociology and contextual-relational

---

[1] It should be noted that one of the "searchers" is not a sociologist but a developmental psychologist. This may make childhood sociologists cringe because childhood sociology was launched as the very critical counterpoint to the classical "grand theories" of developmental psychology.

developmental psychology are very broad in scope, however, encompassing more than just one approach, and space constraints prohibit a comprehensive presentation.[2] For the purpose of this book, the search for various child perspectives and children's perspectives, those positions are selected, which are most likely to enhance our knowledge.

But why look within childhood sociology and contemporary developmental psychology for child perspectives and children's perspectives? First of all, over the past decades, the childhood sociology has established an important platform for itself within the social sciences. In a brief amount of time, the sociology of childhood has gone from marginalized rebel to a mainstream source of knowledge about children and childhood (Kampmann, 2003). Particularly during the 1990s, this branch of sociology articulated new socially and reality embedded constructions of children and childhood. These theories not only renewed sociology; childhood sociology is now in widespread use within ethnography, educational studies, and cultural studies (e.g. Lloyd-Smith & Tarr, 2000; France, Bendlow, & Williams, 2000; Kampmann, J. 2000; Tufte, Kampmann, & Juncker, 2001; Carlsson, 2003; Halldén, 2003; Warming, 2007). However, childhood sociology has had relatively little influence on social and developmental psychology.[3] Hence, we should also look within the so-called contextualist relational developmental psychology for a possible child perspective in order to revitalize developmental psychology, not least since childhood sociologists seem to agree to use classical grand developmental psychology as their "scapegoat" in legitimizing their theories.

Secondly, the same period has witnessed a remarkable, parallel unfolding of the child perspective in society. Childhood sociology as well as recent developmental psychology and various humanistic approaches claiming a child perspective reject the classic dogma about children as passive recipients. But whether child perspective and childhood sociology in fact reflect one another is far from certain, although many researchers and professionals seem to take this relationship for granted. Thus, the paradigm of childhood sociology has been applied as "the new view/perspective of children" in various contexts as synonymous with a child perspective (e.g. Lewis & Lindsay, 2000; Ottesen, 2002; Eide & Winge, 2003; Halldén, 2003). Also architects of childhood sociology have specifically used the concepts child perspective and children's perspectives and related them to their work: The Norwegian Centre for Child Research arranged in 2003 the seminar *Children's Perspectives in Childhood Research – Prospects and Challenges.* Here Jens Qvortrup delivered a lecture titled "A Child Perspective and Childhood in the Welfare State" and William Corsaro contributed with "Gaining Children's Perspectives and Using Them to Interpret Children's Agency in Their Peer Cultures".

But current developmental psychology is not synonymous with the grand developmental theory paradigm, so the assessments and considerations put forth in this book will not be based on such an approach.

[2] Readers wishing a more comprehensive insight into these theories may consult the reference list.

[3] Although childhood sociology has carved a niche for itself in sociology, it has had little influence on sociology in general.

It remains an open question, however, whether there is any real basis for this. Is it possible to deduce, directly or indirectly, essential understandings that are relevant for a child perspective? As will be demonstrated later specific statements from childhood sociologists clearly point in that direction.

The same can be said about recent contextual-relational developmental psychology. But whether these qualify as actual child perspectives requires further examination. It is, however, important to note the following: Contextual-relational developmental psychologists do not necessarily claim to offer specific child perspectives. For Example, one does not find any chapter or substantial section describing how recent developmental psychology defines and does research within a "child perspective" or "children's perspectives". These terms are not to be found in the detailed key word indexes of standard updated works that represent the state of the art (e.g. Berk, 2006a). But obviously, this does not mean that one cannot search for a child perspective; it may be present, implicitly or explicitly. Therefore, it is of important academic interest to make such an inquiry. As mentioned, researchers and professionals have used theories on childhood alike as though they represent a child perspective – probably because these theories articulate important statements that suggest a possible child perspective, as we shall demonstrate later.

The search for a child perspective and children's perspectives will be guided by the following key questions:

- *Is a child perspective apparent in selected aspects of childhood sociology?*
  If yes, in what ways are children conceptualized that enhance adults' recognition and awareness of children's perceptions and experiences of their worlds?
- *Is a child perspective apparent in selected aspects of contextual-relational developmental psychology?*
  If yes, in what ways are children conceptualized that enhance adults' recognition and awareness of children's perceptions of experiences of their worlds?
- *Do children's own perspectives have a central position within these bodies of theories?*
  If yes, in what ways do the respective disciplines show and present children's own perceptions and experiences of their worlds?
- *What common conceptual platforms and potential for future integration can be identified?*
  What concepts appear to be particularly important for an interdisciplinary integration of concepts from childhood sociology and contextual-relational developmental psychology?[4]

---

[4] It is our impression that there is a growing opportunity for an interdisciplinary integration. New openings have been possible, because some fundamental views of children have interacted with each other in sociology and psychology.

In Search of Child Perspectives and Children's Perspectives in Childhood Sociology

From the second half of the 1980s–1990s a number of groundbreaking new ideas about children emerged within sociology. It is fair to talk about a *new sociological childhood paradigm*. Until then, the paradigm implied in classic sociology was largely that the individual and person were equal to the adult. In classical socialization theory, children were typically reduced to "emergent" members, i.e. immature uncivilized humans on their way to maturity. Guided by the thinking of teleological finality childhood was reduced as a transitional period on the path to the end-goal: adulthood (Sommer, 2005b). Frustrated with classical sociology and developmental psychology, some sociologists began to treat *children and childhood as conceptually independent categories in society*. These sociologists explained the specific social conditions of childhood, with the ambition of constructing a new sociology of childhood. As described in the Introduction, various disciplines and childhood sociologists themselves have drawn on the new sociological paradigm of childhood and have used it heuristically as a legitimate representation of a child perspective. However, the authors of this book have not been able to find any analysis that investigates the validity of this. Here, we will consider key theoretical aspects as well as the preferred empirical methods of the sociology of childhood.

Childhood sociology consists of various theories with certain commonalities. But they differ, too, in their specific emphasis on various aspects of research into children and childhood[1]. According to Qvortrup (2002), however, there is common agreement on the following three basic views:

---

[1] These sociologists constructed their theories as counterpoints to the grand, universal developmental psychology, where the child was detached from history and society. At this time, Psychoanalysis and Piaget were still in vogue in many textbooks on children's development, with universal stage theories as the prevailing paradigm. What these sociologists overlooked was that a shift in paradigm within developmental psychology was already underway. However, this groundbreaking research had not yet been pooled in the late 1980s or early 1990s. Hence, there was only a limited understanding of the revolutionary consequences of this shift in child paradigm in psychology among sociologists. To illustrate: Anthony Giddens (1994) bases much of his influential theory about the living in a radicalized modernity on Erik H. Erikson's outdated classical-modern theory of psychoanalysis. Giddens, too, is the author of a textbook on developmental psychology. But it only addresses the major classical theories that ignore the new view of children after the shift in paradigm.

D. Sommer et al., *Child Perspectives and Children's Perspectives in Theory and Practice*, International Perspectives on Early Childhood Education and Development 2, DOI 10.1007/978-90-481-3316-1_2, © Springer Science+Business Media B.V. 2010

- *First*: Childhood is essential as something that can be *perceived, experienced, and documented for children here and now* (rather than a view of children as future adults).
- *Second*: *Childhood is an element in the social structure* (rather than a period in an individual lifespan).
- *Third*: Children are important actors in their own and society's development (rather than objects of socialization and teaching).

How may these three points be of importance in relation to a potential child perspective? In point one, one should note the phrase "for children" in the sentence "... childhood is essential as something that can be perceived, experienced, and documented *for children* here and now". It is by no means trivial that the phrase is "for children" rather than "by children". "For children" implies that it is someone else, not the children themselves, who perceives, experiences, and documents on behalf of them. In other words, this is a matter for the adult researcher. This is clearly not about children's perspectives, i.e. their experiences as subjects in and experts on their own lives. But whether this paradigmatic statement offers a child perspective where adults reconstruct children's perceptions, experiences, and actions is not immediately discernible. To determine that we will in this section further examine the substance of various childhood sociologies.

The second point, where "childhood is an element in the social structure", has not much to do with a child perspective and children's perspectives as defined in the Introduction of this book. Although the existence of childhood is based on real children it is clearly abstracted from any child and children living their childhoods.

The third point describes children as "actors in their own and society's development". This suggests, perhaps, the outline of a child perspective, i.e. a philosophy that gives adults a greater appreciation of children's *agency*, a being with perceptions and experiences of their life-worlds. The notion of agency in society's and one's own *development* even suggests a reference to developmental psychology. However, this view of children as developmental actors is not explored or explained further. Hence, it is not possible to follow up on this otherwise promising clue.

Childhood sociology addresses many aspects of the interrelatedness of childhood, children, and society. To mention just two Examples: Children should be "made visible" in society through specific statistics. Not with the usual focus on *families* with children but in statistics where *children are the unit of account* (Qvortrup, 1994b, 2002). Children's economic living conditions differ so much from those of their parents, even when they live at home, that it affects our general understanding of society.

However, one risks throwing the child perspective out with the bathwater if one thinks that contemporary childhood sociology in itself offers the child perspective within sociology. As discussed in the Introduction part of this book, the definition of a child perspective may become so broad as to become meaningless. Hence, in the remainder of Part I will address only those aspects of positions within childhood sociology that hold potential relevance for child perspectives and children's perspectives.

Childhood as a Social Structure

The Danish sociologist Jens Qvortrup has developed a prominent sociology of child-hood (e.g. 1994a, 1994b, 1999, 2002). His theory involves the following key theses, among others:

1. Childhood constitutes a specific structure in society. This means that sociology must examine and describe the specific architecture of childhood.
2. Despite the differences between children and adults, they are exposed to the same social influences. However, these influences often have very different effects on children and adults, respectively. It is well known, for Example, that working conditions in society affect families with children, but that does not mean that working hours and income levels affect parents and children in the same way.
3. Children are actors who should be studied in their own right. They are partici-pating co-constructors of childhood and society. Hence, children are not passive objects of institutional or adult purposes.

Qvortrup's theory does not address the fact that children – as they develop – change both physically and mentally, since his branch of childhood sociology rejects the usefulness of studying *individual changes across the lifespan*. It ignores the verifiable fact that individuals develop from early childhood to old age – develop-mental chronology (Wrosch & Freund, 2001). In this respect, Qvortrup's sociology of childhood is very different from classical developmental psychology and from contemporary views that emphasize the importance of the human lifespan and its transitions (Boyd & Bee, 2006; Sommer, 2001).

But perhaps children's perceptions and experiences of their life-world have in fact made it into this sociology of childhood? One may think so, since the term "a child's perspective" actually occurs. In outlining some fundamental principles of the theory Qvortrup (2002, p. 65) coins the importance of "... *seeing society from a child's perspective*" and "... *adopting a child's point of view*". But what do those clearly child-oriented key phrases "seeing", "perspective", "adopting", and "point of view" mean? Contrary to what may be expected they do not refer to a child perspective, seen as an attempt by the adult to perceive the world through the eyes of a child, or any effort to come closer to understand a child's point of view. According to Qvortrup (2002), this would be an illusion, since adults are not chil-dren and therefore do not have access to a child's perceptions, just like a man would be incapable of fully comprehending a woman's way of thinking. So, instead the sociological study of "children in their own right" implies that researchers use sci-entific objective approaches to describe, explain, and interpret objective aspects of children's life-worlds. This is what "seeing society from a child's perspective" is all about, and this is the way for "adopting a child's point of view". This purely top-down structuralism use clearly misleading conceptualizations about the nature of a child's perspective and point of view, which is crucially different from the nominal definitions proposed in this book, shared by other proponents.[2] Surely, at first glance some of the statements in the theory appear to embrace a child perspective. But in fact, the theory does not involve concepts that expand our understanding of children as perceiving, experiencing subjects in their social world. To Qvortrup, studying "children in their own right" means giving childhood *conceptual autonomy*; it does not mean that adults should even *attempt to approximate* a child's perspective. The study of the phenomenon of children in their own right is an undertaking by specially qualified adults who take it upon themselves to describe and interpret children's unique position in society. This childhood sociology therefore deliberately distances itself from the psychological constructs of the generalized child and individual development:

> ... while psychology focuses on the *child* and the child's *individual development*, sociology focuses on *childhood* and its *historical, cultural, and social dynamics*. (Qvortrup, 2002, p. 46)

Thus, childhood exists independently of individual children, a point that is difficult to dispute. But a general structural theory about childhood without any interest in actual people's feelings and thoughts is just as problematic as the classic de-contextualized child psychology with its lack of interest in historical, cultural, and social dynamics (Sommer, 2005a, Chapter 7). This type of childhood sociology deals with the objectification of the children, which is important. Psychology is deliberately excluded, but in doing so, childhood sociology is cut off from the contributions from psychology in the integrative appreciation of children as subjects living in historical, cultural, and social dynamics. An Example of the importance of including the subjective dimensions: It is useful, but impossible to fully explain violence committed against people with "different" views or lifestyles purely in sociological, objective terms. Experimental research documents the importance of including subjective views of individuals as well as group identities – polarized "us" versus "them" perspectives (Zimbardo, 2004). There has to be enough individuals to create collective feelings of fear, anger, and hatred, feelings that are also affected by and interact with historical, social, and collective conditions.

If all the individual children in the world do not exist, the superstructure of childhood would be gone – so the individual level has in principle some kind of relationship with the macro-level. As spelled out in a later section this is a key proposition in the contextual–relational developmental approach (Witherington, 2007). It is very complex indeed to relate an individual's real-life existence to macro-oriented sociological phenomena such as childhood. However, ignoring the very existence of the individual and his or her subjective perceptions and affecting society mediated through interpersonal relations seem to repeat the failures of the classic "top-down" narrative of structuralism where the individual is reduced to a passive reproducer of society. Another Example may illustrate the importance of the subjective experience

---

[2] This should not be seen as criticism of the theory as such, which has offered groundbreaking insights into the social construction of childhood in society.

for active (defensive) social participation: 9-year-old John refuses to go to school. When dad asks why, he replies:

I'm afraid to go. The bigger boys hit me. Peter (the class teacher) doesn't do anything about it. They are waiting for me when I get there.

Bullying can be meaningfully explained in both sociological and cultural terms, for Example as the result of structures of dominance that have been transferred to children's groups in an individualist and competitive society. Research into the active production of hierarchies in peer groups through child–child interactions may also offer important explanations of bullying. Here, relationships and interactions among the children take priority over the individual child's thoughts and feelings (see Sommer, 2005b). Yet, this is not sufficient to explain why John refuses to go to school. John is telling his dad about an unpleasant internal psychological state – fear. This is the personal motivation behind his refusal to go to school. Even with the best possible sociological and cultural interpretations, John's perspective ("private anxiety") cannot be explained without an interpretation on the individual level. Thus, even the most careful social and historical analysis is unable to fully elucidate actors' dynamic transactions with other individuals in society if the individuals' own perspectives on their life-world are ignored.

This type of childhood sociology, however, does not totally ignore the dialectics between society's structuring influence on childhood and people's ability to actively change their society. Let us therefore review the previously quoted third point in Qvortrup's sociology of childhood, which articulates the basic view of children in the theory: "Children are *active actors*, and children *construct* society and childhood." As a minimum, active agency and the ability to construct presuppose that children are capable of comprehending and making sense, that is, rather sophisticated and competent organisms that are mentally capable of processing social and cultural information. Childhood sociology raised justified criticism of the classical view of socialization where children are seen as passive recipients of information (see also similar criticism from developmental psychologists: Sommer, 2005b). But despite the rejection of psychology, Qvortrup's theory implicitly *presupposes psychological structure and activity*. Logically it follows that children encompass psychological structures and processes, because without someone who remembers and comprehends any sensible talk of children as constructors becomes meaningless. Unless children are to be seen as robot-like "constructors" of society and childhood, their active agency must, at the very least, presuppose both awareness and intentionality.[3] In a few cases, Qvortrup actually writes "the child" rather than childhood or children. This indicates that a given child may in fact choose to initiate acts or choose not to act – this possibility is coined in the phrase "by choice" (Qvortrup, 2002). For this to make any sense, a choice presupposes intentions and

---

[3] Active agency and processing capacity depend on age. Apart from primitive stimulus-response processes, active agency requires internal states – i.e. intention and volition. Conceptually, this brings us close to an actual child perspective.

the will to act in certain ways – an individual or a group of individuals choosing to do "this" rather than "that".

The underlying presupposition of some important psychological phenomena in this childhood sociology is also evident in this quote:

> Unless children are given a constructive role in school, i.e. unless their *capacities, intelligence*, energies, *creativity*, etc. are perceived as useful, one would be forced to opine that children only *learn* and *know* what has been transferred to them. (Qvortrup, 2002, p. 57, our emphases)

Intelligence, creativity, learning, and knowing are hard to understand without an appreciation of the existence of some phenomenological, psychological phenomena. Unfortunately these terms are not elaborated further, they are scattered as isolated conceptual particles in this grandiose theory spelling out the architecture of childhood. Here, elements in contemporary developmental psychology could have contributed with important knowledge about children's cognitive capacities, intelligence, and creativity, in order to enhance adults' understanding of children's approaches to learning and knowing – in other words, a child's perspective.

But where may children's perspectives be found in this theory? As already stated, they are absent, despite it being explicitly claimed that this childhood sociology includes a child's point of view. Qvortrup (2002) acknowledges, however, that there is an inherent epistemological conflict in a "sociology seen from a child's point of view" given that its "producers" have a completely different approach to understanding, living, experiencing, and acting. Here he adopts the sociologist Alanen's argument about the unsolved "epistemological conflict" inherent in childhood sociology:

> What remains is resolving the inherent epistemological conflict between a childhood sociology seen from a child's point of view and the fact that its "producers" by necessity have a different way of knowing, living, experiencing and acting in the world. (Qvortrup, 2002, p. 74)

This statement highlights the dichotomy between the theory's adult-centred macro-level construction of the child's point of view on the one hand and children's qualitatively different perspectives on the other. This conflict may be addressed through applying an interdisciplinary approach: Childhood sociology has the conceptual devices for carrying out a social analysis that objectivate children in society, but it has not developed concepts for grasping children's unique ways of experiencing, perceiving, and acting in their life-world.[4]

Although Qvortrup's innovative sociology of childhood is a major contribution, it offers little knowledge of relevance to a child perspective. The theory explicitly rejects the notion of bringing adults closer to appreciating children's ways of perceiving and experiencing the world and society, as children's own perspectives are not the goal of the theory. Qvortrup's sociology of childhood reflects

---

[4] Alanen's "epistemological conflict" might be resolved by including psychologically relevant new knowledge about children's and adults' different ways of knowing, living, perceiving, and acting, not as a counterbalance to sociology but as an attempt at an integration. See a later section for this.

a *macro-oriented structuralism*, which leaves no room for experiencing, thinking subjects.[5] Children's thoughts and feelings may be considered irrelevant in a given research context, or they may even, as stated by Qvortrup, be considered outside an adult's reach, but that does not make children's experiences go away. Individual experiences – for Example the "Phenomenological Now" – is present in the consciousness of both children and adults (Stern, 2004). The emotional tone in personal relationships, for Example, is very real for children, and even if adults do not experience things exactly as children do, it is highly possible to approximate children's perspectives in a realistic way. This possibility, however, is deliberately ignored in Qvortrup's theory, despite some promising, but misleading phrases as "seeing society from a child's perspective" and "adopting a child's point of view".

We must therefore conclude that our search for child perspectives and children's perspectives in childhood sociology has been unsuccessful so far. But perhaps another branch of childhood sociology may bring us closer to our goal?

Children's Interpretive Reproduction

From the mid-1980s the American sociologist William Corsaro developed his theory about children as active participants in peer groups (e.g. Corsaro, 2002, 1992). He has also made important contributions to the development of the interpretive ethnographic approach (Corsaro, 1996; Corsaro & Miller, 1992). There are some similarities between Corsaro's and Qvortrup's positions, in particular with regard to their view of the unique character of childhood in society – but there are also distinct differences.

Qvortrup's sociology was described as a structural macro-oriented approach, aiming to map the unique and pervasive character of childhood in society. Despite the fact that every child, by the time that he/she becomes an adult and leaves childhood, structurally in any society childhood will exist, even if it may be constructed very differently in different cultures and historical times. Consequently, Qvortrup's childhood sociology does not include empirical investigations of everyday life, specific observations of children, or any child's statements about seeing society from his or her perspective. When empirical studies of children's reality occur (in order to adopt a child's point of view) it is in the form of various statistics that document the present state of childhood in society. This has led to new, surprising, and very useful knowledge about the social architecture of childhood. But this approach does not involve a child perspective or children's perspectives, although certain phrases may have suggested that this would be the case.

As mentioned, Corsaro's sociology also applies a macro-perspective, and like Qvortrup he devotes considerable attention to historical, demographic, and

---

[5] A macro-oriented theory addresses a societal and sometimes a historical level, unlike the micro-oriented view, which focuses on social and cultural processes emerging and distributed in everyday life. Micro-oriented types of childhood sociology will be introduced in the following sections.

socio-economic aspects of childhood. But in addition, Corsaro includes children's *interpersonal world, especially the everyday routines in peer groups.* That gives his theory a much more social psychological and ethnographic touch compared to a purely sociological one. This reflects that Corsaro's sociology of childhood developed gradually out of a longitudinal study of American and Italian preschool children's everyday interactions in peer groups in daycare settings.

So, Corsaro's sociology concerns both a macro-oriented childhood level and a micro-oriented group analysis level. This is clearly expressed in the following:

> Another challenge in writing about children concerns doing justice to both micro (social psychological) and macro (structural) approaches to the sociology of childhood. My main theoretical orientation of interpretive reproduction is clearly social psychological; however, at times I felt I needed to write two books (...) to cover both micro and macro issues. (Corsaro, 2005, p. xii)

This is another Example of the lack of a systematic merger of macro-/micro-perspectives and of object/subject approaches in the sociology of childhood. As discussed above, Qvortrup is not interested in the micro-level, and Alanen pointed out the unresolved epistemological conflict between a childhood sociology formulated by adults and the fact that its "producers" experience and act in a different way than their subjects. Corsaro points to the dichotomy between the macro- and the micro-levels. As pointed out in the Discussion of Qvortrup's childhood sociology, no theoretically founded links have been established between the overall childhood perspectives on the one hand and children's life-world on the other, let alone any link to children's own perspectives of their life-world. When Corsaro addresses childhood on a macro-level, his theory resembles Qvortrup's. Consequently, the same Conclusion applies here concerning the lack of relevance of this type of childhood sociology for the conceptualization of a child perspective and children's perspectives.

The theory, however, is more promising in its distinct micro-orientation, which is evident in the key concept *children's interpretive reproduction.* Let us take a closer look at this key point: Like Qvortrup, Corsaro criticizes traditional developmental psychology for its individualist doctrine, i.e. its method of explaining social development as the individual child's passive internalization of adult socialization. From a micro-sociological point of view, children are *actors* who actively "acquire", "rediscover", and "reproduce" culture. The main focus here is on the collective activity where children "negotiate", "share", and "co-create" culture (Corsaro, 2002). Cultural routines are the essential "anchors" for children's interpretive reproduction. Cultural actors gradually establish daily routines that provide a sense of security, predictability, and familiarity in everyday interactions with others by virtue of reducing ambiguity.

Corsaro (2005) assumes that cultural routines develop soon after birth. In Western cultures, according to Corsaro, social interaction between adults and babies is governed by "as-if" assumptions. In accordance to that adults approach babies "as if" they are able to take part in social communication, even before they in fact possess this capacity. The baby "replies" by responding to this cultural idea, thus the infant is co-producing the first micro-cultural interaction routines together with the parents. Corsaro points to the game of peek-a-boo as an Example of a prototypical cultural social routine:

1. *Shared attention* is established: Mom smiles and establishes eye contact as she says, "Hi, honey!"
2. *Disappearance*: Mom hides her face, for Example with her hands or behind a pillow, and says, "Where's mommy?"
3. *Reappearance*: Mom shows her face to the child.
4. *Contact is re-established*: For Example "peek-a-boo" or "There you are!" Smiles and laughter.

How does Corsaro interpret this key event? According to him, mom acts *as if* her baby is socially competent. To Corsaro, this expectation of children reflects a cultural (Western) view, where parents' "as-if" assumption initiates and drives the interaction. This is clearly stated as a *theoretical assumption* about the child's (non-existing) capacities. But does it represent a child perspective? That would require that the adult's attention is directed at a realistic (conceptual) understanding of the infant's perception of his or her world and his or her actions in it, for Example in the infant's own expressions in interactions with the mother in cultural micro-routines. The "as-if" assumption plays a key role in the epistemological view of infants in this theory, and it is therefore well suited to revealing the realism or lack thereof in this type of childhood sociology, and its basic assumption of whether or not children possess early capacities for engaging as actors in cultural micro-routines. Once this has been clarified, we will be able to conclude whether or not the theory expresses a child perspective in this respect. Corsaro's definition of the "as-if" assumption is as follows:

> ...assumption or attitude in person-to-person interaction where something that is potentially true or possible is treated "as if" it is really true or possible, For Example, infants are often treated by adult caretakers as though they are socially competent (that is, capable of social exchanges). Because of this, children eventually progress from limited to full participation in cultural routines. (Corsaro, 2005, p. 340)

We are now able to deduce the theory's essential view of human socialization early in life: Infants are socially incompetent and hence incapable of establishing, maintaining, and affecting interactions. Why else would parents act as if their baby had these capacities? As described earlier, Corsaro in principle views children as social actors and co-producers of cultural routines, but apparently this is not the case early in life. In the section quoted above, infants' participation in cultural routines is described as "limited", while Corsaro's several empirical presentations and analyses of the interpretive reproduction of 5-year-olds describes children as competent actors. This leaves a crucial question to be answered: When in onto-genesis, and not least, how do humans turn into co-creating producers of cultural routines? Ironically, by claiming that early human ontogenesis is characterized by limited or absent social capacities, Corsaro's sociology of childhood adopts the same basic assumption about the passive receptive child as the traditional socialization theories that it criticizes. Furthermore, the distinction between "limited" and "full participation" in cultural routines suggests what childhood sociologists have criticized in traditional socialization theories: that in their social limitations, children are "emergent" members, on their way to "full participation". This theoretical construction of early life may well have been implicitly influenced by traditional historical and philosophical conditions underlying various social theories as a sort of common Zeitgeist (Sommer, 2005a). But the "as-if" assumption does not represent a realistic approach to children in early ontogenesis. It is an assumption that lacks any conceptual grasp of infants' actual experiences and actions with others, and it is overlooked that babies act in ways that make it unnecessary for parents to act "as if" infants were socially active and competent. This argument is supported by groundbreaking knowledge about babies' basic social nature: Theories strongly based on empirical documentation support hypotheses about babies' primary and secondary intersubjectivity and their early capacity for taking part in finely attuned social routines (e.g. Trevarthen, 1988; Aitken & Trevarthen, 1997; Stern, 1985, 2004). This makes it essential to adopt an approach to even the earliest social encounters between infants and their environment that takes agency and reciprocity into account. Human beings are social actors who engage in attuned relationships from the first days of life (Stern, 2004). The attempts by childhood sociologists (including Corsaro) to distance themselves from developmental psychology have led them to ignore groundbreaking new knowledge about very young infants' (and older children's) socio-cognitive capacity. This knowledge has the potential to effect constructive changes in the micro-oriented sociology of childhood and its basic views of early cultural routines. It also offers an appropriate basis for a more consistent general view in childhood sociology of the fundamental social character of human nature. Additionally, it offers a conceptual basis for an actual child perspective on early cultural routines, which Corsaro's infant-approach does not.

What further problems does Corsaro's "as-if" assumption hold? From repeated experiences with early social interactions with their infants, parents learn to know that even very young infants are relatively socially competent and active participants in interactive routines. Hence, adults do not have to act "as if" the infant has social capacities that it has not. More fundamentally, the "as-if" assumption has crucial consequences for the understanding of human *agency* in early micro-cultural interaction, and hence for the basic feasibility of a child perspective in Corsaro's theoretical framework.

"What you know – you see" and "What you don't know – you don't see". "Seeing" highly affects what we notice; it reflects the eye of the beholder (Dahlgren & Hultqvist, 1995). Furthermore, seeing something means missing something else, which points to the researcher's eternal dilemma between the fundamental necessity of having specific knowledge and the limiting effect of this knowledge for one's interpretation of what one sees, or perhaps more disturbing do not see. Not only does the "as-if" assumption in itself lead to mistaken assumptions about infants' social skills but also has crucial methodological consequences for taking a child perspective or not. For Example what does Corsaro "see" and "does not see" in the peek-a-boo game: Throughout steps 1–4, presented earlier, the mother is described as the actor who drives the process. The infant, however, renders invisible, because his or her possible replies, initiatives, and activities are not included in the case. This negates the possibility of a child perspective that involves infants. Accepting the "as-if" assumption eradicates the infant's social agency – it is not "seen" and therefore excluded from the description – although the peek-a-boo game is in fact an activity that involves two social partners. Ironically – and unintentionally – the basic "as if" conceptually and empirically renders invisible the very children that the principle of interpretive reproduction intents to highlight. Within the relational framework that characterizes contextual-developmental psychology, this one-dimensional Mother→Child direction and Corsaro's interpretation of the peek-a-boo game would be inconceivable. Once again, this underlines the urgent need for interdisciplinary integration.

Despite the problem with agency in early ontogenesis, Corsaro's paradigm of the child as an actor in everyday encounters is a crucial parameter in this sociology of childhood. Without that, the basic axiom of children's interpretive reproduction will not make sense. According to Corsaro children "negotiate" and "create" culture when they interact with other social actors, but this clearly applies only to older preschoolers. As for non-infants, Corsaro does have rich documentation for his thesis of agency stemming from detailed observations of daycare preschoolers in the USA and Italy (Corsaro, 2002).

Language plays a key role in Corsaro's sociology of childhood. Language is essential for children's cultural participation, and the function of language for the child's interpretive reproduction can be summarized as follows:

- Language is a "symbol system" that encodes local, social, and cultural structure.
- Language acts as a "tool" for maintaining and creating social and psychological realities.

Thus, language does not exist for its own sake but as a useful tool for executing and comprehending specific routines in social life. Language is also anchored in children's intimate world. Interestingly, Corsaro, a sociologist, refers directly to some "psychological realities" that are both created and maintained through language. This conceptual framework brings us one step closer to a child perspective. But only if it encompasses adults' deliberate attempts at constructing realistic concepts about the types of articulation and symbols children use as experiential and action tools to create and maintain social and psychological realities. One searches in vain, however, for a more in-depth elaboration and Discussion of the function of language- and symbol-use in relation to the psychological realities mentioned. A way to fill this lacuna of knowledge is to turn to cognitive-developmental psychology. The ability to use symbols as "tokens" for real-life events requires the development of internal representations (Westcott et al., 2002), which necessitates the integration of *mental models* into Corsaro's theory of interpretative reproduction. Mental models, however, are not the same as the child's own experiences or perceptions; rather, they are analytical tools that may help adults develop a realistic understanding and explanation of children's experiences, perceptions, and actions. Hence, with adequate content specification, mental models may enable the development of a child perspective.

A child's ability to comprehend what goes on in another person's mind is a crucial prerequisite for acting in a socially attuned way, being a competent social actor in the peer group. This ability should not simply be epistemologically assumed as Corsaro does, it should be explained theoretically and verified empirically. Promising concepts from contemporary developmental psychology such as "theory of mind" and "perspective-taking" and the empirical research that these concepts are based on (e.g. Baron-Cohen, Tager-Flusberg, Cohen, 1993) may prove to be useful mental models in relation to a child perspective. Participating as an integrated and co-creating social actor in cultural routines requires a mental ability to "take the other's perspective", reading the other person's mind. Corsaro's detailed documentation of 5-year-olds in complex interactions (involved in interpretive reproduction) would be unthinkable without a more or less implicit assumption of sophisticated socio-mental competencies. Corsaro's fundamental thesis of children's "interpretive reproduction" has documented children as actors, but revealed little knowledge about *subjects as interpreters* of social interactions. Understanding a situation implies a subject that makes inferences and allocates meaning to events. This *presupposes some sort of mental activity* – for Example linguistic and symbolic processes. As mentioned above, Corsaro treats language as a tool that both creates and maintains social and "psychological realities". However, one looks in vain for any elaboration on the *psychological structures, processes, and mental content* of these realities.

Unfortunately, this interpretive childhood sociology stops exactly where a child perspective that enhances the understanding of children's unique interpretation strategies could be unfolded. For Example this sociology of childhood does not contribute much in answering the following questions:

- What enables children to interpret and comprehend, engage in, and affect their own social interactions?
- What socio-mental skills does it take to be a co-producer of everyday culture?

Socio-cognitive mental models stemming from psychology have documented and conceptualized how children interactively experience, understand, and act differently from adults. A child perspective is only truly in place if it manages to conceptualize how children use *their* interpretation strategies and *their* actions to engage in everyday cultural routines. In the closing section of Part I, which discusses possible common platforms of a child perspective, this Discussion will be revisited.

The Study of "Real Children" and the "Experience of Being a Child"

A third influential theory within the new sociological childhood paradigm comes from the English researchers James et al. (1998) and James and Prout (1990). Their sociology of childhood has been seen as offering a child perspective; for Example Ottesen (2002, p. 16) describes the theory as "the new child perspective" (see also Eide & Winge, 2003; *Pedagogisk Forskning i Sverige*, 2003).

But what is it exactly in this type of childhood sociology that makes others consider it a child perspective? Like Qvortrup's and Corsaro's theories it is highly critical of classical child psychology and developmental psychology with their abstract, universal child. In some respects, these sociologists agree with Qvortrup, for Example in their reflections on "children and work". But there are also important differences, for Example in their social-constructivist reservations towards the structuralist view that Qvortrup's theory so clearly relies on.

This type of childhood sociology is explicitly launched as *the reality-oriented* counterpoint to psychology's de-contextualized child paradigm. In the following, only aspects of the theory that have formulated promising concepts relevant to our search for child perspectives and children's perspectives will be examined: In what ways does this type of childhood sociology offer or imply conceptual formulations relevant for a potential child perspective? Which elements of the theory may enhance our understanding of children's own perspective of their childhood? To answer these questions, we will examine the construction of the child in this type of childhood sociology.

Classical child psychology, as represented, for Example, in Jean Piaget's stage model, viewed the child as a solipsist, alone in his or her world, on the way towards adulthood – "becoming". By contrast, this childhood sociology views the child as "being":

> The child is conceived of as a person, a status, a course of action, a set of needs, rights or differences – in sum, as a social actor. (. . .) this new phenomenon, the "being" child, can be understood in its own right. (James et al., 1998, p. 207)

The terms "a course of action" and "social actor" reveal clear commonalities with Corsaro. The term "the 'being' child" implies an interest in children and childhood in their own right, as this perspective does not view the child as someone on their way to becoming someone else. James et al. (1998) quote Wartofsky in attributing children agency; not as passive imitators of adults but as actors in their own construction; with equally natural agency as any adult and with the ability to initiate actions based on volition. This hints at a Western voluntarism, where agency is at the core of what it means to be human. Unfortunately, the authors do not elaborate on this interesting point about agency and volition. However, "volition" does spark human activity and action, and activity and action in turn edit "volition" in an ongoing, dialectic process. Theoretically, this point is expanded far more in contextualist-relational developmental psychology (e.g. Fogel, 1993;

Rogoff, 1990; Witherington, 2007). In the closing section of Part I, which discusses common platforms for child perspectives, this Discussion will be revisited.

Traditional theories on developmental psychology represented neither a child perspective nor children's perspectives because they constructed children "in the abstract", that is constructs which are created through a relatively small set of general concepts and universalities and then projected on the child. May not a move by this type of childhood sociology be away from this and towards an alternative view? One that directs the adult's attention towards a deeper understanding of the child's perceptions, experiences, and actions in the real world – require the study of "real children"? And may an understanding that represents children's own perceptions, understandings, and experiences in their life-world not require studies of "the experience of being a child"? We are not far from the mark, as this childhood sociology explicitly sets out to study exactly that:

> To summarize: the epistemological break that we have claimed for new sociological approaches to the study of childhood is the move to *study real children or the experience of being a child*. (James et al., 1998, p. 207, our emphasis)

Few theorists would want to be seen to address "unreal children", but as mentioned above, the grand developmental theories of child psychology did just that. For Example, psychoanalysis was not about children "as they are" but rather reflected adults' projections and fantasies about the essence of the child[6] (Stern, 1985). There is more rhetorical power in the above monopolizing the study of "real children" and "the experience of being a child". Perhaps this is where our search for child perspectives and children's perspectives should be taking us?

In clarifying the child perspective we need to examine how "real children" are constructed in this narrative of childhood sociology. It turns out to be a construction fraught with internal contradictions: On the one hand, a general *adult-centrist social-constructivist Foucaultian analysis* is applied in the describing and explaining of children's worlds. This childhood theory reflects a very strong element of a Foucaultian analysis of power, time regulation, and school-discipline in society. On the other hand it also constructs the *child as a subject*: This child has a "private self" – a unique inner world, one must consider. The child is presumed to have *agency*, i.e. children are actors, able to affect their surroundings.

These remarkable contrasts do not really match up in this type of childhood sociology, and indeed, the authors address this obvious conflict and ambiguity:

(1) The social forces that structure the mind, and which are outside the child's influence, versus

(2) The child as social actor – *someone who affects his or her surroundings.*

---

[6] Proponents of classical developmental psychology might reject this claim. To them, this naturalized, universal child is very "real". But if one is able to monopolize "the real child" you have earned a strong rhetorical position – hence, when such terms are introduced, critical readers beware.

This theory fails to close the gap between "structures-shaping-people" and "people-creating-structure-through-processes". As discussed earlier, this was also a problem for Qvortrup, Alanen, and Corsaro. So, this question remains still to be answered in the various childhood sociologies which apply both as a macro- and as a micro-perspective: If children with their subjective perceptions and private selves act in a social world and in a society, how effectively does this promote change – and at what levels of society?

It is still uncertain whether this type of childhood sociology represents an actual child perspective and/or children's perspectives. Possibly yes, if the theory's notion of the *child as subject* forces adults to attempt to understand (and empathize with) the child's world, professionally as well as personally. Possibly yes, if the child's own experiences, knowledge, and perceptions are in focus (we will revisit this issue in the closing, integrative section of Part I). But a resounding no, if the general sociological categories are imposed on the child. In Foucaultian analysis, the "real child" is reduced to an abstraction, residing in society's more or less hidden power structures – the child as the (un)disciplined prisoner of society in Foucault's lens. As shown previously this sociology of childhood perceives itself as distinctly different from classical child psychology and developmental psychology, which indeed is borne out in the very different content of these theories. But, despite that, in the general approach to children the similarities are glaring. In the application of the Foucaultian perspective, the analysis of "real children" is in principle not essentially different from the generalized "top-down" rhetoric of the grand developmental theories. The general analysis uses non-child-oriented conceptual categories that can be used to "explain" practically any (child) phenomenon of our time in society.[7] Thus, the explanation of "real children" or "the experience of being a child" manifests itself as a sociological, adult-centrist projection on children and their childhoods. The experience of being a child, thus, is reduced to a Foucaultian critique of humans living in contemporary society, which is far from children's actual experiences. This approach is no closer to real children and their experiences than the much-criticized traditional disciplines of child psychology and developmental psychology. In fact, it does not even give room for adults' potentials for having qualitatively different life-experiences within Foucault's social order. In this respect, this type of childhood sociology does not represent a child perspective – or for that matter an adult perspective on life – although this is suggested in statements mentioned above. The general Foucaultian analysis imported and applied on children does not direct the adult's attention towards any specific understanding of children's experiences, their unique life-world, or active agency (i.e. child perspective). Nor does it explain how children as subjects perceive and comprehend themselves in their world (i.e. children's perspectives).

---

[7] Foucault did not discuss children at all, and the theory does not contain any specific concepts concerning children in society. So, as mentioned in the Introduction part, such a type of theory is "imported" because it is used to explain what is not its primary goal. Unfortunately, James et al. do not legitimate its relevance in relation to children.

As mentioned previously, researchers and professionals consider James, Jenks, and Prout's type of childhood sociology as an actual and useful child perspective. But after the analysis of the theory's "top-down" approach this assessment does not seem verifiable. One unfortunate consequence of accepting it would mean that any type of general sociological point of view that discusses children could qualify as a genuine child perspective.

But the presence of a child perspective depends on which aspect of the theory the assessment is based upon. Let us therefore address another more potentially promising dimension of the theory, the one that focuses on the *child as a subject*. Perhaps this dimension of childhood sociology will expand our knowledge about children's unique perceptions of their own life-world by including children's perspectives? One may think so, since the quote mentioned above describes this sociology of childhood as the study of *the experience of being a child*. Taken at face value, this statement would have to mean that the focus is on the child's phenomenology. But how is the experience of being a child described? What additional insights into children's own perspectives of their world does the theory offer?[8] After thorough analysis, the Conclusion is: virtually none. Interestingly, *childhood as a subjective space* is explicitly mentioned – i.e. an inner psychological space of the self is (perhaps) subject to the strict societal time regulation of childhood, for Example in school. Additionally, it is emphasized that girls and boys construct radically different *subject identities* (James et al., 1998, p. 54–55). This introduces some powerful constructions concerning subjective phenomenology and raises expectations of further elaboration. For Example:

(1) How do schoolchildren experience their life in (the analytical construction of) time schedules as digital regulation?
(2) How is the "experience of being a child" constituted in the person's inner psychological space?
(3) How do "real girls and boys" experience their subject identities as different from the other sex?

These issues are not addressed and analysed, however. The self as an inner-space-construct in the subject is rather empty and acts almost as a sort of empty-Box construction in the theory. Another Example of the serious conceptual problems that childhood sociology faces in its attempts to explain obvious psychological realities. In discarding psychology (or not using new developmental research) the possibility of offering a detailed explanation of the life of "real children or the experience of being a child" is lost, i.e. studying the complex relationship between and within subjects in society.

Thus, taking a child perspective is presumingly an important part of the programme, but only in what appears to be a declaration of intent with little substance.

---

[8] The focus here is on *theory*. In the following section we will examine the *method* of the micro-oriented childhood sociology, the ethnographic interpretive approach, for its potential as a possible child perspective and/or making manifest children's perspectives.

Nevertheless, the theory does propose a number of basic theses concerning *subject, self,* and *psychological realities* in children, which invite specification, for Example through self-theories from contemporary contextual–relational developmental psychology. This possibility will be explored in the closing section of Part I.

The Ethnographic, Interpretive Approach of Childhood Sociology as Child Perspectives and Children's Perspectives?

So far, our search for child perspectives and children's perspectives has focused on key elements in three theories of childhood sociology. Now, we will turn to a closer examination of the presence and impact of these perspectives in the empirical approach of the micro-oriented childhood sociologies – the ethnographic, interpretive approach.[9]

Three positions which can be identified to guide the evaluation of the ability of the ethnographic, interpretive approach to offer insight into informants' perceptions[10] are the following:

- *The pro-position*: Argues that the method offers privileged access to the participants' points of view.
- *The sceptical/rejecting position*: Doubts that it is possible to truly gain insight into children's subjective perceptions of their world. At best, adults may achieve a child perspective, but even this possibility is viewed with scepticism.
- *The mid-seeking position*: Adults are able to approximate an understanding of children's perceptions of their world. But children's statements and actions cannot be taken at face value: Sociological interpretation is required.

The pro-position: Some micro-oriented versions of childhood sociology view the ethnographic, interpretive approach as uniquely suited to accessing children's experiences and knowledge (Corsaro, 1996; Corsaro & Miller, 1992). Corsaro (2005) uses it in his many observations of children's interpretive reproduction in order to "see" from the children's point of view. James et al. refer frequently to the method and its particular advantages in studies of subjects' perceptions of their world (e.g. James et al., 1998).[11] However, they do have certain reservations concerning how "close" to children's experiences the adult is able to get. At best, the adult

---

[9] Qvortrup's method excludes the possibility of a child perspective because the work is based on statistical data about childhood. Therefore, Qvortrup's empirical approach is not featured in this section.

[10] This method uses fieldwork, among other things, in an attempt to gain real insight into people's everyday life, but reflected, analytical distance is also a key aspect of the interpretive approach.

[11] However, they do have certain reservations concerning how "close" to children's experiences the adult is able to get. At best, the adult may become a "semi-participant", which places these childhood sociologists in a mid-position.

may become a "semi-participant", which places these childhood sociologists in a mid-position (see later).

Thus, in the micro-oriented childhood sociology, it is a clearly stated purpose to study children not only as objects in society but also with methods that capture children's subjective perspectives. According to Corsaro (2005) the interpretive approach offers direct access to subjects' perception of their life-worlds. Thus, it appears to be *the approach* for not only achieving a child perspective but also reflecting children's perspectives. In Corsaro's words:

> ... interpretive research methods stress the importance of understanding social processes *from the participants' perspectives*. These methods involve the careful entry into natural settings like families and peer groups, observing over long periods of time, and capturing the meaning of social processes *from the perspective of those studied*. (p. 113)

Substituting the phrases *from the participants' perspectives* with "from the children's perspectives", and *from the perspective of those studied* with "from the perspective of children studied" clearly encourages a children's perspective paradigm. This is probably one of the main reasons why researchers and professionals have adopted the sociology of childhood and its ethnographic approach as both a child perspective and a means of "hearing the voice of children" as a minority group (e.g. Lewis & Lindsay, 2000). But is this in fact borne out? Corsaro does not help us answer this question, since he does not criticize and evaluate his own empirical approach; instead he argues that it is a way of capturing children's perspectives. Ethnography has concepts in favour of this point of view, for Example "children as natives" and "tribal children" (this is discussed in James et al., 1998, and in Gulløv & Højlund, 2003). Here, empirical research is viewed as a child-centred attempt to present children's very different (exotic) experiences and knowledge in contrast to an adult point of view. This may be seen as a parallel to the ethnographic attempts to offer authentic portrayals of exotic tribes and cultures in order to limit white, Western scientists' projections on other cultures. This may be attempted, for Example, by living with and like the "natives", or by "climbing into the sandpit with children" to adopt their perspective. Corsaro does not suggest, however, that it is necessary to act like a child to take children's perspectives. Instead he advocates acting as *an atypical adult*, that is, an adult who pretends to be little and who puts the children in charge (Corsaro, 1996). One may also act "strategically ignorant" in relation to children's experiential world in order to encourage them to correct one's misperceptions from their point of view. According to Corsaro, these field study approaches make it possible to understand social processes from the perspective of the subjects that one is studying.

Furthermore the *sceptical-rejecting position* questions whether an authentic representation of informants' points of view is really possible. Before the childhood sociologists adopted the ethnographic, interpretive approach, the method had been used for years in empirical anthropological and ethnographic research. Here, its possibilities and limitations have been under close scrutiny. Let us therefore turn to anthropologists and ethnographers who reflect on the ethnographic, interpretive approach as a possible source of a child perspective and/or a true reflection of "native voices" as a direct way to access children's own perspectives. Gulløv and Højlund (2003) speak a word of caution:

> There has even been a tendency to view ethnographic methods as *the way to achieve a child perspective*, which may lead one to conclude that ethnographic methods necessarily capture children's perspectives. We find this Conclusion problematic, however, as we remain skeptical of the analytical potential of concepts like the child perspective and children's culture[12].
> (p. 28)

They base their scepticism on a number of arguments. An implicit assumption in the child perspective is the idea that informants have a particularly privileged access to the "truth" about their own lives and the world. Naturally, in practice children are experts on their own life and know their environment better than any (adult) fieldworker ever will. But as Gulløv and Højlund (2003) point out, there is an essential difference between *knowing* a culture and *understanding* it. That is, the difference between intimate and implicit native knowledge (= a child's understanding) on the one hand, and an external, explicit expert's knowledge of that culture and its inhabitants (= adult understanding) on the other. Adult researchers may gain insight into children's world, but their knowledge must inevitably be of a different order than the experiential knowledge that children act on in their daily practice. In this view, adults' awareness of children's reality will inevitably be both limited and selective. Since the method is *interpretive* it makes no sense to examine the phenomena as such, because there is "no way to approach reality without interpretation" (Gulløv & Højlund, 2003, p. 24). Thus, there can be no naked, true, realistic recording of children's perspectives. The very observation of children's acts involves an element of inference, for Example of children's intentions, in order to even begin to make sense of the chaos of movements and interactions that plays out. According to the sceptical-rejecting position any observer will perceive and describe human-patterned movements as "directional" and "intentional" forms of communication. Thus, there is

> ...no way to escape the subjective slant in the selection and favoring of certain aspects over others and the idiosyncratic and adult-centered character of this interpretation. Furthermore, when we transform these observations to text, we reshape the ambiguity and simultaneity of activities and statements that we perceive to a manageable and comprehensible form of information. (Gulløv & Højlund, 2003, p. 24)

According to this rationale, the interpretive approach does not enable a loyal representation of children's perspectives. This is in contrast to Corsaro and followers in general and in particular the brand of anthropological research that seeks to "turn native" in an attempt to see the world through the eyes of the native subjects, i.e. children.

---

[12] Gulløv and Højlund use the term "child perspective" as synonymous with "children's perspectives". It is therefore somewhat unclear whether they in fact reject adults' ability to adopt a child perspective or whether they only reject the idea of capturing children's subjective perspectives through ethnographic research.

This highly relevant theoretical and methodological Discussion in ethnographic child research has important implications for our search for a child perspective and children's perspectives in the micro-oriented sociology of childhood, which applies the same interpretive approach. Gulløv and Højlund (2003) reject the notion of an identifiable immediate reality. As they see it, there is no "pure data" about children, only one or more adult-selected perspectives on children. They conclude that the anthropological approach is not aimed primarily at a distinct child perspective, let alone the representation of children's knowledge in any unambiguous sense: "Anthropological research targets children's (cultural) knowledge and actions, not a representation of children's perspectives, because adults never get close enough to be able to claim that they share children's experiences or know what children are thinking" (ibid., p. 31). Thus, children are always viewed through an *interpretive* filter, but the anthropological research method does not promote the voices of children as an oppressed group with "rights" in a political sense. This is in clear contrast to supporters of the convention on human rights and the convention on the rights of children, who call for "children's voices" to be given prominence and heard, and who believe it is possible to ensure this by including children as informants. This is clearly a contentious issue.

Thus, the sceptical-rejecting position clearly rejects the notion that adults (researchers) are able to produce *children's perspectives*. But is the *child perspective* even recognized as an analytical possibility? Let us examine this question:

> A child perspective is not an empirical entity that can be produced through the study of children's statements and actions alone, but rather an analytical construction related to the theoretical considerations concerning the planning, execution, and analysis (of fieldwork). (Gulløv & Højlund, 2003, p. 29)

This statement resembles the definition proposed here in this part, in that the child perspective is seen to stem from adults' construction and views of children. However, it differs in its point about whether adults directing their attention towards and seeking to understand children's perceptions, experiences, and actions are present or not. In this sense, a genuine child perspective does not reduce children's utterances to purely cultural manifestations, as may be an inherent tendency in ethnographic and cultural research. It also implies that adults – through certain scientifically realistic child constructs – are in fact capable of understanding how children perceive, experience, and know the everyday culture of their world. Although the quote above suggests some acceptance of a child perspective (as an analytical construct), Gulløv and Hastrup (2003) remain sceptical of the concept, because, in their view, it overemphasizes common features, putting all in a children's Box, at the cost of differences, inequalities, and conflicts among children. This is clearly a risk, and researchers should strike a vital balance when studying groups of children. On the one hand, researchers should be able to identify common features in their perspective on children (or risk disintegration into particularism). On the other hand, they should remain open to plurality and conflicts in co-existing perceptions, positions, and interests within the group (or risk a rigidly monolithic view).

The sceptical-rejecting position questions the basic ability of the ethnographic, interpretive approach to describe the world "from the participants' points of view" and from "the perspective of the subjects". This is at odds with the points raised by both Corsaro, the "turning native" approach, and the advocates for children's rights. Accepting the sceptical-rejecting position would force anyone engaged in the search for a child perspective and children's perspectives in the sociology of childhood to conclude that this empirical method does not represent children's perspectives.[13] But after a careful reading of Corsaro's (2002) many observations and descriptions – what children communicate verbally and non-verbally to each other, how they act in social contexts – this radical Conclusion is hard to accept. As mentioned earlier, Corsaro presents his observations as reflective and evidence of "children's interpretive reproduction". That is, he focuses more on children's statements as purely cultural interpretative reproduction than manifestations of their subjective governed perceptions and actions. However, more subject-individual-oriented interpretations of the same observations reveal that individual children clearly express their own, private views. Naturally, the children's statements have been observed and thus selected by an adult (the researcher). Nevertheless, Corsaro's observation material has so much "empirical resistance" that it reduces the risk of far-flung and wild interpretations. Furthermore the observations are open to re-interpretation by other researchers in a way that focuses more on individual children's (non-cultural) utterances and actions that stick closely to reality and to subjects' idiosyncratic perceptions. The "can you eat chips"-observation is only one Example of this (Corsaro, 2002).

The sceptical-rejecting position is contradicted by extensive psychological empirical research of younger and older children's *testimony*, including their credibility as informants. Provided that they are questioned in a qualified manner, children can be as credible as adults in their testimony about events and they are fully able to *express their particular perception of events* (Thomsen & Berntsen, 2002; Westcott, Davies, Bull, 2002). According to this research, it is possible to produce children's own perceptions and experiences, for Example in their capacity as witnesses in court cases. But it is also possible to "induce false memories", i.e. to make children believe in events that never took place in real life. But this, too, is a case of *children's (incorrect) perspectives*. The fact that children can be made to believe a lie is just as important for our understanding of children's perspectives as perceptions that reflect the truth. The feasibility of a method that presents children's perspectives is therefore not a matter of whether children's subjective perceptions are true or false; it is instead a matter of children's ability to *express their perceptions* and adults' ability to understand and interpret children's statements on the children's terms.

Now it can be concluded that there are differing views on whether it is possible to achieve an authentic presentation of children's perspectives within empirical research. Some – within childhood sociology, anthropology, and psychology – believe this is indeed possible, while others remain sceptical or even reject this.

---

[13] This illustrates how binding basic analytic axioms are for one's empirical approach. The ethnographers in question apply the hermeneutic approach.

The mid-seeking position: This Discussion will be incomplete without the inclusion of a third position. James et al. (1998) are clearly positive towards the ethnographic, interpretive approach as a child perspective. Still, they occupy more of a mid-seeking position with regard to the ability of that approach to reflect informants' points of view; they discuss this point under the theme "the tribal child" – a position embraced by ethnographers who act "as un-adult like as possible" by assuming the role as a child in order to achieve a better understanding of their world. James et al. (1998) are sceptical of this approach and propose a more balanced semi-participatory role relationship:

> Might not more, or at least different, things be learned about children and their social world by adopting the more middle ground of semi-participant or friend? (...) if we admit the inevitability of the differences between children and ourselves as researchers, acknowledging that, however friendly we are or however small, we can only ever have a semi-participatory role in children's lives, then we might develop tools and techniques specifically for work with children on those occasions when our adultness prohibits our full participation. (p. 183)

There may be a methodological benefit in maintaining the distinction between adults and children. Being aware of the differences between adults and children may be more informative than adults' attempts to "turn native" in order to understand children in a tribal sense. If anthropologists do not have to "turn native" in order to understand culture as perceived from a native inhabitant point of view, then childhood researchers need not pretend to "turn childish" in order to get closer to children's perspectives. In all, James et al. (1998) seems to believe that the *ethnographic, interpretive approach may be suited as a child perspective* because it may direct the adult's awareness of and an understanding of children's perceptions, experiences, and actions in their worlds. This resembles the definition of a child perspective that was proposed in the Introduction section of this book. The child perspective and the approximation of children's points of view are not in their view established by acting like a child nor by providing an uncommented summary of children's statements and actions but rather by taking, for Example, the role of friendly, engaging adult.

But are James et al. (1998) also saying that the ethnographic approach represents children's own perceptions, understandings, and experiences of their life-world – i.e. *children's perspectives*? On the one hand, they approve of direct, verbatim presentations of children's statements in research reports. They also approve of the sincerity in the notion of the "tribal child", that is, that the researcher listens to the child as a representative of a different reality than the one inhabited by adults. Furthermore, they emphasize that insightful anthropologists avoid imposing their concepts and phrasings on children's actions, instead they attempt to accept children's own stories at face value. On the other hand, they are critical of "extreme reproductions" of children's statements, i.e. representing these statements "as they are", without interpretive comments (James et al., 1998, pp. 185–186). Extremely naturalistic reproductions of children's perspectives would not bring us any closer to a sociological understanding of children's life, because children ("the natives") do not have this understanding of themselves in the world. These key statements indicate that the goal of the ethnographic, interpretive approach is less about reproducing children's subjective world as such and more about including empirical findings in an adult's (but child-focused) sociological narrative about children's lives. Thus, these mid-seeking childhood sociologists do not reject a child perspective, but children's own perspectives will always be "wrapped" in adults' interpretations of children's life-world. In other words, they do not see the approach as a means of presenting children's perspectives in an unfiltered form.

To conclude, whether the ethnographic, interpretive approach is suitable for achieving child perspectives and/or representing children's perspectives in the sociology of childhood *depends very much on the applied position*. We identified the following three positions:

1. *Pro-position*: William Corsaro's micro-oriented sociology and empirical findings, the "tribal children"/"children as natives" approach and psychological studies of children as witnesses all argue in favour of the method, each with their respective rationales. For Example, Corsaro's many empirical Examples – as well as empirical findings in psychological studies of witnesses – support the possibility of establishing a relatively credible subject perspective.
2. *Sceptical-rejecting position*: The ethnographers Gulløv and Højlund represent a voice in ethnographic research, arguing against the approach as a means of capturing children's perspectives. They are more ambiguous with regard to the child perspective: On the one hand, it is used in adults' analytical construction of children. That is to say, researchers interpret children's statements and actions in ways that direct the adults' attention towards understanding children. On the other hand, they are sceptical of the term per se, because it suggests a generalized understanding of children.
3. *Mid-seeking position*: James, Jenks, and Prout's argumentation implies that the ethnographic, interpretive approach is appropriate as a child perspective. It directs adults' attention towards the understanding of children's experiences, perceptions, and actions. But is it in fact useful as a means of capturing children's perspectives? On the one hand, insightful researchers must avoid imposing their concepts on children and accept children's stories at face value. On the other hand, James et al. are sceptical of uncommented "extreme reproductions" of children's statements. Thus, the mid-seeking childhood sociologists do not reject the notion of a child perspective, but children's perspectives are always "an approximation", woven into adults' interpretations of children's statements and actions. These interpretations, however, should be kept as subject-focused as possible.

Conclusion: Child Perspectives and Children's Perspectives in Childhood Sociologies?

In the Introduction child perspectives and children's perspectives were discussed and defined. Additionally it was argued that analytical concepts should not be allowed to grow too wide and inclusive in scope. A scientific definition means that concepts as theoretical building blocks should be relatively precise, specific, and, thus, with distinct boundaries to other scientific constructs. Further, we determined that childhood sociology is not one theory but rather a body of theories that contains common as well as contrasting positions. It has also been emphasized that child-hood sociologists do not necessarily define their positions as child perspectives, and that this does not constitute a scientific problem. Earlier in this book, it was stated that the reference book that deals with the child perspective per se without the use of "imported theories" has yet to be written.

However, it was also documented that research and professional practices in the social sciences and the humanities – often outside sociology – increasingly draw on childhood sociologies as if these represent a child perspective. This is no sur-prise, since our search until now has revealed that *specific statements by childhood sociologists* in fact point in this direction. Thus, the terms and concepts that in partic-ular suggest a child perspective and/or children's perspectives have been analysed and assessed in the search for these perspectives in various positions within the sociology of childhood. It is now time to draw Conclusions: What has this search produced? Was it in vain, or did it contribute useful knowledge?

In Qvortrup's macro-oriented approach, childhood is viewed as a particular struc-ture in society, which always exists independently of any individual children or groups of children. On the basis of this "top-down" structuralism, it was not pos-sible to find neither a child perspective nor any concepts that convey children's perspectives. On closer inspection, specific statements that may have appeared to reflect a child perspective – for Example that this sociology of childhood studies *children in their own right*, views *society from a child's perspective*, and adopts *a child's point of view* – proved more to be declarations of intent on behalf of children rather than applications of an actual child perspective. In Qvortrup's very consis-tent line of argument, the notion of "studying children in their own right" implies that childhood is viewed as having conceptual autonomy. Adults should not attempt to approximate a child's perspective, just like a man, according to Qvortrup, could never fully comprehend a woman's perspective! Nevertheless, as shown, there are statements that clearly *presuppose a subject perspective*. Qvortrup's theory implies inherent concepts of children as *actors*, involved in *constructing* society and child-hood. Agency and the ability to construct are human characteristics to be combined with a subject perspective of children, or else it becomes mysterious as to what makes a child able to act in and construct society. But the theory does not attempt this at all. Besides, Qvortrup holds the important notion that the child have opportu-nities to *choose* to initiate actions – a so-called by choice argument. But surely, does an act of choosing not imply some volition and intentionality in children? This is not touched upon either. This sociology of childhood also advocates giving children a more positive role in school, which as said requires that adults understand children's *capacities*, *intelligence*, and *creativity* and that children are better able to *learn* and *know*. However, the theory does not elaborate further on those promising mentalist, psychology-loaded formulations.

William Corsaro's childhood sociology is on the one hand macro-oriented, like Qvortrup's, in addressing key historical, demographic, and socio-economic aspects of childhood. On the other hand, the theory is far more micro-oriented when it conceptualizes and understands children in their intimate world and everyday routines in peer groups. As for the macro-sociological side of the theory, Corsaro's theory resembles Qvortrup's: It contains neither a child perspective nor children's perspectives as these terms are nominally conceptualized and defined in this book. Arguing that child perspectives are present in a macro-theory ultimately implies that any general theory concerning children, old or new, can be construed as a qualified child perspective. That would render the scope and logic of the concept so all-embracing that it would cease to be useful.

In the theory's micro-oriented approach to interpretive reproduction, children are portrayed as *actors* who *acquire, rediscover*, and *reproduce* everyday culture. They are also active as *negotiators* and *creators* of cultural routines that serve to reduce social ambiguity and increase predictability and security in everyday life. This is less true of the youngest infants, who according to Corsaro are not capable of active social participation. This lead him to invent his *"as-if" assumption*, meaning that adults in interactions with the baby pretend that the infant is actively socially competent, although this is not the case, according to the theory. This construction demonstrates that neither a child perspective nor children's perspectives are present in the case of the youngest infants. It can be concluded, too, that this approach is highly out of touch with recent research in developmental psychology.

As for the older preschoolers, who make up Corsaro's core research area, the theory applies the important notion of *children's interpretive reproduction*. This basic micro-sociological thesis produces a number of interesting theoretical (and empirical) details about children acting and interacting in peer groups. However, Corsaro's theoretical interpretations of the empirical findings do little to expand our understanding of a subject, which we interpret, reproduce, and create, not only culturally, but in personal perspectives as well. Corsaro's numerous observations of 5-year-olds actually have the potential to do this, but that would require a different approach including a more psychological analysis. Corsaro's interpretations of his observations of preschool peer groups in the USA and Italy often (but not always) reflect the adult's attempt at approaching and understanding children's utterances and actions in their social world by applying a theoretical perspective to these observations. Thus, the theory's micro-oriented approach does hold Examples of a child perspective, but these are not consistent because the theory paraphrases and interprets children's actual, subjective utterances and actions solely as *cultural* reproduction. A full-fledged child perspective requires, however, a conceptual explanation of the ways that children perceive themselves as active participants in cultural routines on the basis of *their personal* perceptions and *their personal* actions in social relationships. As we shall see in the following section, concepts from recent developmental psychology could help the micro-oriented childhood sociology go the last part of the way to include and explain in detail the subjects' own perceptions of their life-worlds.

Language plays a crucial role in Corsaro's theory, as a symbol system for encoding local and cultural structures. Language also creates social and *psychological realities*. But as we found the position of language in the theory offered no deeper explanation of what are "psychological realities". This interpretive childhood sociology stops short of an elaborate theoretical understanding of how subjects create and experience themselves and other people in negotiation and interpretation processes. It is therefore problematic to conclude that the *theoretical* part of this type of childhood sociology contributes to the understanding of children's own perspectives on their social worlds – i.e. children's perspectives. On the other hand, Corsaro's *empirical work* contains many case Examples reflecting children's points of view. And indeed, we have showed that Corsaro himself views the ethnographic, interpretive approach as a valid way of uncovering participants' points of view, although he applies a specific "filter" to the children's utterances and social communication and interprets their activity as solely cultural reproduction. With a more direct subject focus (and less emphasis on children only reproducing culture), however, many of his observations could be re-analysed as expressions of specific children's perspectives of their own social life and particular subject perception. (The observation "can you eat chips?" is just one Example of this.)

In line with the other childhood sociologists, Allison James, Chris Jenks, and Allan Prout view the child as a social actor and as a *being*, not as in traditional developmental psychology as a *becoming*. Their ambition to study *real children* and *the experience of being a child* clearly suggests both a child perspective and an interest in looking into children's perspectives. However, our search in the theoretical elaboration on these two basic concepts reveals that this is not the case. In using a Foucaultian lens "real children" are reduced to a sociological abstraction, living, like adults, within society's more or less hidden power structures. Similarly, "the experience of being a child" is converted to a general analysis and critique of society, but far removed from children as subjects. In fact children's "experiences" are constructed precisely as if they were human adults living in the modern world. Replacing "child/children" with "adult/adults", or vice versa, does not alter this type of analysis in the least.

However, childhood is also viewed as a *subjective space* that involves the notions of *the inner psychological space* of the self and the construction of *subject identities*. Thus, children's subjective world is declared as important, but with little substance, it seemingly has the function as serving as an empty-Box to be filled with sociological-societal content. But James, Jenks, and Prout (and Corsaro) have proposed promising basic theses concerning children's subject, self, psychological realities, and language that suggest a possible integration with recent research in developmental psychology. This possibility will be explored further in the last section of Part I.

So far, our search for actual child perspectives and children's perspectives – as the concepts were defined in the Introduction of this book – has yielded little when it comes to the *theoretical approaches* to children in the sociologies of childhood presented. We did conclude, however, that a child perspective may be derived from some arguments concerning the ethnographic, interpretive approach. Thus, fieldwork may direct adults' attention towards a deeper understanding of children's experiences, perceptions, and actions. For Example, adults should be hesitant not to bring pre-conceived notions of children into their fieldwork and they should be sensitive towards children's utterances in the interpretation process. However, there is a duality and ambiguity here, because when children are constructed through generalized sociological theory — for Example concerning the study of "real children", "the experience of being a child", or explaining children's lives in school and society — the methodological-driven sensitivity to take a child perspective and children's perspectives evaporates.

Therefore, the result of our search for possible child perspectives and children's perspectives in these particular childhood sociological positions is this: If we are dealing with the theoretical positions per se, the answer is predominantly negative. If, however, we are talking about some articulated rationales behind the empirical approach used, and the character and content of empirical findingsbecomes more affirmative.

In Search of Child Perspectives and Children's Perspectives in Contextual–Relational Developmental Psychology

This section will discuss selected aspects of recent developmental psychology in our search for child perspectives and children's perspectives. Can contextual-relational developmental psychology contribute to a theoretically founded child perspective and deepen our understanding of children's own perspectives of their world?

A Child Perspective in Developmental Psychology?

Current developmental psychology encompasses all human life stages, cf. Lifespan Development (Berk, 2006b). The discourse in contemporary developmental psychology expresses a multitude of theoretical and an empirical approach to the study of children and the paradigm of the grand developmental theories is history. In fact the grand developmental unifying theory does not exist, which has been the situation for decades. The present situation reveals *developmental psychologies* consisting of various "domain-specific" research activities with a strong tendency towards empirical studies and theory building based upon an empirical basis (Sommer, 2005a). In fact just recently a unifying meta-theoretical approach has been suggested in the form of a contextual dynamic systems approach (Witherington, 2007).

However, developmental psychology still has a clear emphasis on children in the description and explanation of important milestone changes in emotions, cognition, and social relationships during childhood. This may perhaps give the impression that developmental psychology represents a specific child perspective. But is this in fact a prominent feature of mainstream developmental psychology, as it is represented in recent international standard texts?[1] Are concepts such as "child perspective", "children's perspectives", and "children's perceptions", for Example, frequent occurrences? Are children's own expressions presented when the discipline presents itself through generally acknowledged insights? Are child perspectives or similar terms evident in chapter headings or major section headings on important

---

[1] Mainstream textbooks present the essential and reliable knowledge available – "the state of the art".

D. Sommer et al., *Child Perspectives and Children's Perspectives in Theory and Practice*, International Perspectives on Early Childhood Education and Development 2, DOI 10.1007/978-90-481-3316-1_3, © Springer Science+Business Media B.V. 2010

professional topics, in fact Boxes or keyword indexes of recent textbooks? Is it possible to look up a specific nominal definition of child perspective? A careful survey of leading international standard textbooks and recent handbooks shows that this is not the case (see Berk, 2006a; Lerner, 2006; DeHart et al., 2000; Feldman, 2001; Hetherington & Parke, 1999).

In reviewing the knowledge base of this discipline, however, it seems to be much more *about* children and much less a specified scientific activity *involving* children.[2] Both current and earlier paradigms of developmental psychology tend to construct children in objectified form through adult and scientifically reflected terms. Children are rarely presented as subjects with a focus on their direct experiences of the world.[3] Still, a phenomenological (subject) focus is more or less implicitly understood (when relevant), even if it is not evident in the presentation.

So, it will be rather problematic to claim that mainstream developmental psychology expresses an explicit child perspective just because it deals with the investigations of children. It would, however, also be too hasty to conclude that (certain aspects of) recent developmental psychology does not represent one or more child perspectives. One may argue that a child perspective is present, albeit relatively implicit, and that one simply has to look for it.

Although mainstream developmental psychology textbooks do rarely express a "child perspective" as a key term or discuss the term in any length, one may argue that since the main focus of developmental psychology is children, it does contain perspectives on children. But this would imply that most classical and modern approaches are legitimized as (different) perspectives of children. For Example, Piaget wrote about children throughout his professional life, in the beginning rather close to a child perspective, but later applying a highly abstract structuralist stage-bound approach to children's development. Freud preferred not to deal with children, but he does offer a psychosexual stage theory – derived from therapy with adults – that addresses allegedly universal stages in children's development. According to this line of (problematic) reasoning, children are seen in different "perspectives", not only by Piaget and Freud but also by any other child theory and empirical child study. In this very broad and inclusive view, the entire childhood period becomes synonymous with a child perspective – regardless of the position of this approach in relation to the child (i.e. the child psychology domain of lifespan developmental psychology = a child perspective).

Despite key difference, this bears striking resemblance to the presentation of theories in the sociology of childhood as child perspectives (e.g. Qvortrup, 1994b). Here, children are embedded in a structural category based on age (0–18 years) and social position. Childhood has its own structural features compared to adulthood.

---

[2] The point of view changes considerably depending on whether the talk is of a perspective *on* children or *with* children.

[3] Later in this part we will provide specific Examples of recent key concepts in developmental psychology that have introduced a completely new paradigm of children and their development. However, it still remains an open question whether and when such concepts may be referred to as actual child perspectives. Whether this is a case or not will be pursued later on.

Despite the differences between psychology and sociology, in both cases an entire discipline can be claimed as constituting a child perspective. The same can be said of the distinction between adult culture and child culture (Juncker, 2006). The child culture angle, then, is the perspective that deals with children, for Example, their play behaviour. Within a theoretical framework, this reasoning may be plausible and reasonable, but not in comparison with a nominal definition of a child perspective and children's perspectives.

The broad and inclusive application of the child perspective that is outlined above resembles the commonsense everyday understanding presented in the Introduction. The common feature is this: If an adult makes any statement about children, this will be sufficient for claiming a child perspective. That is not satisfactory, however. The issue here is not the scientific content of various theoretical perspectives, but the logical and conceptual status of the term "child perspective". The justification of a conceptual construct is weakened if it can be readily replaced with or is synonymous with any given child discipline. As a consequence one may refer anyone interested in a child perspective to the child domain of psychology, i.e. the "department" of classical and modern developmental psychology, or to sociology's "department" of childhood, or to the child culture niche within cultural studies. Undoubtedly, these areas offer important insights about children − but is that the criterion for a child perspective? Someone interested in learning about child perspectives may expect a more specific content definition of the concept.

The Child Paradigm in Contextual–Relational Developmental Psychology

Basic views of the child in modern developmental psychology are close to approaches in both the interpretive approach (see Part II) and developmental education (see Part III). In all three approaches the child is generally perceived as active and sense making, and the focus is on the child's tangible life world and phenomenology. This is considered an actual child perspective in education, partly because the child's own experiences and perceptions form the essential basis of learning (Johansson & Pramling Samuelson, 2003). This resonates well with the shift in paradigm − the so-called new view of the child in developmental psychology[4] (Sommer, 2005a). Thus, psychology's new perspective of the child may contribute to the ECE-learning approach. This new view of the child in developmental psychology may perhaps lead to a specific inclusion of child perspectives. Or may it? Let us take a closer look with a focus on

---

[4] Please note that this "new" change in research was developed in the 1970s and 1980s. The same argument goes for the "new" child paradigm within childhood sociology that took place back in the 1990s. Anyway, the term "new" has obviously come to stay. For childhood sociologists, anthropologists, historians, and others *outside psychology* the paradigm shift within developmental psychology may represent new knowledge.

recent infant research. This research has been chosen for two reasons: (1) it has revolutionized the understanding of human nature and (2) it is in the non-verbal period of human life that the notion of the phenomenological child perspective can be tested.

During the past 25 years or so, a growing amount of documentation has shown that children are more competent in many developmental domains than previously assumed (Sommer, 2005a; Stern, 2004). A child is not born as a *tabula rasa* as proposed by classical behaviourism or as in Mahler's psychoanalysis equipped with a *stimulus barrier* that isolates and protects the infant psychologically from the environment – metaphorically speaking as a chicken in the egg. Instead, the child arrives prepared for active communication and social participation. A key aspect of this new view is the theory about the child's primary and secondary *intersubjectivity* (Trevarthen, 1998). Similarly, Reddy et al. (1997) review the research behind the groundbreaking notion of man's inherent communicative capacities in their theory of mutually regulating minds. This basic research holds important implications for philosophy, psychology, cultural studies, and education. Trevarthen (1998) describes the groundbreaking perspective of the child:

> ... the image of the biological newborn needing 'socialisation' to become a person does not apply when attention turns to evidence for complex psychological expressions in the responses of contented healthy newborns to people who take them as persons with intentions and feelings of companionship, and who feel pleasure when an infant responds. (Trevarthen, 1998, p. 16)

The infant's innate communicative competences are built into the human brain from birth, but they continue to develop and be refined throughout life (Aitken & Trevarthen, 1997). This theory is not just a fabrication; it is based on in-depth studies and observations of timing and turn taking in adult–infant interactions and studies of joint attention and social referencing. These studies support the view that the infant comes equipped with a certain attitude and perspective towards the environment: "A *taking into account* of the other by the infant" (Meltzoff & Moore, 1998, p. 48). This marked a crucial step away from Piaget's influential view of the newborn child as "solipsist". Piaget believed that the newborn infant possesses no inner urges or capacities for social dialogue. Furthermore, classical Freudian and Behaviorist theories have been left since recent research has undermined those points of views (Berk, 2006a).

The Phenomenology of Contextualism

Research contributions to the new view of the child by no means come only from one theoretical framework. During the past 25 years, however, the contextualist approach has gained influence within developmental psychology. The basic research that led to the new perspective on children can in fact be traced to a contextualist approach to development (see Sommer, 2005a, 2005b). But can contextualism be considered a new child perspective? If so, and in what way, then? Here, it should be noted that contextualism represents neither a new "grand theory" nor a single specific theory. Instead it consists of a number of relatively loosely related professional perspectives with the common belief that psychological phenomena must be embedded in time and space (see, e.g. different versions: Bronfenbrenner, 1979; Fogel, 1993; Witherington, 2007). Bronfenbrenner (1979) was a pioneer who had substantial influence on developmental psychology with his ecological model of the individual's nestedness in micro-, meso-, exo-, and macro-systems. This may give the impression that he deemphasizes the child's inner phenomenological world. The objective system-theoretical aspects have, indeed, been dominant in the presentation of the theory in mainstream developmental psychology, at the cost of subject phenomenology (e.g. by Berk, 2006a), but without subjective experiences, contextualism loses its theoretical validity. And Bronfenbrenner has in fact emphasized the subject perspective on several occasions, for Example, in defining *ecological validity*:

> Ecological validity refers to the extent to which the environment experienced by the subjects in a scientific investigation has the properties it is supposed or assumed to have by the investigator. (Bronfenbrenner, 1979, p. 29)

This phenomenological criterion is important for our attempts to pursue and specify a child perspective. It is a crucial feature of the contextualist approach, which does not isolate the subject from his or her "nested" environment. It takes more than that; however, an attempt must be made to achieve correspondence between the child's experience of his or her situation and the adult's understanding of it (Krøjgaard, 2001[5]). The infant's experience is distinctly different from that of the adult. But as far as possible, they should have a "shared" understanding of the given situation. The adult is responsible for approaching and taking the infant's perspective to ensure this correspondence. The younger the child, the more difficult it will be to live up to this requirement of approaching the child's perspective. But this challenge does not make the requirement any less essential.

Bronfenbrenner (1979) refers in the quote above to the experimental situation and its properties and the requirements it places on researchers in terms of understanding and adapting to the test person as a subject. But the argument goes far beyond the scientific context, however. For Example, Stern (1985) emphasizes the same point with his notion of "affective attunement", which takes place in everyday relations: The emotional correspondence between infant and adult "tells" both of them something about the other. The infant senses the adult's perspective and the adult understands the infant's perspective. This provides a promising basis for an actual psychological understanding of a child perspective. Therefore, let us now address the following question: What constitutes an actual psychological child perspective?

---

[5] Krøjgaard uses this Example in his Discussion of ecological validity in relation to experimental infant research. Here, it is used in a different context: in a Discussion of the criteria for identifying a child perspective in contextual developmental psychology.

A Psychological Child Perspective – Criteria and Challenges

It is difficult to offer a conclusive answer to the question above, but the particular view of human nature inherent in psychology may offer a good point of departure. Psychology is devoted to the study of the mind and addresses human experiences and actions in environments. Notions, perceptions, thinking, memory, intention, emotion, motivation constitute the core subject of the discipline, although various psychological disciplines differ in research. Thus, a psychological child perspective will specifically address one or more aspects of the subject's experiential world, including the way it is construed in behaviour and actions. This phenomenological criterion distinguishes a psychological approach to the study of the child from a sociological one, where children are reduced to social categories, mainly without personal experience, feelings, and thinking (although as shown previously some concepts hint at psychological phenomena and concepts). Hence, a sociological approach to children could be referred to as a "childhood perspective", while a psychological, phenomenological approach may be called a "child perspective". That may be evident in an interpretive attempt to understand the child's inner world and/or in research that makes a direct attempt to express the child's experiential world. This means that external behavioural descriptions are only meaningful if they are part of an attempt to understand subjects and their mutual relationships. We may now conclude the following:

- In a psychological child perspective, a *phenomenological criterion* is essential.
- Another key requirement is *coordination* between childrens' and adults' perspectives.
- The *responsibility* for ensuring this correspondence rests mainly on the adult.

But these requirements alone are not sufficient, partly (but not exclusively) because they fail to address the link between the child's inner experiential world and the conversion of these experiences to actions. This connection therefore has to be added: Children express themselves (and their selves) through social practices, and this enables them to grasp other people's intentions and share experiences with them. Adults and other children attribute intentions and agency to the children, which enables them to understand the meaning of their actions. But what is meant by children's "intentions" and how are these "converted" into actions? Intentions are to be defined as specific goals, objectives, and purposes. Intentions and purposes can be observed through frequently occurring social practices – realized through action as endeavours. An intention is not immediately visible to an observer, as it is an inner, psychological urge – a purpose, a goal. In social practice, however, intentions are made visible as purposes in social interactions, i.e. as endeavours. In their interactions with others, children constantly propose suggestions, desires, ideas, and goals. Thus, intentions are expressed in social practices and can be inferred from them, but it's a twofold process because experience in social practice also gives rise to intentions.

Meltzoff and Moore (1998) argue convincingly for the empirical evidence behind the revolutionizing idea of man's inherent intersubjectivity and intentionality. The paradigm of children as active, intentional subjects has crucial impact on descriptions of observed behaviour. In this connection, they point to the key influence of a given scientific perspective on the way that human "movements" are described. Kate sits at a table with a cup in front of her. Now, the following happens:

> 1: Kate's hand touches the cup and the cup falls over.
> OR
> 2: Kate attempts to pick up the cup, but accidentally drops it.

Here, the "same" behaviour is filtered in two essentially different ways. Example 1 is a pure, objectified (physical) description of behaviour. The child carries out a movement ("touches"), which causes the object to move ("falls over"). Example 2 describes the time–space sequence as an intentional act ("attempts"), and here, the toppled cup is not merely the result of a physical causal movement but rather the consequence of an unintentional act ("accidentally"). In our search for a child perspective in child psychology, not the first, but the second Example meets both the basic phenomenological criterion and the criteria of intentionality and agency. According to Meltzoff and Moore (1998), Kate's relationship to the cup is based on a fundamental view of the child that characterizes recent developmental psychology: "Evidently, infants are not behaviourists" (p. 52). Even young infants can discriminate between dead objects and living humans, and they expect different relationships with them.

Although it may seem that we are steps closer to capture a child perspective and children's perspectives in psychology there are more steps to be taken. For Example, it is not sufficient pursuing valid information about a child's actual experience by declaring a paradigm that celebrates children's phenomenology, agency, and intentionality. Gaining actual, truthful insight into children's actual experiences of themselves and others, either through direct everyday interaction or by empirical research studies, poses a very different set of challenges. For decades, Stern (2000) has done both empirical and theoretical research into infants' understanding of the relationship between self and other. He presented his theory on this relationship in his milestone work *The Interpersonal World of the Infant*. Here, Stern expresses the attempts of developmental psychology to carry out research to understand the world from the subject's point of view and points out the main inherent difficulties:

> The problem of how we can know the nature of the infant's subjective experience is always lurking in 'The Interpersonal World of the Infant'. Of course we can't know it. And even with the onset of speech, any close mapping of narration to experience is uncertain and fraught with difficulties. (p. xxxiv)

This quote may serve as a constant Warning when a true child perspective from developmental psychology stems from.[6] Research into a child perspective – in the

---

[6] This sort of critical examination should not only apply to developmental psychology but also to any discipline that claims to be a child perspective.

sense of getting as close as possible to children's own psychological processing and understanding of their world – is fraught with methodologial problems. Interviews and direct observation of behaviour and actions are always subject to an interpretive adult perspective, despite the best attempts at maintaining data authenticity: We have to arrange the observational material, not only in the subsequent analysis but even during the initial registration phase (Kvale, 1996). Furthermore it is not possible to record all the events that are part of a social situation in one go. The observer also has to attribute meaning and direction to children's actions and statements by categorizing behaviour into patterns to make children's utterances appear coherent and meaningful. Besides, children are not understood solely as themselves but through a given perspective and/or theory.[7] Nothing is wrong with this, provided there is a professional reflection and acknowledgement of these constraints. If not, a child perspective risks being little more than clichés about "seeing the child through the child's own eyes" as paraphrased by Reimer et al. (2000).

The Pre-verbal Child's Intersubjective World – An Empirical Example

Let us now take a closer look at the possibilities and challenges facing adults as they seek to assume and understand the infant's perspective through empirical studies. Observation of children is a key element in psychological research attempting to achieve a "reality-based" understanding of children's experiential world. The contextualist perspective states, as do Bruner and Haste (1987), that subjects have intentions. One may ask and learn about these intentions, provided the child has developed sufficient language skills. But, as mentioned, intentions are also externalized as endeavours, and these can be observed as meaningful acts. Thus, observations (and/or conversations, once the child has acquired speech) may in principle give the well-prepared adult phenomenological information that corresponds with the child's perspective – thus, according to the psychological definition one may approximate an actual child perspective. But naturalistic observation, too, is selective and subject to adult interpretation. Let us examine this challenge through a selected prototypical Example from observation research with infants. How can we learn about the infant, the pre-verbal child's experience, and perception of his or her environment? How do we know that 2-month-old children perceive themselves and others in systematic ways?

This groundbreaking experiment (described in Murray & Trevarthen, 1985) took place in the infant's home, that is, in familiar surroundings. The mother was asked to interact with her child as she normally would. The sequences were as follows:

---

[7] People construct configurations out of what they perceive, even of phenomena that are unrelated. We "see" the constellation the Big Dipper, even though we know that the seven points that form the constellation are millions of kilometres apart in three-dimensional space. In fact, the seven stars are no more related to each other than to any other stars in the sky.

1. *Initial phase:* Typical mother–infant interaction.
2. *Interruption:* After thirties, the mother's interaction with the child was disrupted for thirties as the researcher came into the room and asked her a couple of questions. The mother turned her face away from the child and looked back over her shoulder.
3. *Blank-face:* After a renewed period of normal mother–infant interaction the mother was asked by the researcher to be non-responsive for forty five seconds. During this period, she displayed neither positive nor negative facial expressions.
4. *Final phase:* Normal mother–infant interaction was resumed.

A film recording began as soon as the initial normal interaction between mother and infant was established. The recording lasted for 3 min and included the brief episodes described above. This made it possible to study whether the child's changing facial expressions[8] and body movements were in any way synchronized with the mother's acts and her emotional expressions. Separate analyses of the film recordings were then carried out, and independent observers scored the child's social–emotional reactions: direction of regard, communication, positive/negative affect, activity level. All these categories were operationalized to describe the child's specific behaviour. For Example, positive affect was recorded when the following four types of behaviours occurred in the child: (1) open palm, (2) raised eyebrows, (3) relaxed eyebrows, and (4) smile. There were distinct, non-random differences in the infant's attention direction and positive/negative affects in the normal situation versus the blank-face situation. Analyses of the infant's behaviour patterns in the blank-face situation also revealed that the infant displayed frequent arm movements and other communicative acts in the beginning of the episode, while he or she looked at the non-responsive mother. But with time the infant began to look away, frown, and showed signs of negative affect. Murray and Trevarthen (1985) offer the following interpretation:

> ... the patterning and organization of acts in the blank-face condition gave an impression of solicitation or effort oriented to the mother to reinstate mutually responsive interaction...
> (p. 191)

Note the phrase "gave an impression of", which implies an interpretation of the infant's intentions. This is probably as close to the infant's inner world as adults can get. This interpretation seems very convincing, however, since the study is able to trace the infant's finely attuned acts, reactions, and initiatives in relation to the mother second by second.[9] To support their interpretation, Murray and Trevarthen

---

[8] One premise underlying this research was that the face is more than a "social medium". The face also directly reflects the infant's inner emotional states. Thus, long before children are able to express their feelings verbally, their facial expressions (and accompanying gestures) mirror their phenomenological constitution.

[9] A reminder from the earlier Discussion: Intentions turn into endeavours, and this makes it possible to observe the infant's inner states. These chronological interaction sequences therefore enable us to observe how the infant's intentions are converted to acts within the social context.

(1985) compare their findings with studies of infants of depressed mothers. These infants' facial expressions and body language bear a striking resemblance to the behaviour of the infants in the blank-face situation. Based on this study, Murray and Trevarthen (1985) draw a number of far-reaching Conclusions about infants' competences.

- *Intersubjectivity*: Humans are capable of social reciprocity at a very early stage in life, as mother and infant interact to "share" their subjective worlds with one another.
- *Agency*: At a very early stage, humans attempts to affect the interaction partner.
- *Mental organization*: At an extremely early ontogenetic stage, human mentality represents phenomenological structure and process. Infants remember, expect, recognize, and enjoy typical everyday interactions.

Altogether, emotions and gestures appear to make up a powerful "first language", and non-verbal humans use this language effectively to communicate their inner states to other people, converting their intentions into endeavours.

Conclusion and Closing Reflections

Revolutionizing ideas concerning the competent child stem from a number of observation studies of infants, with the blank-face study as only one among many. Thus, fundamental concepts about inherent human characteristics – for example "intentionality", "curiosity motivation", "agency", and "socio-emotional competence" – were not handed down from above as a new "grand theory". Instead, they are based on empirical evidence and there is a relatively high degree of consensus concerning the Conclusions (Sommer, 2005b). There may, however, be disagreement when a given set of findings is interpreted rather differently. In any given study it is the rule rather than the exception that there is room for a number of different logically consistent interpretations,[10] but often, controlled experiments can clarify which of two or more competing interpretations appears most convincing (Krøjgaard, 2001).

There is a limit to how different the interpretations of a given type of study can be, however. For Example, observations that demonstrate infants' early interest in objects are rarely disputed. Disagreement relates more to the age at which the infants grasp object permanence. Some believe it happens at the age of 2 months, while others argue that it is in place at a somewhat later ontogenetic stage. While there may be a room for disagreement, there are not an endless number of different interpretations about the way that infants experience and perceive their world, because of some "empirical resistance" against wild speculations. This is also true of the

---

[10] Infant research uses studies in natural situations as well as lab experiments. The contextual approach does not rule out lab studies per se. The criterion is rather whether or not the lab setting is "ecologically valid" (Bronfenbrenner, 1979). The lab offers a different type of physical and social setting for studying children and infants, which is different from the natural situation.

groundbreaking research concerning early human intersubjectivity. A condition for mastering intersubjectivity is that the infant has a feeling and a sense (rather than "cool cognition") of/about himself or herself and the other as subjects. In addition, the infant must be able to distinguish between animate and inanimate "objects" and treat them accordingly. But even when Conclusions are based on observations of infants' external behaviour, the goal is to maintain a phenomenological child perspective as, for Example, in Meltzoff and Moore's (1998) attempt to understand the ontogenetic sources of intersubjectivity. They acknowledge how difficult it is to understand the children's perspective:

> In investigating the origins of intersubjectivity one is immediately confronted with the question of how to 'ask' infants whether they read below surface behavior into the minds and hearts of others. This seems a difficult question to pose without language, because all we can do is show the infants' behavior and measure their behavioral (or physiological) responses. (Meltzoff & Moore, 1998, p. 50)

Note the phrase "how to ask". This is impossible for the adult, because the subjects are non-verbal infants. Hence, "asking" has to be construed in another sense, that is, as a given empirical method, for Example, the blank-face Procedure. Here, the researcher "asks" the infant by observing him or her in a situation where various incidents happen both spontaneously and by arrangement.

The typical interaction – the one that the infant expects – forms the basic motif. This is then altered experimentally, and something happens that the infant did not expect. The non-verbal infant's "reply" is derived through the careful observation and analysis of systematic changes in the infants' responses. This is then presented as systematic research findings and interpretations. This is not identical with the infant's actual experience, but it is probably the closest an adult can get to the experiential universe of the non-verbal infant.[11] With this reservation in mind, we may now conclude as follows: The previously stated *phenomenological criterion* for qualifying the psychological child perspective is not fully met in the study of these very young infants. It is, however, possible to approach the infant's inner world through empirical studies where the risk of adult projections on the infant is minimized.[12] The second principle, the *requirement of correspondence* between infant and adult, can also only be an approximation with subjects this young, but one should attempt to meet this requirement.

Developmental psychology at large should not be considered an explicit child perspective. The concept of a child perspective is simply not on the agenda; therefore, it is absent in recent international "state-of-the-art" textbooks. Furthermore, it

---

[11] In *Diary of a Baby* Stern (1991) avoids scientific jargon. The book is a wonderful, poetic attempt at describing an actual infant's experience of himself or herself and the environment.

[12] Infancy is particularly prone to be a projection mirror. One Example among many is the psychoanalyst Mahler's (1988) theory of the existence of a "normal autistic" phase early in human life. This notion has been swept away by current empirical research and should be seen as a theoretical projection on the infant (Sommer, 2005a). Indeed, Mahler had no systematic empirical findings from earliest infancy to support her assumption. Careful studies of infants and children do not eliminate the danger of theoretical projection, but they are able to reduce it.

is unsatisfactory to consider developmental psychologists' interest in children as a reflection of a child perspective, as this would mean that practically all theories and research concerning children in the diverse history of developmental psychology could be coined as child perspectives. Such a broad definition of child perspective would render it meaningless, as it will cease to be a specific and useful professional concept. Deriving a child perspective from developmental psychology is therefore not the obvious thing to do. Nevertheless, contextualism and the research that led to the so-called new view of the child do offer some basic scientific terms that may suggest the outline of a research-based child perspective.

A mundane, commonsense child perspective is not a sufficient basis for professionals. A professional-based view of children may act as a "meaning interpretive filter" as adults observe and assess the ways children's intentions are reflected in their actions. Psychology has much to offer education with its well-documented new view of the child, but psychology does not constitute an explicit child perspective. As we have demonstrated, such a perspective has to be deduced. It has been pointed out that there are inherent possibilities, but also major limitations in grasping non-verbal humans' experiences of themselves and their world. Nevertheless, we should strive for an approximation. In that respect, a well-reflected child perspective based on the new view of the child may prove helpful.

Childhood Sociology and Contextual–Relational Psychology – Common Platforms for a Child Perspective?

This section will discuss some possibilities for integrating key child perspective concepts from the sociology of childhood with certain elements of the new type of developmental psychology that arose after the breakdown of the grand developmental narratives. How is it possible to establish common professional platforms in order to construct an integration? We have stated repeatedly that the positions presented that make up the sociologies of childhood have not only many key features in common, but also important differences. However, modern developmental psychology is characterized by internal disputes to a much higher degree, because the discipline has grown in scope, added a multitude of new dimensions, and appears rather fragmented. Therefore, it does not make any sense to compare childhood sociology and developmental psychology as two clear-cut monoliths. Instead, we should select those concepts from recent developmental psychology and childhood sociology, respectively, that hold integrative potential of particular relevance for child perspectives and children's perspectives. In order to determine whether an integrative child perspective is even possible, however, first some fundamental concepts are examined, although they may not address a child perspective or children's perspectives per se[1] – just to name a few: the view of children as actors and the self presented as an inner psychological space. We will examine and assess the relevance and consequences of these concepts for a potential child perspective.

This section first briefly points out what the sociology of childhood has to offer developmental psychology – and vice versa. The next point will be to identify promising common conceptual platforms for a child perspective. Each section opens with an excerpt of the specific statements in various positions within the sociology of childhood that may promote integration. Next, similar concepts and theoretical elements from recent developmental psychology are presented and discussed, and we will discuss prerequisites for the establishment of a child perspective. The structure will be as follows: First, we discuss the paradigm of "children as intentional sense-making actors" as a potential common platform. Then follows a Discussion

---

[1] Once again, this brings up an earlier raised issue. Neither childhood sociology nor modern developmental psychology has presented directly applicable child perspectives. These can only be derived through careful analysis.

D. Sommer et al., *Child Perspectives and Children's Perspectives in Theory and Practice*, International Perspectives on Early Childhood Education and Development 2, DOI 10.1007/978-90-481-3316-1_4, © Springer Science+Business Media B.V. 2010

of the "self as an inner psychological space". In closing, we look at future possibilities for integration. But before that we will seek to answer: What challenges is raised by childhood sociology for developmental psychology – and vice versa?

Challenges Raised by Childhood Sociology for Developmental Psychology – and Vice Versa

Childhood sociologists had no use for the de-contextualized child from classical child psychology and developmental psychology. As late as the 1990s, the model of "the developing child" in developmental psychology was pointed out as in absolute opposition to the "new" sociological paradigm of childhood that was

> ... in part a response to the overwhelming dominance of the model of "the developing child" in which children's incompetence is assumed, research within this tradition begins from an understanding of the child as socially able. (James et al., 1998, p. 180)

Anyone, however, with a minimum of insight into developmental psychology research at that time will recognize the misleading argument quoted above. At the time, developmental psychologists had spent more than 20 years building a thorough and detailed empirical and theoretical foundations where the child was viewed as a highly socially able and active being (Sommer, 2005a).[2] This new insight has made developmental psychology a potential integration partner. But despite the current accessibility of this groundbreaking knowledge, Qvortrup (2002) and James et al. (1998) still claim that the new sociology of childhood springs, to a large extent, from dissatisfaction with the concept of the universal child in developmental psychology.

To support the childhood sociologists' new self-image as "the good guys", the bearers of the classical developmental theories were portrayed as "the bad guys". In his review of childhood sociology, Kampmann (2003) characterizes the situation as follows:

> It was important from the outset to posit precise and effective arguments that portrayed the contributions from the sociology of childhood as different from the approaches that had dominated the area until then, based on the vocabulary of developmental psychology. This undoubtedly led to a new form of dichotomist thinking. (p. 79)

This dichotomist view undermines the possibility of exploring potential interdisciplinary inspiration from more recent developmental psychology. The childhood sociologists' bold challenge to developmental psychology resembles Don Quixote's fight against imaginary enemies. As we shall soon see, there are important points of paradigmatic agreement between (some aspects of) psychology's and (some aspects of) childhood sociology's new child paradigm, for example children as actors in

---

[2] In the beginning, this research did not enjoy much attention outside the closed circuit of the research communities. But the situation was very different when childhood sociologists launched their theories as the antithesis to the model of the incompetent child – a paradigm that a growing number of developmental psychologists had long discarded.

their own world. On the other hand, differences still remain. These differences and similarities have an impact on the contributions from each discipline in order to enhance our understanding of child perspectives and children's perspectives.

How may we characterize the period leading up to today, beginning with the shift in paradigm in the view of the child in various social sciences? What may the main future professional challenge be?

First Period: Parallel Processes of Redefining Childhood, Children, and Child

Some decades ago, new insights about children emerged in various social sciences and the humanities – with the child perspective more or less in focus. The so-called new views of the child were characterized by a pronounced critical stance towards preceding views, misconceptions, or the total absence of children within their own respective disciplines. In ethnography: the forgotten people (James et al., 1998), in feminism: an oppressed minority group (Alanen, 1988), in sociology: a neglected age group in society (Qvortrup, 1999). Another common characteristic was a rejection of the deterministic view of the socialization process in classical social psychology and sociology (Corsaro, 2005; James et al., 1998). During the same period (and even before), some psychologists heavily criticized developmental psychology's grand universal theories, and a new child paradigm emerged (Parke, 1989; Sommer, 2005a). These were important professional changes that took place within the framework of each respective discipline relatively isolated from other disciplines.[3] This relatively independent, parallel course of reinventing the child that took place in different disciplines at the same time probably stems from a complicated reciprocal exchange between innovation and changes in Zeitgeist in late modern society, culture, and science (Pramling Samuelsson & Asplund Carlsson, 2003). This first parallel phase can be characterized by its relatively high degree of theoretical purism and professional self-sufficiency.

Second Period: Integrative Redefinition of Childhood, Children, and Child

Perceptions of acceptable Procedures for knowledge production in late modernity have moved away from the classical-modern ideal of disciplinary monism towards a growing acceptance of the benefits offered by a multidisciplinary approach. One does not have to be a dyed-in-the-wool social constructivist to acknowledge that there may be more than one scientifically sound route to insight. Some strands (but not all) of psychology have now become open to multidisciplinary narratives

---

[3] It shall be pointed out, however, that some childhood sociologists had links to ethnography from the outset. This is evident, for Example, in their use of the ethnographic, interpretive approach.

(Jørgensen, 2002). Studies of whether theories can be fully or partially combined (with due consideration for their unique properties) have become less controversial, and "creative theoretical kleptomania" may open doors to new interdisciplinary studies of child perspectives and children's perspectives. One Example that this integrative tendency is both desirable and possible is the stated goal of the Nordic conference *Børn og kultur – i teori og metode* (Children and culture – in theory and method):

> ... the idea behind the conference was to bring together and foster dialog among Nordic researchers across disciplines. (BIN Norden, conference invitation, April 2005)

But changes towards an interdisciplinary approach require serious professional redefinition, not least from the sociology of childhood, which has positioned itself in a counter-position to developmental psychology. Thus, a main goal with this section is to suggest and start the implementation of an integrative redefinition of children with a focus on child perspectives and children's perspectives.

Phase two, then, will hopefully in the future be characterized by the examination of promising similarities between fundamental child perceptions shared by contemporary psychology and sociology with the overriding goal of looking for possible common platforms for integration. The tradition within the respective disciplines to work in parallel on their own insights should be supplanted with more interdisciplinary synthesis and integration.

Like other childhood sociologists, James and Prout (1990) reject the grand theories of classical developmental psychology. Still, they leave a door open for psychological approaches that include an interpretive perspective, which study children in their historical and cultural contexts (see Part II in this book). They mention explicitly that voices of doubt within psychology were heard as early as the late 1960s, for Example in the English psychologist Richard's radical criticism of "naturalism" in psychology, with its universal regularities claimed to exist in all societies and throughout human (pre)history. Here, childhood sociologists declare a willingness to include insights from psychology. Unfortunately, however, James and Prout's proposal ends here, and the future of any further integrative research activities remains wide open.[4]

But what does (childhood) sociology have to offer psychology, and what does (developmental) psychology have to offer sociology? Let us briefly consider this in a larger perspective. The notion of an individual that can be studied independently of society and culture has rendered obsolete, and childhood sociology is able to offer child psychology a much broader view of children's everyday, cultural, and societal existence. Sociology can provide important knowledge about the huge social and cultural variations in children's living conditions. Thus, sociology raises essential doubts about the universality of development, which developmental psychologists have taken (and some continue to take) for granted. Still, the child in sociology remains an abstraction; in a sociological optic, children – even as actors

---

[4] To our knowledge, the sociology of childhood has made no further overtures to developmental psychology since then.

– become generalized "bearers", "producers", and "reproducers" of social, societal, and cultural categories. In fact the consequence is "that the child is thrown out with the bathwater" (Warming, 2007). There is a modest interest in the variation in children's responses, perceptions, and experiences within the "same" macro- or micro-cultural context. As argued earlier, psychological phenomena are more or less implicitly *assumed*, as reflected in the conceptual vocabulary of childhood sociology. But the mind is perceived from an "outside" point of view, reflected in what children *do* in interactions with their environment. This ignores *what children are* in the phenomenological dimension. Sociology offers a detailed explanation of the "conditions" of children's actions, while psychology offers more sophisticated and precise explanations of the ways that children orient themselves in relation to society. Individuals experience and act differently, even when the social and cultural conditions appear to be identical. Thus, there are substantial and important differences in the ways that sociology and psychology approach children. Still, the "common object" is the child, children, and childhood. If we accept that no single discipline has access to the full knowledge of its object-of-study, it may be more promising to move the spotlight from differences and instead turn it to potential similarities or complementary dimensions. In line with that we will in the following start to identify specific and promising common child perspective conceptual platforms.

Children as Intentional, Meaning-Making Actors

First, a brief summary of some specific statements from childhood sociologists that suggest a promising common interdisciplinary platform for child perspectives: In the chapter "In the search for child perspectives and children's perspectives in childhood sociology", these key common features were localized in the three presented positions: Children are *actors in their own and society's development* and they are *co-constructors*, not passive objects of adult and institutional socialization (Qvortrup, 2002). Corsaro (2005) also considers the concept of the active child as a cornerstone in his theory: Children *acquire, rediscover, negotiate, share, create,* and *reproduce* culture.[5] According to James et al. (1998) children are described as *social actors in their own right*, involved in their *own construction*, and *possessing agency*, which in the theory is attributed to the subjects' own volition.[6] This is highly similar to other social science disciplines paradigmatic views of the child, for Example interpretive and socio-cultural approaches (Hundeide, 2003a) (see Part II)

---

[5] With Corsaro, we saw, however, that this is not the case in the early stages of ontogenesis. Here, according to Corsaro, parents must pretend "as if" it is the case in order to initiate the activity. The questionable nature of this thesis was pointed out in the Corsaro section.

[6] Qvortrup's "by-choice" phrase also suggests this latter point, i.e. that children have real choices in childhood. Accepting a "choice" presupposes volition, and that brings us close to the Discussion about the more or less free will of the individual. However, this is not addressed in Qvortrup's theory.

and Pramling Samuelsson and Asplund Carlsson's (2003) theory of developmental pedagogy (see Part III). The same fundamental child conceptions lie behind a contextual–relational developmental psychology position as well (Sommer, 2005c, 2007). Here, we glimpse the beginnings of a common interdisciplinary platform for a child perspective, where – as we are about to see – selected elements of recent developmental psychology have contributions to make. However, the establishment of a child perspective presupposes the acknowledgement of the following requirement: The agency perspective has to support the interpretation of children's social acts so it enhances adults' understanding of children's perceptions and experiences in their life-world. Thus, it is not sufficient to sTipulate children as active creators of mini-cultural meaning if their actions are not associated with *their construction of meaning and their intentions* with the interaction. However, we searched in vain within childhood sociology for phenomenological-focused Discussions explaining how children are capable of being their own developmental actors. Nevertheless, the agency perspective offers a promising platform for an emergent interdisciplinary dialogue with selected elements within modern developmental psychology. Thus, the purpose of this section is to pursue this track further, but difficulties should be expected.[7]

The heading of this section introduces three key terms that characterize children: They are *intentional, meaning-making actors*. We will now take a closer look at these basic concepts. How should they be understood? What is their mutual relationship? In what way do they characterize child perspectives and/or children's perspectives?

Intentions represent inner urges (desires and assumptions), while *intentional acts* refer to purposeful activities with a goal that is either in the future or here and now. Thus, intentions are essentially phenomenological of nature (the inside of the mind), but they are often materialized in behaviour, affecting other people, affected by them, and adjusted to other people's intentional acting.[8] Intentions act as a kind of engine that drives and targets acts in social contexts, but children cannot function in attunement with other people without continuously realistically decoding their motives and intentions (Stern, 2004). To pursue intentions effectively, a child has to be able to act in social-regulated ways in everyday life relationships involving many different people. This requires that children develop a "theory" that humans possess *mental states*.[9] But in their understanding of social practices, micro-oriented childhood sociologists do not refer to intentionality and specific mental states.

---

[7] These difficulties do not just stem from the different views of the child perspective in sociology and psychology, they are also present for Example in research concerning child culture. Tufte et al. (2001) acknowledge that there is no common understanding of the concept of child culture. They suggest that the agency perspective might offer a potential common platform, but this interesting idea is not pursued further. We will attempt to do that in this section.

[8] It is important to note that intentions often "start" from the outside derived from an interpersonal process and then within the child as an intra-psychological category that might both drive and direct new behaviour.

[9] Age differences in the development of intentionality are not addressed here; see Krøjgaard (2002).

However, children's active expression of intentions and purposes and their under-standing of other's as intentional beings with minds constitute the foundations for all types of human social communication. If children, engaged in Corsaro's "cul-tural reproduction", are unable to understand and interpret other's intentions and read their minds, they will act outside the realm of humankind. Any socially coordi-nated activity requires an ability to *mind-read* — to understand the communicative intentions of other's. The gradual development of children's understanding of their own and others' intentions has been researched within *Theory of Mind* (TOM) – a rapidly expanding domain-specific topic within social cognition (Harris, 2006). But in relation to a childhood-in-context approach, a problem with TOM research is its character of de-contextualized basic research. Nevertheless, it may prove use-ful, lifted into social and cultural theory embedding the essential insights from this research agenda in a type of contextualized theory that is close to micro-oriented sociology of childhood. However, this integrative work has to be done in the future.

A fundamental condition for our ability to understand others' intentions is the ability to discriminate people from objects; this knowledge is at place in a surpris-ingly early period of ontogenesis. The key difference is that "living objects" have relative complex and unpredictable behaviour compared with "dead objects" that simply adhere to the laws of nature. Legerstee (1992) summarizes the research as follows: Even 2-month-old babies treat humans and things differently. It seems that the infant's understanding of people develops *before* the understanding of non-living objects – a conceptual system that emerges immediately after birth. Social and non-social objects are acting differently, and the infant's emerging conceptual systems function as interpretative fundaments, which make the infants able to understand the characteristic properties of living and dead "objects".

A characteristic property of animate objects is their display of spontaneous agency and relative unpredictability until one learns to read their intentional minds. As children gradually learn to interpret others' intentions, their acts come to be perceived as meaningful. Such insights stemming from psychological empirical research into human intentionality add scientific flesh and blood to James et al.'s "agent", Qvortrup's "co-constructor" that "chooses", Corsaro's "negotiator", "cre-ator", and other agency-related concepts in childhood sociology. Children affect others (and are affected by them) by communicating intentions, which they adjust on the basis of their readings of others' intentions in active everyday cultural practices.

An approach that holds promising integrative power is the developmental psy-chologist Allan Fogel's (1993) relational social and cultural theory. According to this theory, children construct their interpersonal selves and simultaneously create and reconstruct culture in everyday life verbal and non-verbal dialogues. Clearly in line with this is Bruner (1990), who presents his interpretive cultural theory in *Acts of Meaning* and elaborates it further in *The Culture of Education* (1996). Bruner's main point is that mental processes, learning, and experience are essen-tially *situated*, i.e. constructed in the social context where they are created and shaped through active participation. Making sense and finding coherence are char-acteristically human urges from the beginning of life (Bruner, 1990; Stern, 1985; Trevarthen, 1998). The search for meaning is closely linked with our inherent and inexhaustible urge to "wonder" and "take an interest" (Gopnik, Melzoff, & Kuhl, 2001). Bruner (1990) links the paradigms of agency and intentionality directly, saying that agency implies the conduct of action under the sway of intentional states. Bruner further links agency closely to the social and cultural nature of man. In other words, action, activity, and intentionality are fundamental human characteristics. He does not ignore that children experience, sense, and perceive the world in their own way, but the emphasis is moved from the child's individual phenomenology to the interpersonal and cultural construction of knowledge and meaning. Hence, when the "mind" manifests itself, this happens in an action context. The child perspective is therefore a matter of being able to "read" the intentions behind children's patterned behaviours. But how is intentionality, active sense-making, and social affirmation interrelated? Bruner and Haste's (1987) contextualist view establishes the relationship in arguing that there are many possible developmental directions. Bruner and Haste's (1987) establishes the relationship by arguing that children are attributed intentions and confirmed as actors by others which make them realize the importance of their own actions. They also get access to the intentions of other's and can share experiences with them. According to this view, children express themselves as intentional actors within social communities, a feature that in turn is intimately related to the capacity for "mind reading".

What does this mean for the child perspective and our understanding of children's perspectives?[10] The basic perspective described above neither ignores nor focuses exclusively on the inner phenomenological world of individuals; rather, it interprets children's (co-)actions as a reflection of their particular understanding of the world. Thus, interpretations of the *social distribution of children's expressed intentions* become essential for a child perspective and for adults' access to children's perspectives. *Children's perspectives* are expressed through their active externalization of intentions. In such a contextual developmental psychology, *child perspective* is established on the basis of a realistic conceptual understanding of continuously expressed and negotiated intentions, that is, adults' insightful approximated insights into children's desires, motives, and assumptions. This does not preclude the application of other "filters" to the "same" acts, for Example by a Corsarean interpretation of children's social expressions as cultural reproduction, that is, where the focus is not on the interpretation of children's intentions.[11] This marks a key difference between the "child as actor" paradigms seen in the sociology of childhood and relational psychology. In micro-cultural childhood sociology, the agency

---

[10] It should be noted that the theories mentioned here do not claim to be specific child perspectives. Any inherent child perspective therefore has to be derived by analysis.

[11] The classical-modernist definition of the "object" of the discipline is often based on dichotomies. An Example: An ethnographic approach views children's statements as "cultural signs" and rejects the notion of interpreting children's activity as "psychological signs" (Gulløv & Højlund, 2003). As previously mentioned, traditional child psychology takes the opposite view. But applying just one interpretive "filter" to children's activity does not imply that the phenomena that are not studied are non-existent or unimportant, which only means that the purist scientific lens ignores them. This does not support attempts at integration.

point of view is an a priori premise concerning children's "external representation" – that is, the child's social engagement or *actions*. This precludes a child perspective, because the actors' behaviour is solely interpreted as cultural reproduction. Culturally based contextual–relational developmental psychology, however, addresses this external representation too, but also relates it to and views social activity as externalized mental expressions.

In an effort to reach an integrative understanding of the agency paradigm, it is not helpful to embed human activity in dichotomies, for Example as "external" versus "internal", "private" versus "social", "individual" versus "group", "idiosyncratic" versus "cultural/social". These dichotomies should instead be viewed as dimensions, intricately related and relevant on different analytical levels. An integrative study of child perspectives should move away from dichotomies and towards an analysis of the *relationships* between these dimensions and interpretive perspectives. Some promising integrative potentials lie in analysing the connections between the paradigm of intentionality, activity, and sense making in children's everyday life. Would it benefit the exploration of a child perspective to combine developmental psychology's research into children's understanding of mental states/intentionality with the agency paradigm found in the sociology of childhood? Yes, if the *external* agency concept from childhood sociology is combined with the complex *external* ←→ *internal agency* concept from developmental psychology. Sense making and the creation of intentions take place in social groups as well as within subjects, since one would be unthinkable without the other. Empirical research using a contextual–relational framework can demonstrate and explain how mental processes as desires, beliefs, volition, expectations, experiences *within the child* (although most often external of offspring) *manifest and thus become observable in children's social activity* with peers (Sommer, 2005b, Chapter 6). Thus, with *alternating interpretive filters*, adults may hold dual perspectives that view children's acts as signs of "cultural reproduction" as well expressions of subject's materialized intentions. Thus, access to and insight into children's intentional expressions become synonymous with knowing what is going on in children's minds – interpreting their perceptions and intentions. Thus, the child perspective is possible to construct through the same empirically based observations about children's relationships with others.

The Inner Psychological Space of the Self

Previously, we concluded that the search for a child perspective in James et al.'s (1998) general Foucaultian analysis of children and society was in vain. This was also true for the macro-oriented sociological approaches to children. But the approach to the child as a subject did introduce some promising concepts such as the *inner psychological space of the self* and *subject identities*; sound constructs concerning the presumed phenomenology of subjects. However, we also found that the self appeared as a theoretical empty-box construction. Thus, one does not learn how James et al.'s promising child perspective statement – the experience of being a child

– is constituted within the subject. Nevertheless, the inner psychological space of the self is of integrative importance in that it recognizes the existence of something "mental" – promising as a possible common platform and a link between micro-oriented childhood sociology and recent self-theories in psychology. But as the self in this childhood sociology is empty it has to be "filled out" with a richer conceptual understanding from psychology. Let us therefore pursue this by including selected self-theories that in detail explain how the subject's *inside* environment, mediated by an *in-between-side*, is inextricably linked to the subject's *outside* environment. Hence, the selected theories do not sever the close ties between the individual and his or her social and cultural environment, as classical developmental psychology does.[12]

Viewing a person's relationship with his or her environment as a *dichotomy* – "inner versus outer", "subject versus object", "individual versus environment", "self versus other" – is quite common in classical, Western, Descartes-inspired philosophies. Psychology, however, has undergone a significant change, as theoreticians are now, relatively independently of each other, focusing on the major importance of relationships. *Interpersonal relationships* are essential for explaining, for example, socialization, parenting, and learning. In developmental psychology, the traditional split between individual and environment has been acknowledged as problematic, which has even led to the emergence of a discipline called *The developmental psychology of personal relationships* (Mills & Duck, 2000). This branch acknowledges that people live in both *changing and stable relationships*. But what professional terms may support this relational notion of the self as a less isolated inner space? Let us take a brief look at three points of view from self-theory.[13]

Fogel (1993) developed a systemic theory about the *dialogical self* – that is, the self that Results from communication. The self emerges in the earliest pre-symbolic period, long before G.H. Mead and other proponents of classical socialization theory talk about any emerging self. According to Fogel, the infant is socially and communicatively competent. The self is a continuous result of communicative processes in verbal and non-verbal dialogues between people. Thus, the "position" of the self is located more *between people* than within the individual:

> The dialogical self is not an objectively specifiable entity. The self is not entirely "in" the individual, since it embodies the positions of others and can imagine itself in times and places that are not here and now. (Fogel, 1993, p. 141)

Fogel calls this ongoing communicative adjustment between actors *co-regulation*. The ongoing co-regulation, for Example between two interlocutors (verbal or non-verbal), takes place in ways that make it difficult to predict a developmental or socialization outcome of the interaction. One adjusts to the other's input, and vice versa, and unexpected actions may also occur that radically alter the

---

[12] Ironically, James et al.'s (1998) term the "inner psychology of the self" – perhaps unintentionally – reflects the classical polarization between inner and outer worlds.

[13] In this context, there is only room for a brief Introduction. Interested readers are referred to the reference list.

interaction. Obviously, this model rejects fixed goals of, say, socialization. For that, the myriad interactions that people engage in during a lifetime are too unpredictable. However, it should be emphasized that dialogues rarely follow a completely free or chaotic course, since according to Fogel they take place within a so-called *consensual frame*, i.e. the actors' relative agreement on the purpose, topic, and meaning of the interaction. A consensual frame contains both cultural and personal meanings and it regulates which communicative behaviours are relevant and which are not. The frame constitutes meta-communication, i.e. implied communication about what the interlocutors agree to interact about. The frame is related to *customs and everyday routines in a culture*, which provide structure and meaning and typify varied communicative interactions. Thus, in subsequent encounters with the other people, the child does not have to start from scratch. He and she apply (and therefore through socialization must become familiarized with) a large number of cultural consensual customs for when and how we interact, and the meaning of different types of conversations. Corsaro's theory of "cultural reproduction" explains how this happens as Fogel's does, too, but he adds a personal meaning framework as well.

Bruner's (1990) theory of the *distributed self* has similarities with Fogel's dialogical self. Distributed self means that even if the individual's meaningful perception of himself or herself may be perceived as highly private the self is created, distributed, and maintained through daily social and cultural practices. Self-perception is "distributed" as a social product on the various socialization arenas of children. In Bruner's universe, culture and self are simply two different but internally related sides of socialization.

Daniel Stern's *revised* developmental psychology theory (Stern, 2000 paperback version with a new long interesting Introduction, and Stern, 2004), unlike the earlier version, expresses a clearer relational perspective. He explains in detail different self-formative life periods as qualitative different basic *ways of being with others*. Here, too, the child's self-construction is essentially relational when it comes to the understanding of the child's inner mental representation of a personal world:

> Such internal objects are not people; nor are they aspects of others. Rather, they are constructed from the patterned experience of the self in interaction with another: What is inside (i.e. represented internally) comprises interactive experiences. (Stern, 1985, p. xv)

Despite some differences, which are not addressed here, Bruner, Fogel, and Stern agree in the sense that they are all "self-theoreticians" and concur about the basic relational character of human nature. They all acknowledge the existence of the "self as an inner psychological space" and they all acknowledge a phenomenologically perceived self in children – which, for example, Stern analyses in great detail. But "in there", perception and reflection are intimately mixed up with relations to others. Thus, the self-perception of "I" and "Me" will not be possible without the presence of "The Other", "Them", and "Others". According to this logic, any traditional socialization of the self is impossible, if by this we mean the child's passive acquisition. James et al.'s (1998) self as an "inner psychological space" therefore develops in relational co-regulating or counter-regulating processes among child actors, a line of argumentation with which these childhood sociologists would hardly disagree. This continuous process constructs, alters, and regulates children, and the product is not just knowledge and experience. The self is affected (albeit in different ways) throughout the different stages of an individual's lifespan. Thus, the self is constantly changing and affecting other selves.

If we link the assumptions about the self described above with James et al.'s (1998) theses on the subject (e.g. the inner psychological space of the self or subject identities) we can now go all the way: A link can be established between the social/cultural "outside" via mediation in the "in-between-side" and the child's psychological "inside".[14] James et al.'s (1998) empty-Box is not only filled up with analytical content, their metaphor of the self as an intrapersonal "space" (that is, a situated "place") needs rephrasing. Concepts should be constructed to describe the self/selves in children to acknowledge its/their fluent process-like character. Metaphorically speaking, the self can be viewed as a semi-permeable membrane, where the outside and the inside of the filter are intimately related. They are different sides of a structure that filters social processes. This metaphor, however, may give an impression of a huge gap between relational psychology and the objectification of the child that characterizes traditional developmental psychology (and James et al.'s concept). However, it is too vague and too far removed from children's subject perceptions to act as a basis for a child perspective, and James et al.'s empty-Box concept of self and identity also fails to establish a child-oriented perspective unless it is given more detailed and specific content. Here, Stern (1985) provides a detailed description of children's formative self-periods, which enables a realistic interpretation and understanding of children's perceptions and goals in social interactions. Furthermore, a child perspective can be established on the basis of self-theories: When children as subjects externalize themselves and internalize others in communicative interactions they are producing and reproducing culture. But they are doing more than that: At the same time, they are expressing *their unique subject identities and selves* in social practices.

Perspectives and Future Integrative Potential

If childhood sociologies ignore that action-related expressions reveal children's personal emotions, experience, and thinking – by *only* addressing children's involvement in cultural reproduction (Corsaro), Foucault's prisoners in society (James et al.), and as non-existing subjects in childhood (Qvortrup) – the theoretical basis ironically suffers under inherent problems as classical de-contextualized developmental psychology. One ambition for a child perspective could be to apply a dual view of children as subjects (in their own right) and objects (of/to something/someone), where child perspectives and children's perspectives belong

---

[14] In relational self-psychology, the child's self is not a "nucleus" but a relational experiential product. The existence of multiple selves is a possibility, although this is still being debated (Sommer, 2005a).

on the subject side. This is not sufficient, however, unless the object/subject discourse addresses the complicated relationship between *outside, in-between-side,* and *inside*. In other words, children's thoughts and emotions have to be included (although open to various interpretations) as materialized in interactions.

The previous sections have stipulated some potential common platforms for future integrative research. The aim has been, therefore, to stimulate an integrative holistic understanding of the *interrelatedness of* childhood, children, society, culture, and mind, specifically with a focus on child perspectives and children's perspectives. The future holds more opportunities. Here, we will outline just a few of them.

The relationship between the use of language/symbols, "psychological realities", and *children's micro-cultural reproduction*: Corsaro did not elaborate on his views of the role of language in relation to "psychological realities". He also does not explain the essential role of children's growing capacity for symbol and language in relation to the complex social interactions in children's culturally reproductive activities. Many of his observations of Italian and American 5-year-olds reveal that the analysis of *language dialogues* is a key to understanding what is going on. Linguistic research is a vital part of psychological developmental cognition research: The future challenge lies in embedding selected parts of linguistic research in a culturally contextualist approach. For example, linguistic research may help determine the structure and processes of mental models, which helps point towards a child perspective.

Volition and the "by-choice" argument: James et al. (1998) attributed children with the ability to initiate acts based on volition. Qvortrup's "by-choice" term also suggests this capacity. Still, neither of them pursues these interesting ideas. They may be meaningful discussion topics in the context of the above section on children as intentional, active sense-makers. On a more general level, these notions may also help us answer the following question: Where are the boundaries of children's (and indeed man's) "free will" and of our "potential for change"? The macro-oriented and micro-oriented approaches in childhood sociology have been shown to produce very different answers to this question, which is not surprising. However, we need a more in-depth analysis of the *relationships between the macro and micro approaches* and their links to subjects' potential free will and agency. How this integration of analytical levels may be linked to child perspectives and children's perspectives is wide open as a future area of research. European social studies and studies in the humanities have a long tradition and a vital scientific interest in "self", "volition", "volitional acts", and "consciousness" as phenomena. This is not the exclusive domain of neither sociology nor psychology and thus offers a potential for establishing more common platforms for future research.[15]

Part I has pointed out the necessity of relatively clear definitions of child perspectives and children's perspectives. Otherwise, the terms would include such a wide

---

[15] One contemporary example of interdisciplinary and integrative endeavours is the EUROCORES Programme (2005): "Consciousness in a Natural and Cultural Context" (CNCC).

array of theories and empirical findings about children as to lose their usefulness. We also established that "the new view of the child" that we encounter in both childhood sociology and developmental psychology today is not directly constructed as a "child perspective" or as a source of "children's perspectives" – they have to be derived. We have also seen that theories on children can be localized as *closer to* or *farther from* children's experimental realities. The theories differ in the emphasis they put on understanding and explaining children's particular experiential and perceptual world (although some terms proved deceptive in this regard). The *theoretical positions* within the sociologies of childhood are localized relatively far from children's own reality, while theories from relational (developmental) psychology are relatively closer and take a stronger interest in explaining and understanding children's mental worlds. As for the micro-oriented ethnographic, interpretive *empirical method* that was found in two versions of childhood sociology, the Conclusion is less straightforward, because a pro-position, a sceptical-rejecting, and a mid-seeking position were localized.

Part II
A Child Perspective to the Care for Children in Practice: A Humanistic and Interpretative Approach

Introduction

As pointed out in the introductory part of the book, a child perspective approach is not something fixed that is once and for all defined by some historical and professional authority, but is rooted in a humanistic and interpretative orientation to children that can be specified in different ways. In this part, a child perspective approach to human childcare will be explicated – a position that is strongly influenced by a humanistic, cultural-dialogical, and interpretative theoretical orientation. It builds on several of the fundamental child perspective assumptions laid down in the introductory part of the book – for example the ethos of humanization, children as citizens, as persons, child-centeredness, and child–orientation as paradigmatic cornerstones. Furthermore, the two concepts, child perspective and children's perspectives as they were defined in the Introduction, will be explored in more detail in the context of interactive care with children. Also Part II presents a conceptual framework that is in agreement with the contextual-relational developmental psychological paradigm as presented and discussed in Part I.

The first part of Part II presents a brief Overview of some selected core features and assumptions about the nature of children and child development implicit in a humanistic and dialogical context relating to care. Secondly, an analytic model of the components involved in sensitive human care as a communicative or interactive process, where both child and caregiver contribute to the final outcome, is presented. This model is further explicated with examples from research in developmental psychology. A key issue in this context is the conditions that facilitate or obstruct empathic identification with the child – which is assumed to be a precondition for sustained sensitive human care. As an extension of this understanding, the concept of "zone of intimacy" is introduced. This is the zone into which a child can be included and cared for through empathic identification and sensitive availability of the caregiver to the child's needs. But a child may also be expelled from the zone of intimacy with subsequent blockage of empathic identification, affective withdrawal leading to neglect, and possibly abuse.

A series of cases are presented from fieldwork in extreme situations illustrating how this analytic model can be used as an interpretive device for exploring the processes involved in sensitive human care – or opposite, in abuse and neglect of children.

Finally, the conditions facilitating empathic care are summarized and related to the newly emerging field of "ethics of closeness" and Levinas' idea of the "appeal of the face" (Bauman, 1996). Throughout this chapter, a key point is the caregiver's perception of the child, his ability to read the child's signals, and respond appropriately, or to quote Levinas "to read the child's 'face' and respond appropriately without conditions..." This is the essence of a child-oriented humanistic approach.

Part II is closing by summing up in a simple model of the conditions leading to inclusion into the zone of intimacy with ensuing sensitive care, or to empathic blockage with consequent neglect or abuse.

Most of the examples in the first part of this chapter are taken from the author's extensive fieldwork with children in extreme need in developing countries. A reason behind this is that in extreme situations, the potential usefulness of key psychological concepts and child beliefs and their relevance for practice can be tested. It is in extreme situations that what is taken for granted as normal, is coming into a new focus and awareness: The child as a person – is this trivial? When we experience the dehumanization and objectification of children on a large scale in slums and refugee camps, we also become aware of what it means to be human. It is the contrast of extreme deprivation and dehumanization that produces the awareness of what we take for granted in our privileged position, as Pramling points out in the final chapter. It will be argued that such a paradigm is of outmost importance in practice enhancing in a simple and practical way the essential core features of a human caregiver–child relationships – this is child perspective in practice.

In Part II an interpretive approach, as part of a child perspective orientation, is explored in great detail. The whole idea of child perspective implies an interpretive approach to children where the child's subjectivity is explored without imposing the preset standards and fixed Procedures of normal testing and experimentation. The basic principles of an interpretive approach are spelled out and discussed in relation to a critical analysis of diagnostics in tests and experiments with children. From an interpretive perspective, a child's reply in a diagnostic situation is not only a reflection of a child's inner cognitive capacities but as much a reflection of how the child perceives the situation ("why am I here?"), the task, and the experimenter. Examples from classical Piagetian experiments are presented to illustrate this point. At the same time, criticisms are presented regarding the naive testing approach, where children's deviant replies are interpreted as some inner deficiency like low IQ. In such approaches, the child's perception and understanding of the situation is ignored. This is called a competence-oriented approach, in opposition to an interpretive approach... The interpretive approach would involve looking for deficient understanding (or intersubjectivity) between the experimenter's and the child's conception of the situational context and the task. The child is assumed to respond rationally to "another question"...

An interpretive methodology is then introduced where the focus is on the child's reconstruction of how she or he interprets the diagnostic situation. This methodology is illustrated with examples from experimentation with children, preschool communication, and everyday practice. Part II ends with a description of how the "intersubjective space" emerging in the classrooms between teacher and pupils subtly and implicitly regulates the communication between them. A final Conclusion is reached by presenting a summary-model showing the markedly different consequences of using an interpretive, child perspective versus a normative competence-oriented approach. The examples from practice in the interpretive part of Part II are taken both from experiments with children and from non-extreme everyday situations in both daycare and school.

Fundamental Features Embedded in a Humanistic Dialogical Approach to Children

Now five core features and professional beliefs that pervade the presentation in Part II will be sketched. The features have been supported by recent research and shall be seen as specific child perspective-oriented, panhuman beliefs about a child's "nature" and potentials. Guiding the understanding of the caregiver–child as dyad, such professional beliefs will have serious consequences for the relationship.

1. *The child as a person*

This point may seem trivial and obvious. But a look into the history of childhood, institutionalization, neglect, and abuse will show that children often have been treated as non-persons or as objects. The idea of "person" implies the recognition of each child's *uniqueness* with the individual's specific experiential endowment, history, and genetic constitution. But at the same time, it also implies *panhuman similarity* because despite cultural differences, the human child shares the same fundamental needs, and for that reason humans have a common basis for reciprocal understanding. From this point of view, a child's need is not only for sustenance and survival, love, and security, it also includes the need for dignity and self-respect. As a child grows older, he or she develops a self-identity and agency based on the codes of respect in the local community. Treating a child as a person involves recognition and confirmation of the need for respect and dignity, as opposed to humiliation and disrespect. Implicit in a humanistic approach is also the idea of compassionate participation and understanding of our shared human existence and destiny, where we all are at some stage vulnerable and helpless. For that reason, humans have the potentiality to understand and react humanly to others in a similar situation (Bauman, 1996; Hoffman, 2000; Vetlesen, 1999).

2. *Dialogicity as a primary disposition*

Dialogicity as the key to human development is a radical claim because it entails a rejection of the traditional monological assumption of dialogue as two isolated human beings trying to reach each other. Rather it assumes that there is both a

D. Sommer et al., *Child Perspectives and Children's Perspectives in Theory and Practice*, International Perspectives on Early Childhood Education and Development 2, DOI 10.1007/978-90-481-3316-1_5, © Springer Science+Business Media B.V. 2010

(A) pre-adapted pattern of organization and a
(B) shared cultural collective basis

from which attunements and participation with the other can take place as part of one self-organizing communicative system (Rogoff, 1990; Rogoff, 2003; Cole, 1996). This implies that there is always an addressee (or an audience), explicitly or tacitly (also in our thinking and feeling) towards whom humans direct and adjust their actions and utterances, both in form and content. Through reciprocal attunement and adjustment, a common basis for intersubjectivity is created (Trevarthen & Aitken, 2001). An *intersubjective space* is developed between the interlocutors with its own "invitational structure", which regulates what is fitting and appropriate (plausible) to express in the interaction within the situation (Hundeide, 2002). Through dialogues with other significant persons in the vicinity, a child gradually builds up a conception of self and identity, social belonging, and what kind of person he or she wants to be.

3. *Emphatic identification and participation with the other*

In order to know what the other person needs, sensitivity is needed. What seems to be latently available in human beings is the capacity for *empathic participation*. This is a mechanism that can be observed already in babies according to research in caregiver–infant communication (Trevarthen & Aitken, 2001). Human beings seem to be equipped with a mechanism or capacity for spontaneous and direct imitation of and identification with other peoples' emotional states and intentionality. Egotism may develop, but humans are brought into the world with a fundamental capacity for *altero-centric participation* (Bråten, 1998, 2007). This means that in a child perspective approach, there is a deeper and universal basis for empathic sharing and dialogue with children – even with babies. Through this capacity, the adult is able to join in and share empathetically a child's stress and suffering and also to respond appropriately with a "complimentary reply" that is tuned in to the child's state of stress and suffering, in order to provide consolation and reduce suffering.

4. *Learning tacitly through direct participation: spontaneous didactic child rearing*

Evidence indicates that didactic rearing can occur on a pre-adapted, non-conscious basis from the earliest stages of preverbal communication. Without being aware of it, the caregiver assesses, and if necessary, influences, and stimulates the infant's attention with slow, repetitive patterns which are finely adjusted to the infant's response, encourages and rewards mastery, adapts and metes out stimulation according to feedback from the child's behaviour (Papousek & Papousek, 1991). A predisposition seems to exist in both the infant and the sensitive and engaged caregiver for intuitive child rearing. Caring, then, becomes more a question of triggering already existing communicative patterns (as a disposition) rather than learning a set of new caring actions and communicative skills. This means that intervention becomes a question of facilitating and sensitizing of something that is natural and emerges spontaneously, and which the infant invites under normal circumstances through its expressive initiatives (Hundeide, 2000, 2001). When the child grows up, however, more cognitive and conscious governed upbringing and didactic learning practices will gradually become more prominent (for example after infancy, in day care and school), but the primary learning mechanism will still be in place in several everyday situation, because every situation constitutes a potential learning event.

5. *Guided participation into a world of meaning – companionship*

Babies and young children are "natural apprentices" – spontaneously seeking adult guidance. By responding to the child's social initiatives, the caregiver is fulfilling her caring role, not only as a source of consolation and trust but also as the child's guide into a shared socio-cultural world. This guidance starts first as a sensitive dialogue between caregiver and child, where the caregiver attends to the child as a person – as communicative partner – and responds sensitively and contingently to his/her initiatives. This is very much an emotional expressive exchange through face-to-face interaction in the very early stages. Gradually, as the child starts to focus more on objects in the surrounding world, the dialogue takes on a more supportive and guiding form. The caregiver and the child are then jointly involved in the same episode by shared attention to the same topic and by "guided participation" (Rogoff, 1990, 2003). The caregiver becomes a "mediator" between the child's experience of the surrounding world and the world of cultural knowledge and tradition. Through confirming enthusiasm, through pointing, demonstrating, labelling, questioning, and expanding on the child's initiatives, and by filling in, modelling, and keeping the goal present, preparing the setting, the caregiver assists the child to perform better than he or she would have been able to do alone. Thus the adult is operating within "the zone of proximal development"; an important concept in the Vygotskian tradition (Rogoff, 2003; Valsiner, 1989).

Care as a Sensitive Communicative Process: The Primary Circle of Care

Recent research within early communication has shown that human care is not always a one-way process in which the caregiver provides and the child receives care, independently of the child's initiative and responses (Sameroff & Fiese, 1990; Dunn, 1978; Papousek & Papousek, 1991). Rather it seems that sensitive care is a communicative or dialectic process in which the caregiver's actions toward the child are dependent on the expressive appeal of the child's utterances, and conversely, the child's responses are dependent on the caregiver's actions, on how they are attuned to the child's state, and on how they are received and apprehended by the child. This indicates that sensitive care is a dynamic, dialectic process in which the child (in this case) is an active co-creator of the care it receives – or more correctly: the care that emerges and is created between them. Care cannot be reduced to static Recipes for "what one should do when...", nor care is a skill that can be attributed to the ability for caring inside one person or the other. It is rather a process that is created between them (Hundeide, 2002).

In order for such a caring process to arise, a reciprocal and mutual sensitivity and an ability to apprehend and recognize the quality of each other's expressive initiatives and responses are necessary. What do the child's initiatives and responses express? What is the purpose and meaning of a caring action?

Attunement to the Attunement of the Other...

Sensitive care therefore requires that the caring action itself is adjusted to the quality and meaning that the caregiver attributes to the caring expression or appeal of the child. On the other hand, the recipient, in this case the child, must be able to receive and understand the intention of the caregiver's caring action, i.e. both must interpret and adjust to each others' expectations in order for the care process to function optimally; there must be an "attunement to the attunement of the other" (Rommetveit, 1998). According to one of the most distinguished researchers in the field, this facility for interpreting the expression of others appears to be a fundamental ability existing in all of us:

> ... human perceivers have a remarkable sensitivity to beings with animacy and intentionality ... they can readily detect parameters of motivation in other subjects' behaviour, such as «emotion» of an action, or its «effort» and «vitality»... But the ability to detect and observe qualitative differences in actions of others, and thereby to perceive their motives, is but a small part of the capacity for imitative identification, emotional empathy and reciprocal communication that all human possess. Most importantly, a communicating subject is trying to make an effective complementary reply, to enter into, and jointly regulate, a dyad of expressive «conversational» exchange with the Other. This is what Bråten (1988, 1999) means by the term "dialogic closure". (Trevarthen, 1999, p. 8)

Such an effective complementary reply in an exchange between a committed caregiver and an infant will normally lead to a mutual exchange of smiles and positive expressions. This "proto-conversation" is temporally precisely synchronized to a turn-taking schema, which the infant appears to be able to follow at the age of 5 weeks, and to which it responds with distress if disrupted (Trevarthen, 1989).

But this disposition (inclination) may also be apparent when one of the partners responds by expressing human care, empathy, and comforting in a situation where the other is experiencing pain and suffering. This does not only apply to adults; one sees the same response in infants of less than a year old. One of the leading researchers in this field, Eisenberg (1992), mentions as an example that when the father expresses sadness, the 13-month-old infant responds by giving him her favourite doll. There are many such examples (Eisenberg, 1992; Bråten, 1999).

This demonstrates that the primary cycle of care is a dialogic response of a fundamental and immediate character, which can be seen in the committed caregiver's spontaneous and unpremeditated responses to the infant's expressive initiative. It has also been shown that children respond three times as strongly to such expressions in people they are closely attached to than to strangers (Eisenberg, 1992). As we shall see later on, this shows that spontaneous caring responses in both children and adults are associated with psychological attachment, with being inside of a zone of intimacy.

The Component of Dialogic Caring Behaviour

Let us take a closer look at the different components entailed in such dialogic caring behaviour. Figure 1 describes care and caring behaviour as a reciprocal dialogic process. Each component of the figure is described and is exemplified in the following text:

Let us start with the expressions and initiatives of the child (1a, Fig. 1). When a child for one reason or another experiences discomfort, suffering or need, this will usually be apparent in the child's general expression – facial expression, gaze, body stance, movements, and utterances. These expressions may have a greater or lesser aspect of an appeal for care.[1] This is a crucial aspect of the caring process, since a child who gives weak signals, or no signals, for example because of malnutrition, runs a greater risk of being neglected and ignored when no one can see or interpret its signals and identify its needs.

For this reason, the caregiver's perception and ability to interpret the child's expressive signals (2, Fig. 1) is crucial for the subsequent development of the caring

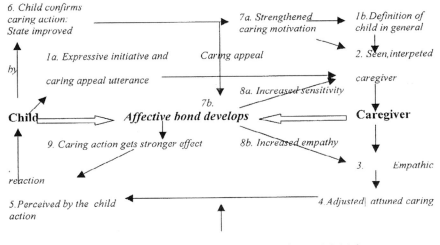

Fig. 1 The primary circle of communicative care

---

[1] This is what in Levina's term is called "the appeal of the face".

process. As Stern (1995) points out, parents experience their children as "understandable beings". This entails that they will always attempt to project meaning into their children's actions. When, for example, an infant expresses some inarticulate sounds, the mother answers in this typical manner:

> Oh, listen to him! Yes! That's right. Tell me all about it – oh, yes, you have so much you want to say. (Trevarthen, 1998, p. 11)

The mother continually seeks to find intentions, wishes, and emotions in the child's utterances, and she responds accordingly – to her interpretation of the child's expressions. Thus, guided by the mother's interpretations, a dialogue develops, which is normally a positive and joyful exchange for both parties. This is another important point, because when one speaks of care, one usually thinks of the negative experiences in which one person needs the help and support of the other. However, good caring has its origins in shared positive and joyful experiences which create the strong bonds between those involved: a smile or another attractive expression from the child has an immediate and direct appeal to a sensitive caregiver, who usually responds with a similar joyful expression in turn. At the same time, she imitates the child by making a similar sound or movement, often pitching her voice high, and she comments on the child's utterances as if they were expressions of intentions or wishes. It is this form of joyful exchange, which is also called "motherese register" that consolidates the mutual bond between them. In a context of intervention, it is important that this early form of dialogue is supported and facilitated (Bråten, 1999; Rye, 2003).

There may be considerable differences in caregivers with respect to attitudes and the ability to see and interpret children's expressions, however. As we shall see later on, the interpretations and actions of a caregiver towards the child may at times lead back to her more general definition of the child (1b, Fig. 1). It may be the case that a child is perceived as being difficult, wilful, or spoiled. In that case, it is quite likely that the interpretation of the child's expressive signals will be influenced by this general negative definition or stigmatization. This is a critical stage of the caregiving process. If the child's appeal for caring is not recognized and experienced by the caregiver, the entire process comes to a halt or is rejected. Thus, we can see that the caregiver's definition of the child *in general* can open or close her sensitivity to the child's expressive signals. This can in turn lead to an obstruction or limitation of the care-giving process. This demonstrates the necessity of the caregiver to hold a (intuitive or reflected) child perspective that direct the adult's attention towards an understanding of the child's perceptions, ways of experiencing, and actions.

If, on the other hand, the child's appeal for care is seen and experienced, an empathic affective response (3, Fig. 1) will normally follow in the caregiver: She is moved and emotionally influenced by the child's expressions, which convey an emotional message that she can recognize, perhaps as an echo from her own childhood. She sees the helpless child needing her assistance – my child needs me. This is what activates a spontaneous caring response, or what Trevarthen calls an effective complementary response (1996, p. 2).

This is usually an immediate, unreflective participatory reaction, different from Piaget's concept of reflective decentration – thinking about the other (Hoffman, 2000). In most people, this spontaneous empathic response leads to an immediate wish to help and to care. This again leads to an adjusted/attuned caring action (4, Fig. 1) where the caregiver adjusts her response (i.e. her caring action) to the child in line with how she has interpreted the child's expressive initiative, and according to her empathic reaction to it. Thus, there are no "correct" responses to children's expressive signals; the same expressive utterance can be interpreted and experienced differently, and thus elicit different empathic responses in different people. For example, is a child's crying an appeal for food or comforting? Is the child stubborn? Does it want attention? The caring action depends on the interpretation.

Box 1 gives a series of examples of which types of care actions are generally applied when a person – regardless of age – seeks the help of another. Nonetheless, the caregiver's ability for attunement and synchronization of her caring actions will naturally vary (Stern, 1995), probably reflecting both differing cultural standards and different models for caring as these are transferred from the caregiver's own childhood. But in the Box, a selected list of child perspective founded responses is shown:

Box 1 Examples of child perspective directed caring actions

- Acknowledgement and recognition of the other's pain or suffering.
- Help to alleviate pain, accommodate physical needs, survival: medicine, food, and money.
- Comforting (consolation) and support when there is fear and traumatic experiences – to ensure security.
- Comforting and understanding when there is loss, sorrow, or longing.
- Support, attention, and contact when there is loneliness.
- Support when there is loss – create new hope.
- Help to negotiate the realities of daily life.
- Help to create new meaning.
- Confirmation of and support for the other's self-confidence.
- Empowering a person's positive initiatives for coping.
- Counselling and instruction within a particular area of expertise.
- Help to engender optimism and joy.

However, the communicative caring process is not ended when the caregiver produces an attuned caring action. A crucial next stage comprises the way in which the child experiences and receives this caring action (5, Fig. 1). Does the child accept to be comforted? If a child rejects the "reply" or focuses in another direction, or if the caring action is misplaced and not attuned to the child's state and situation, it will not be apprehended as a relevant response and overlook the child. Let us take a look at a description of the opposite, where the caregiver adjusts and provides responses that are relevant and attuned of the child:

> In harmonious face-to-face interaction with infants, parents will reduce their tempo, exaggerate and repeat their movements, respond by imitating and enhancing their behaviour, turn taking and respecting the infant's coincidental interruptions of the exchange. The infant appears attentive and contented. (Field, 1990, p. 124)

As noted by Stern in his rich casuistic material (Stern, 1985, 1995), there are often clinical cases where the caregiver is so badly synchronized and attuned to the child's state and emotional needs that care-giving actions are rejected or are counterproductive, thus worsening the child's state (ibid.), for instance, in the case of a well meaning but domineering and insensitive mother or father imposing her or his own initiatives on the child, in conflict with the child's needs, rhythm, or state. When, on the other hand, the caring action is experienced as being a relevant and attuned response, which accommodates to the child's needs and suffering, it will have a healing and comforting effect. The child's state is improved, it stops crying, and it often shows approval of and satisfaction with the care he or she has received. In this way, the child confirms and signals the reception of the caring action (6, Fig. 1). It has understood the reply to its own "question" (the expressive utterance), and the caring action (the reply or response) has been effective. This confirmation is crucial for the caregiver's subsequent relationship both with the child and to the further development of the caring process.

As shown in Fig. 1 of chapter "Changes in the Developmental Ecology of Infants and Young Children", such confirmation has two parallel effects: on the one hand, it strengthens the motivation of the caregiver (7a, Fig. 1). The child feels better, or it shows happiness, gratitude, and affection for the care it has received. This strengthens the caregiver's incentive to continue caring, but it also strengthens the affective bond between them (7b, Fig. 1). From being an indifferent person, the caregiver now becomes a person who can lend help, one who understands the child's state and suffering, one who is sensitive and who can adjust to the child's state. As Ainsworth et al. (1974) point out, these are the qualities that are needed for the development of attachment, that is, not only for the child to establish a bond with the caregiver as a dependent recipient (attachment) but also for the caregiver to become bonded to the child as a provider of care. These are two complementary and interdependent roles, having their own unique motivations for their sustenance. But as the child grows older, they need to be adjusted in order for the child to develop as an independent and autonomous being.

The mutual bond in turn leads to an increased sensitivity in the caregiver (8a, Fig. 1), that is, she becomes increasingly sensitive to the expressive initiatives of the child, and more empathic in her responses (8b, Fig. 1). This state of enhanced sensitivity is what Winnicot describes as "early maternal pre-occupation", in which the mother continuously follows the infant with her gaze, responding with imitation and empathy to all of the infant's responses as if the child were a part of herself (Stern, 1995). This is a state of extreme sensitivity and empathic attunement to the child. As concerns the child, this newly strengthened bond with the caregiver has the consequence that the caring actions become much more effective when they are initiated by people to whom they are attached (9, Fig. 1). Mere comforting of the child is not enough; the comforting must come from the mother (Eisenberg, 1992).

As an example of this, a young sensitive mother's relationship with her first-born was observed over a period of time. Her absolute accessibility at all times was amazing, as well as her participation in everything the child did. When the child was eating, she participated by opening her own mouth when the child did. When the observer played with the child and made it laugh, the mother participated all along, laughing with the child. When the child tried to attain one goal or other, such as putting something into a Box, the mother was attentive and participating, and she made small movements as if to help the child to carry out the activity. She was sensitively accessible throughout, participating in everything the child did.

This example of the early maternal preoccupation (to use Winnicot's term) can be called *empathic identification with the child.*[2] The caregiver empathizes with the child and participates in both its assumed experiences and its activities as an alternative, supporting self (see Bråten, 1998, 2003 on "the virtual other").

At the bottom of Fig. 1, external situational conditions or circumstances are included (10, Fig. 1), components that refers to the components 2–6. It is a very important factor in all social interaction, but it is often overlooked or taken for granted. This is because we always function in situations that have particular *affordances* or invitations (Reed, 1993). In our case, there may be affordances that may promote or prevent good quality of care between the caregiver and the child. Thus, the accessibility of the caregiver in terms of attention and emotionality in relation to the child's initiative is often dependent on the situation, for example situational stress and to how many other tasks the caregiver is committed to in the same situation. The same applies to the child: How it experiences the caregiver's caring actions (components 5 and 6, Fig. 1) also depends on whether the child's attention is accessible in the situation, for example in relation to how many other distractions or attractions are present.

From Caring Ability to Caring Processes

This account of a child perspective oriented care as a communicative, dialogic process has important implications for how we understand and analyse care. In the context of childcare, the caring capacity of a parent is very often mentioned as critical. It has even come to the point of using intelligence testing as an indicator of the caring ability of mothers! This is an example of a misguided conceptualization of caring capacity. If caring were only a matter of the abilities of the caregiver, for example sensitivity, one could talk about caring capacity or ability. But this is not

---

[2] Certainly fathers may have a similar commitment to the child as mothers. It is all about emotional investment and sensitization through experience.

the case. The quality of caring that emerges between the caregiver and the child is a dialogical product to which the child, the caregiver, and the situation all contribute; it cannot be attributed to some ability in one or the other partner. The quality of caring, as opposed to an individualized ability for caring, is a two-sided process in which both the child and the caregiver contribute. This means, as has been confirmed by empirical research (Dunn, 1993), that the same caregiver can show completely different caring qualities in the interaction with and in relation to different children, even within the same group of siblings. The caring is dependent on the dynamics that are elicited between those involved, and the situation they are in. In this interaction, the child is an important contributor to the care he receives, and not merely a recipient (see Sameroff & Fiese, 1990).

Therefore, the caregiver alone does not sustain the caring process. It also depends on the impact of the child's appeal-signals for care, and on the child's response to the caring action (6, Fig. 1) whether the caring action has the expected effect and whether the child responds back with acknowledgement and approval (even gratitude) for the caring action. A child who openly expresses approval and joy on receiving care from the other is well liked. This may in turn lead to a stronger mutual bond (7, Fig. 1), with increased motivation and sensitivity to the child's needs (8, Fig. 1). But if the child does not show the expected approval and satisfaction on receiving care, this may reduce motivation in the caregiver. In the context of social work with street children and child soldiers, one often sees examples of this: When these children are placed in foster homes, they often have considerable problems of adaptation because they are adjusted to a completely different life. In addition, they have not learned the codes for mutual politeness, and this causes the caregiver to experience disappointment with the lack of gratitude and approval from the "care victim". The famous American pedagogue Holt (1975) phrases it in this way: "the helping hand strikes back" with the demand for gratitude for "everything I have done for you". In this situation, it often happens that the former street child escapes back to the streets, where they are free from the pressures of such implied demands and expectations. Also this is a part of the caring process that is often overlooked.

The caring cycle builds on a child-oriented perspective that has been elaborated in such detail because the aspects that have been mentioned above represent critical points at which the process can be disrupted or stopped completely. Such a model can therefore be helpful in the development of a dynamic conceptualization, which may have diagnostic value, and in the sense of providing new ideas for interventions, an aspect I will discuss later. Table 1 shows a diagnostic schema that corresponds with the model.

The Primary Caring Cycle

The model *the primary caring cycle* expresses the fundamental aspects of the mutuality and reciprocity of caring, corresponding to what Trevarthen describes as "primary intersubjectivity". This expression refers to the early, un-reflected and

Table 1 Diagnostic scheme of the functional components in the cycle of care between caregiver and child

Components in the cycle of care	Very positive/strong	Positive/medium	Bad/weak	Very bad/weak
The caregiver's general definition of the child				
The caregiver's understanding of her role and task				
The child's expressive initiative and appeal for care				
Is seen, interpreted by the caregiver (sensitivity 1)				
Empathic response in the caregiver (sensitivity 2)				
Adjusted/attuned caring action (sensitivity 3)				
The child confirms the caring action: improved state				
Affective bond develops between them				
Care motivation increased				
The child prefers the caregiver				
Situation/setting and circumstances				

immediate "musical" interaction between mother and infant, as one can see in the proto-conversation, in early imitation and in what Papousek and Papousek call *didactic child rearing*.[3]

> We have collected evidence, which indicates that what we call didactic rearing can occur on a pre-adapted, non-conscious basis from the earliest stages of preverbal communication. Without being aware of it, the caregiver assesses, and if necessary, influences and stimulates the infant's attention with slow, repetitive patterns which are finely adjusted to the infant's response, encourages and rewards mastery, adapts and metes out stimulation according to feedback from the child's behaviour. (Papousek & Papousek, 1991, p. 24)

In other words, Papousek and Papousek claim that there exists a predisposition in both the infant and the sensitive and engaged caregiver for intuitive child rearing. If this is the case, then caring becomes more a question of triggering already existing communicative patterns (as a disposition) rather than learning a set of new caring actions and communicative skills. This means more concretely that intervention becomes a question of facilitating and sensitizing of something that is natural and emerges spontaneously, and which the infant invites under normal circumstances through its expressive initiatives (Hundeide, 2000, 2001).

Not all caring has its basis in the primary care cycle, however. There are forms of caring adapted to older children and adults that naturally require a more reflective approach, mirroring society's varying conventions and values. This *secondary caring* does not have the same immediate and spontaneous qualities as the primary caring cycle; rather it represents the more reflected humanitarian values and principles of human rights that are a part of our culture (Berger & Luckman, 1966). This will be discussed in more depth later on.

---

[3] In other contexts, they call this "intuitive child rearing" (Papousek & Papousek, 1991, p. 25).

When Empathic Care Is Obstructed

So far we have primarily been concerned with the positive sides of the primary caring cycle, but it is also apposite to look at the negative aspects – when care is obstructed. Under normal circumstances, the primary caring cycle functions as described above. However, there are special instances in which grave abuse towards children occur, for Example when children are placed in traditional institutions, when there is extreme poverty and the struggle for survival prevail, when there is brutalization due to wartime violence, when there is family conflict involving alcohol and drug abuse, or when the child triggers negative images in the caregiver, images that may be associated with the caregiver's own problematic childhood. In the following section we will take a closer look at some Examples in which abuse occurs and in which the natural empathic caring mechanism – what was called empathic identification with the child – does not appear to function or has become obstructed (or blocked).

Children in Objectifying, Non-child Perspective-Oriented Institutions

In the book *The Politics of Mental Handicap,* Ryan and Tomas (1976) provide an analysis of an old-fashioned medically oriented institution for mentally retarded children. By way of participant observation, the authors give an inside perspective of the experiences and attitudes of the care-giving staff and the patients (the children). This description is extreme and hardly represents modern institutions for children in Western society today. Nonetheless, three reasons lie behind presenting this: (1) Some typical attitudes are presented that may easily develop in traditional authoritarian regimes, in which control and order are the most important values. (2) It functions as an Example of institutional rigour that is the antithesis to a child perspective. (3) This can sharpen the key concept in this book by using the principle what a phenomenon "is not" is highly clarifying for knowing what "it is".

According to Ryan and Tomas, typical traditional institutions tend to invite a differentiation between "them" and "us". Those who are in charge and are authorized to set limits are also those who determine which treatment is best for the patients;

D. Sommer et al., *Child Perspectives and Children's Perspectives in Theory and Practice*, International Perspectives on Early Childhood Education and Development 2, DOI 10.1007/978-90-481-3316-1_6, © Springer Science+Business Media B.V. 2010

they decide which privileges the patients are to be given and they can determine the nature of punishment for insubordination to the rules that have been set. This is a part of the logic of leadership characterizing traditional institutions. The differentiation of "them" and "us" is sustained by the use of stigmatizing designations (labelling), use of uniforms, physical separation in different rooms, and separation for meals.

Such segregation in which one group controls another can easily lead to exploitation and abuse. This occurs when one simultaneously uses negative and objectifying definitions of the patients, definitions writing them off both as individual persons and as human beings. This is a description of an institution in which patients were defined as "it" or "them":

> In reality we have at least thirty patients we are supposed to have conversations with, play with and entertain (. . . .) all of these are tedious. Making beds, changing bed linen, washing away dirt, cleaning toilets is what work is about. If "it" moves around, put «it» in its place. Wash «it», but don't bother to talk to "it". What is the point? It is a waste of time (. . .). (Ryan & Tomas, 1976, p. 55)

Revulsion for the patients was also apparent in some of the staff:

> They are just like cattle – aren't they? They look like a bunch of fucking monkeys, right? (ibid., p. 62)

This attitude invariably led to abuse and brutality at any disruption of daily routines:

> We have to be a little cruel to be kind. This is the way it has to be. I am not saying we hate any of these patients, but they have to know who is in charge (. . .). Look at that guy over there. He doesn't like any of the staff, but when he sees me, he runs as fast as he can. He knows what's good for him, you see. I can't stand the damned bastard over there. All he knows how to do is stand there staring at you. Can you understand that – damned bastard! (ibid., pp. 50–51)

Negative definitions combined with segregation and distancing create an environment in which brutality and abuse may be experienced as legitimate. When members of the staff were asked about the patients' reactions, they refused to accept that the patients could even have reactions such as fear and anxiety. Maybe for Example one of the patients was anxious about something. A member of the staff, Sarah, answered with a strange expression: Why should he worry? He has nothing to be afraid of. He gets all needs, his clothes, his food is free, and he has a bed to sleep in. He should be grateful. There are many others who are worse off than him. Why should he worry?

> – Interviewer: But don't you sometimes worry about different things?
> – Sarah: Of course I do, but I'm normal, and that's different (. . .). Not like these idiots here. They don't have the brains to worry about anything (. . .). (ibid., p. 46)

According to Ryan and Tomas (1976), an objectified relation in a care context has the following characteristic:

- People are categorized as normal or abnormal, and there is no option for the abnormal to share any of the psychological characteristics of the normal.
- There is no possibility for the abnormal to be anything other than what is designated by their social roles and negative definitions, in this case that they are mentally retarded – and nothing else.
- There is an unwillingness to accept their subjectivity as persons – that they have their own subjective consciousness, feelings and thoughts and inner experiences of themselves and others.

Thus, patients tend to be deprived of human values in the world of traditional extreme institutions. In the worst cases they live in a de-humanized world in which they are being seen as objects (for Example as numbers – not as persons). This again invites abuse. To a certain extent this pessimistic description has been confirmed to a certain degree in institutions in Norway from before the 1960s and from traditional institutions for orphans and mentally retarded children in different parts of the world (Hundeide, 1991; Hundeide & Egebjerg, 2003). In addition to the characteristics that have been mentioned, there is often a shortage of staff in such places, for Example institutions where there were 30 or 40 children to one nurse. Under such conditions care will, at best, be limited to accommodating physical requirements; providing food, washing patients, and keeping institutional discipline and order. There will be few opportunities for individual care and emotional accessibility. The patients are treated in an authoritarian and mechanical manner. Under such conditions people are not individual persons, but beings belonging to the category of "them", which means beings with no need of individual treatment and affectionate care.[1]

In general, there seem to be a tendency within institutions within this category, to be concerned with the managerial, logistic, economical, and controlling aspects of directing an institution. These are the factors that have priority and set the agenda for all other events, and this does not leave much room for the individual needs of the patients, not to mention their psychological needs.[2] They are therefore susceptible to neglect and abuse. In extreme cases, they may spend all their lives in bed, on the grounds of lack of staff.

When Children Are Negatively Defined and Stigmatized

As mentioned above, there are two conditions that are particularly conducive to neglect and failure of care, i.e. *negative definitions* of the child *and distancing.* These often occur together as part of a general pattern of rejection of the child and withdrawal of empathic identification and care (Pelzer, 1995).

---

[1] It is under such dehumanizing condition that the concept of a "person" and a child perspective approach becomes important among professionals, politicians, the media, and citizens in order to change the situation.

[2] This is in fact the same criticism that has been raised against the modern market- and economy oriented trends in education and in society in general: We are in danger that economy and pure rationality will be running human values.

·

Negative definitions in the relationship between parents and children often develop in situations where there is a high level of family stress and where children become a burden, both economically and emotionally. This is visible both in environments with extreme poverty in developing countries and in wealthy Western societies, where children may be experienced as a hindrance to the free career development of the parents. Under such circumstances, negative and objectifying definitions of children, with subsequent emotional withdrawal and distancing in relation to the children, may easily develop.

The anthropologist Scheper-Hughes (1992) gives an Example of this from her studies in the poorest quarters of Recife in Brazil. In the district where she was working, infant mortality was exceptionally high, close to 50%; she discovered that poor mothers under such high survival pressure and high infant mortality sometimes withdrew emotionally from these infants as if to protect themselves from the ensuing emotional shocks and mourning when they understood that their chances of survival were minimal.

A weak and physically vulnerable child was labelled and defined by their mother as "a child who wants to die" or the child looked "ghost-like"; additionally they were described as "small angels". Such children had little chance of survival because of the maternal emotional withdrawal and the ensuing neglect. The negative definition of the child as "ghost-like" started a self-fulfilling process of emotional and physical neglect that usually ended in death. In some cases, it was said, the infants were helped by their mothers to die because "that was what they wanted". When the researcher tried to help some of these children through special assistance, she was warned that this would be wasted efforts, because sooner or later these children would die, which was their destiny and that was what they wanted (Scheper-Hughes, 1992). Figure 1 summarizes Scheper-Hughes' description of care-giving in the slum in Recife.

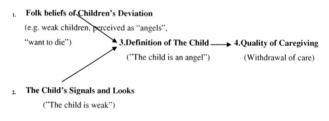

Fig. 1 Folk beliefs and childcare

When the child is born the midwife, grandmother, and mother assess it whether it is resilient and strong or weak and low vitality (2). This assessment is based on folk beliefs that weak children are "angels wanting to die" (1). This Results in a child perceived as weak being defined as an angel (3) – "it wants to die". Consequently, the mothers withdraw emotionally and do not identify themselves empathically with such a child. The child is therefore neglected (4), which again can contribute to the fulfilment of their expectations that the child will die. On the other hand, if the child is perceived as strong and vital, it is included into the family care where the mother (in this case) identifies emphatically with the child and expresses normal caring emotions.

When infant mortality is so high that the mother unconsciously tries to protect herself by withdrawing her emotional attachment, the child will be in danger. It is like an unconscious calculus of risk and emotional investment, and if the Conclusion is withdrawal, the whole caring mechanism is at risk and the chances that the negative assessment of the infant will be self-fulfilling, is considerably increased. Under such conditions, a more pragmatic economical survival approach becomes more feasible. As Scheper-Hughes expressed it,

> Part of learning how to mother in the slum includes learning how to "let go" of a child that "wants" to die. (p. 365)

In this way a self-fulfilling process was initiated on the basis of the mothers' negative diagnosis or apprehension of the child. According to the anthropologist, "there was no expression of great joy nor of sorrow"; at the child's funeral, "the infant was seldom even the focus of the conversation at all (. . .)" (ibid., p. 418). It is nonetheless misguided to interpret this as a general deficiency of empathy and caring ability in these impoverished mothers, because it was evident that the same mothers were sensitive and caring towards the other siblings that showed signs of vitality and robustness. Such emotional withdrawal response can therefore be understood as a strategic reaction of self-protection with the purpose of avoiding repeated experiences of loss and depression following the death of weak and physically vulnerable children. Such reactions may be interpreted as adaptive strategies that emerge under difficult life circumstances where survival, both physical and psychological, has become a challenge (see also LeVine, 1988; Hundeide, 2003c).

In connection with social work directed towards vulnerable children in extreme situations this author (Hundeide) has witnessed similar Examples of the stigmatization of children in relation to local superstition of possession and bewitchment. In the rural districts of Angola there is a prevailing belief that if a child is divergent for one reason or another – it may be anything from physical defects and impairment, to psychological handicaps following traumatic experiences of war – this deviation, is explained, as a result of bewitchment of the child and possession by demons. An evil spirit is thought to have entered the child and it is this spirit that creates aberrations in appearance or behaviour (Hundeide & Egebjerg, 2003). As a consequence of this definition (that was very often performed by the local witch doctor) they are rejected by their families, both physically and psychologically. In the worst cases they are expelled from their homes and left to beg in the streets for survival.[3]

The most extreme Example this author (Hundeide) has witnessed in this context stems from a group of impoverished orphans in North Angola. They had been

---

[3] In social sense these children serve as scapegoats being held responsible for any negative occurrence within the family or in the local community, thus functioning as a scapegoat for uncontrollable misfortunes in the community.

diagnosed (and defined) as being possessed by demons after consultation with the local witch doctor. These children were blamed for most of the local accidents, from deaths to crop failure and drought. They became public scapegoats, thus providing an explanation for the adversity experienced by the local society.[4]

These children were usually expelled from their homes, ending up in treatment centres owned by the same witch doctor that had diagnosed them. Here they were subjected to different forms of torture or exorcisms in order to "drive out Satan". For Example, they had chilli-pepper applied to their eyes, which then became swollen and red, so that they acquired the look of monsters. They were also subjected to painful cleansing rituals in which they were beaten and tormented. This went on for several months. When we were given the opportunity to visit this "institution" following one such treatment, the children were already totally subdued, subjugated, and traumatized. This in turn led to the unwillingness on the part of their parents to take the children back, and most of them ended up as workers on the farm of the witch doctor who had originally "diagnosed" them. An important factor in this context is that the children were themselves convinced of their own possession, and they told the most incredible stories about what they could do at night, all corresponding to the local beliefs about possession. In other words, the children dramatized the expectations, the "diagnosis", and the conceptions they were attributed. It became a part of their understanding of themselves and their behaviour.[5]

More generally, one can say that we approach other people according to our definitions of them. We continuously interpret and attribute characteristics to our fellow human beings and behave towards them accordingly thus initiating a process that can easily become a self-fulfilling process (Bråten, 1999, p. 98). In a context of child-oriented care, this implies that *the most important diagnosis a professional can do is to assess caregivers' definitions of their children and their children's definitions/expectations of themselves.* Rather than making absolute diagnoses of a child's deviations in relation to our norms (which is the normal practice in testing), it becomes more important to gain some knowledge of which the people surrounding it attribute characteristics to the child, as these attributions may become self-fulfilling.

Thus, one of the most important tasks of psychosocial *intervention* in such cases is to attempt to positively influence the caregiver's definition of the child, helping them to see the child as a "person" and fellow human being with the same needs for affection and love, and the same need for respect and inclusion as they themselves have. The most important thing is to activate the mechanism called *empathic identification with the child.* This often occurs when the caregiver sees and experiences the vulnerable and helpless aspects of their child, for Example when its negative attention seeking behaviour is shown to overlie a desperate need for contact with and attention from the parents. When the caregiver experiences this appeal, that "my child needs me", the way towards a new and more sensitive and empathic caring

---

[4] This is a striking parallel to the "lightning rod function" of women (and children and men) pointed out as witches or demons in Europe in the sixteenth and seventeenth centuries.

[5] This appears like a hidden contract between themselves and the healer about who they are, what their symptoms and powers are, and how they can be healed (Hundeide, 2003b, 2003c).

relation with the child becomes possible (Hundeide, 2000, 2003c). The child is then included in what can be called *the zone of intimacy*, an important conceptualization that will be introduced and discussed later on.

Objectification and Abuse

Let's pursue the idea of the importance of people's beliefs for the behaviour towards others. In fact non-human treatment and cruelty has to be followed by mental convictions that legitimizes abuse, and vice versa.

Extreme physical abuse and torture usually involve objectifying and demonizing definitions of the victim. "Traitor" is one such definition that appears to legitimize abuse and torture. Working with child and teenage soldiers in Angola, we[6] learned about extreme abuse in this category. They had been kidnapped as children and re-socialized as guerrilla soldiers in the UNITA. The soldiers were trained according to the principle of "the son of a snake is also a snake", and this implied that the entire family and all relatives were killed if one of the family members were accused of treason. They were also trained in different torture techniques to be used on alleged traitors. In an area on the border of Namibia a group of teenage soldiers participated in the execution of a group of people accused of treason. This was perpetrated by having the victims themselves collect wood for a pyre on which they were subsequently burned alive. These teenage soldiers were highly regarded among the officers because they were "totally loyal, they carried out orders and killed without hesitation".

An interview with a young female soldier from the war in Sierra Leone gives an impression of what they had been through:

> I: Have you ever killed rebels in this war?
> C: Yes, many times. When the soldiers came back to camp with the rebels, I was often ordered to «wash» them.
> I: What does that mean?
> C: Kill them.
> I: Did you shoot them with a machine gun?
> C: No, bullets are expensive. I killed them one by one (with a knife).
> I: Did you feel that you did something wrong?
> C: I was defending my country.
> I: Did you ever feel pity for the rebels you killed?
> C: In the beginning, when I saw their dead bodies I sometimes felt sorry for them, but we had to kill them, otherwise they would have killed us if they had the chance. These rebels killed and cut open the stomachs of pregnant women. They raped all women they could get their hands on. (Peters & Richards, 1998, pp. 87–89)

---

[6] "We" implies collaborators in the ICDP project (see Hundeide, 1991), particularly Pedro and Irina Mendes, Milu and Santana.

This is an extreme case, but it contains some of the following legitimizing components one finds with lesser abuse as well:

- An objectification, and often a demonizing definition of the victim who is seen as morally inferior, non-human, traitors and therefore deserves to be abused.[7]
- That they were following orders – and if they did not comply, they would be killed themselves.[8]
- That this was in fact a noble and necessary action performed in the service of their country.
- These legitimizing arguments seem to absolve the perpetrators from a feeling of responsibility and awareness for their inhuman actions.

For the child soldiers, this ideological rationalization was an important part of their indoctrination and preparation for their role as "under-aged soldier"[9] (Bracken & Petty, 1998). Many of these youngsters sustained serious psychological problems when they were to be integrated subsequently into civil society after having lived for years in brutalizing war conditions with totally different values (Hundeide, 2003b).

The Dehumanizing of "Outsiders"

It is worth noting that in conditions involving dehumanization and objectification, an invisible line appears to be drawn between "them" and "us". "We" who are on the inside of this line may experience mutual love, empathy, and human care and friendship from the others on the inside, while those on the outside are at best treated with indifference, and at worst as objects deprived not only of their rights, but also of their subjectivity – to be understood and viewed as "persons" and fellow human beings with the ability to feel, wish, and need as human beings. Under such conditions it can be important to intervene in order to promote human conditions, particularly between caregivers and children.

---

[7] It is important to note that this type of legitimizing and stigmatization also occurs in violations of human rights and UN conventions in the pursuit of what are called "terrorists" like the abuse of Iraqi prisoners in the Abu Ghraib Prison. One can also find comparable justifications in violence-prone racist gangs, such as new Nazis (Bjørgo, 1997; Hundeide, 2003a, 2003b, 2007).

[8] These experiences were a part of the teenage soldiers' training: in some cases they were instructed to kill prisoners – in some cases members of their own families – while the others were watching. If they were unable to comply with others or showed signs of weakness in crying or clutching, they were themselves shot in front of the other recruits. This is the terrorism that led to blind obedience to "the sergeant", who often exploited them with extreme cruelty (Bracken & Petty, 1998; Hundeide, 2003b).

[9] "Under-aged soldiers" is now the politically correct term as child soldiers is starting to have a stigmatizing effect due to the violence associated with this term.

Dealing with obscured empathy, we have learned that belief systems play an utmost important negative or positive role in defining the relationship to and treatment of other people in general and children in particular. Some pathways seem to lead away from and other pathways towards taking and practicing a child-oriented perspective. Let's have a closer look at this by introducing the "zone of intimacy". The duality of being constructed as an "outsider" (the child as an object) or an "insider" (the child as a person) is in the following section spelled out in detail.

The Zone of Intimacy

Variation in human empathy can be metaphorically described as if we have a zone for intimacy between ourselves and our nearest and dearest. Those who are on the inside of this zone are the people we love and who are close to us – they are a part of our family. With these people we *co-experience* their state and their needs through empathic identification, and we act accordingly. Those who are outside of this zone we do not apprehend in the same sensitive and empathic way. They are surely human beings, although they are strangers, and as participants within a shared community we understand them according to conventional codes and rights that apply among human beings. However, this is *an outwardly conventional* relation (secondary care), different from the spontaneous co-experiencing we have when someone in our family is exposed to a tragedy or a great joy. In that case our experience is inward as if it involves us directly and personally. Tragedies happening to people outside of our zones of intimacy affect us to a much lesser extent and less spontaneously. Although we may on reflection respond to the miseries of the world, this is nonetheless a different matter. Those who are outside of our zone of intimacy may be strangers to whom we are indifferent or show an externalized sympathy. At worst they may appear as enemies we relate to by rejection, objectifying, hatred, or revenge.

As shown in Fig. 2 the zone of intimacy can metaphorically be described as a barrier indicating who is on the inside and who is on the outside, Here we can see how we locate people with whom we have a personal relation ("I–you" relation) within the zone of intimacy. These are people who are close to us, with whom we identify empathically. We co-experience their feelings, wishes, and intentions for good or bad. In relation to them, it is easy to be caring because it is a natural extension of the relationship we already have with them. The impetus for caring itself is already in existence. This is not the case for people who are outside our zone of intimacy, however. These are people we have an external, at worst an objectifying "I–it" relation to, characterized by indifference or rejection. In this situation it is not easy to influence and promote good caring because the relationship does not in itself comprise a natural extension of the relation.

The deepest goal of sensitization and psychosocial intervention in such a situation is therefore to attempt to influence the relation itself, and this means that we try to bring the outsiders in from "the cold" by trying to include them in our zone of intimacy so that they are experienced as persons with whom we can identify empathically (see Fig. 2).

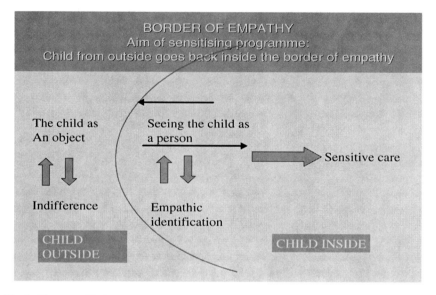

Fig. 2 The zone of intimacy

By including the child in the caregiver's zone of intimacy, it is possible to elicit her empathic identification with the child, which in turn provides a deeper and more sustainable basis for care. When this mechanism functions, the caregiver is always "with the child", and it is therefore easy to influence the relationship between them in a positive way, whether it concerns the child's physical or its psychosocial health. This is illustrated in Fig. 2.

As seen in Fig. 2, both inclusion and expulsion from the zone can occur. Inclusion has already been discussed, but expulsion occurs when, for Example, the child is negatively defined and rejected by the family and forced to leave home and the family to live on the streets. In conditions of extreme poverty and hardship this is not uncommon: Many street children have families still living in the same town, but they cannot return home because they, for different reasons, have been rejected and expelled. Even for those who have not been evicted in the physical sense, life within the family is so full of rejection, humiliation, and brutality that they in reality experience themselves as outsiders. Therefore, to be expelled and to be outside of the zone of intimacy does not necessarily mean that one leaves the scene or home in the physical sense. Rejection and inclusion refers to relationships between people.

As the model shows, seeing the *child as a person*[10] is the first step towards humanization and inclusion. This means that we see the child as a fellow human

---

[10] The concept of "person" as opposed to a non-person, a thing, has been used in social science to indicate the crucial importance of labelling, stigmatization, and negative definitions when violence, terror, torture, massacres, and crimes against humanity are committed (see Buber, Bauman, Bråten, Christie and Smedslund). The concept of "person" is not necessarily limited to human beings; a loved animal, a pet, a dog, or a whale, can become the object for person-attributions, which implies that they are perceived as having similar sensitivity to pain, suffering, and humiliation and also

being with the same needs for security, love, approval, self-respect, and human rights as we have ourselves. When this conception of the child is in place, the crucial mechanism, which I have called empathic identification, can take place. This means, among other things, that we are capable of recognizing and identifying the child's expression and refer it to its mental state, its emotionality, and its intentionality ("mentalizing"). This is how we would have felt ourselves; in this way we become capable of reading the other person's mind (Fogany et al., 1991).

The zone of intimacy is both flexible and permeable. It is flexible in the sense that an episode, such as a moving film or story, can temporarily open up and expand our zone of intimacy so that we may include and identify empathically with a suffering child who is normally outside of our intimate network: "it could have been my own child". But it could just as well have been an account of an enemy that makes us withdraw all empathic commitment so that the person (enemy) remains on the outside of the zone of intimacy – remote as an object. In Fig. 1 of Chapter 5, this definition (apprehension) of the other as a non-person is indicated with a (p), while the included person is indicated with a **P**.

The zone of intimacy is permeable in both directions in the sense that it is possible for a person on the inside to be expelled from the zone, i.e. $\mathbf{P} \rightarrow$ (p). He then becomes a stranger or an object with which one no longer feels empathy and sympathy, but rather distance and remoteness. In the same way, a person on the outside can be included in the zone to become a person who can take part in the human fellowship on the inside, in which one feels closeness and care for one another (p) $\rightarrow \mathbf{P}$.[11]

Finally it should be mentioned that the zone can also be constricted and limited through self-centred commitment, self-stimulation, and hypochondria, or when there is no Other to respond to the child's invitations; a *virtual Other* (or "transitional object") may be created that may serve as a tool for interactive self-stimulation and phantasy-conversations (Bråten, 1999).

Ways In and Out the Zone of Intimacy

In order to arrive at this state of emotional sensitivity to the Other, it is necessary to be in close contact. This can occur by way of what I have metaphorically called the ways into the zone of intimacy. Such ways are

– Face-to-face communication and intimate dialogue
– Bodily contact and touching
– Imitation and direct participation in the activities of the other

---

similar needs for being secure, included, loved, and respected – as we ourselves have. They are, in other words, co-human beings. This makes empathic identification possible.

[11] According to Bauman (1996), this was one of the things the Nazis tried to prevent. Face-to-face contact with "the Jew next door" could be the basis of inclusion into the zone with sympathy and empathic identification.

In the following each of those ways into the zone of intimacy will be treated separately and in more detail.

Face-to-Face and Gaze Contact (p) → P

Face-to-face contact is one of the ways into the zone of intimacy and empathic identification with the child. Face-to-face contact will also provide eye contact and the reciprocal exchange of facial expressions and speech. A strong and direct emotional experience can create sensitivity and openness to the child's attitude. "The appeal of the face" is brought to bear, as Levinas and the ethics of closeness has described it (Vetlesen, 1999). There is a body of literature on the importance of the face and gaze in the establishment of emotional contact that I am unable to discuss here (Ekman & Friesen, 1975; Vanderberg, 1999; Oppenheim et al., 2003).

A close Norwegian friend of this author (Hundeide) recounted the impact of face-to-face contact and gaze contact. It was about his relationship with his son who had Down's syndrome: When after scanning, the doctors told him that they would have a child with Down syndrome he became very agitated and depressed, despite his daily contact with handicapped children at work. In the beginning after his son was born, he had great problems in looking at him, touching and holding him. Despite his explicit ideology about the acceptance of deviations there was something in him that was unable to accept that this was his own son. This continued for some time. He was unable to relate to the child, and he avoided and ignored him. But one day his wife asked him to hold the child – who was then an infant – in such a way as to gain direct eye contact with it. He then experienced that the child looked him in the eye, smiled at him, and reached out for him – and this was what it took to break the ice. It gave him an emotional shock. For the first time he could see his son as a smiling, but vulnerable and helpless person who turned to him. This was a breakthrough in his relationship with his son.

Experiences such as these, where there has been emotional rejection of a child, are not unusual. It is as if the profound feeling of emotional contact and acceptance of the child breaks through when it is experienced as a helpless being, combined with a feeling of "my child needs me". This appears to be a fundamental aspect of all empathic care and a precondition, which in Part II has been called empathic identification with the child. Although this Norwegian father did not perceive his son as "bewitched" or "ghost-like", the Example shows some of the same adult reactions to a child that is not wanted or accepted, for Example in the first phase where denial of seeing and taking-in the "social invitations" from his child was dominating.

This example also demonstrates the strong effect which direct face-to-face encounter and gaze contact can have on the relationship between the caregiver and the child. Since this is a two way dialogical process, it is apparent that expressive children can have a humanizing effect on adults: Through their emotional expressive signals, usually experienced as expressions of innocence, vulnerability, and helplessness, they invite care and empathy in most people – even people who rarely express such feelings themselves.

Not all infants or children have this immediate emotional appeal. Some are unattractive, even ugly to look at. Others are passive and not very expressive; they give weak or ambiguous emotional signals. In such cases it may be important to help the caregiver to establish contact with the child by identifying the signals that are there, gradually supporting a positive redefinition of the child as a person needing care (see the ICDP programme, Hundeide, 2000).

Let's compare two of the Examples we have mentioned and relate them to Fig. 2 of the zone of intimacy. In the Example of the "children who wish to die" mentioned earlier, we see a Brazilian mother who withdraws emotionally from the child because it was defined as an "angel who wished to die". A withdrawal of emotional identification occurs as a consequence of the negative definition, and the child is expelled from the zone of intimacy ($P \rightarrow (p)$). In the Example with the Norwegian father who could not accept his child, but who experienced an emotional breakthrough in contact, we see the opposite. Through gaze and the experience of the infant's expressive appeal, the father gained a spontaneous emotional contact with the child, which in turn initiated empathic identification with the child – "my child". From being ignored and overlooked, the child was included in the zone of intimacy and care (($p) \rightarrow P$). From being a non-person, the child has become a person for whom the father feels protective, i.e. there has been a movement from (p) to P. Furthermore, these two Examples illustrate two important ways into the zone of intimacy, i.e. the importance of positive definitions of the child and the importance of expressive exchange through face-to-face contact and gaze contact. Body contact is also an important way into the zone of intimacy.

Sensitive Touch and Bodily Contact

In the ICDP's work (Hundeide, 2000) with orphans and neglected children in different parts of the world, we have observed the importance of bodily contact and affectionate touching when treating children who have been subject to affective deprivation and traumatization (Field, 1990). Two Examples from Angola will be discussed.

A blind girl in an institution for children with mulTiple handicaps was observed. When she arrived at the institution she was so weak and undernourished that she could hardly walk. After a period of time with supplementary feeding and care her condition improved, and this was when we discovered that she was almost blind. This made communication with her very difficult (the signals for mutuality were ambiguous), and when we met her, she appeared to ignore human contact while the physical care was seen to. Through sensitive physical communication it was possible to achieve contact with her again. We took video recordings of the emerging interaction between the girl and one of our female "facilitators" who first approaches the girl by taking her hand, holding it, and gently caressing the hand with sensitive touch. It is seen how this leads to a change in the girl's expression: she leans back, relaxes, smiles contentedly, and appears to enjoy this intimate contact. The facilitator gradually expands the physical contact by first touching the girl's lips and then her cheeks with affectionate stroking. Finally, she puts her arms around the girl and holds her closely. The girl responds by putting her hands around the supervisor's neck and clinging to her as if a crucial need in her is satisfied. While the supervisor holds her like this, she speaks into the girl's ear, repeating her name and guiding her hands towards her eyes, nose, mouth, and ears while repeating the girl's name and the names of the body parts she is touching. In this way they come to understand one another and speak of the same things – a space for intersubjective sharing is created. All the time the facilitator holds the girl tightly to herself, and there is a contented smile on the girl's lips. The ice has been broken and an intimate contact is in the process of developing between them.

Through sensitive physical contact, touching, and intimate dialogue it was possible to bring the girl into the zone of intimacy – or more aptly, they included each other mutually in their own zones of intimacy. Sensitive, affectionate touching that leads to close embracing is the prototype of closeness and mutual love, whether in relation to an infant or a partner in an adult love relationship. In a situation of sorrow, loss, neglect, and despair, such contact can often release repressed feelings and tears, which may relieve pressure and provide a considerable sense of comfort and security. Nonetheless, this is a powerful form of intervention and contact, and it must be applied with sensitivity and respect for the other's limits – more as a spontaneous response to the other's expression and appeal. Because the danger of infringement is of course great in such situations and in relation to persons having such dependency needs. Therefore, this method must be used with prudence and follow-up in order to prevent new disappointments and new betrayals.

Sympathetic Participation in the Child's Initiatives and Activities

Another way into the zone is by first establishing contact by imitating the child's gestures and initiatives, and then gradually developing this into communication and participation in the child's activities. This is a way of responding by following the child's initiative. As long as a child produces expressive or goal-oriented initiatives and actions, it is always possible to start a simple communicative cycle by imitating the child's actions, following the child's initiative and thus initiate a cycle of turn-taking.

A well-known Example in this regard comes from Hunt's intervention study in Iran. In addition to instructing the caregivers to express an affectionate attitude towards the children, he particularly asked them to imitate the children's gestures and expressions so that a simple communicative cycle could begin. It was this simple, pragmatic instruction that turned out to have a very strong positive effect on the orphans' subsequent development when they were compared with a control group only receiving the so-called responsive toys, in line with Piaget's theory on the important role of self-initiated actions (Hunt, 1982).

In our work in Angola, the ICDP team has occasionally employed the same technique, particularly in cases where there have been contact difficulties. In one case, one of our facilitators was contacted by a father who was an alcoholic and unable to take care of his two and a half year old daughter after his wife died. At that time the girl functioned apparently normally for age and she was able to say a few words. Due to her father's condition she was placed in a very poor foster home with a foster mother who was only interested in the financial benefits of keeping the child, thus subjecting her to extreme neglect.

The child was placed in a small room where she spent the next 2 years without any form of human contact. There was a little window high up on one wall, but no toilet. The room was never cleaned, food was thrown in once a day, and the girl lived in her own dirt for 2 years. When this state of affairs was discovered, one of our facilitators intervened and got the child out of the prison. At this time, the child could no longer walk properly, but crawled about on the floor making sounds like an animal. She had rat bites all over her body. It was impossible to establish eye contact with her or gain contact through face-to-face expressive exchange. She did not respond to normal communicative expressive signals, and her face was closed and devoid of expression. She avoided eye contact and she constantly moved restlessly around in the room. The only thing that caught her attention was when she was given food, at which she produced a specific sound – something like "tchee-tchee". While this went on it was possible to focus her attention on the food for a short time.

When one of our facilitators started working with this girl she was more than 4 years old. The facilitator was deeply committed to help this girl and in line with the ICDP approach she started by looking for expressive signals, initiatives, and actions that she could relate to and imitate in order to start a communicative cycle. In the beginning, these signals were the same sounds that she made in connection with feeding. After a period of time, she was able to distinguish more signals from the child, and began to use them systematically in relation to food, washing, visits to the toilet, and play. Little by little, a rudimentary communicative system based on imitative signs and sounds began to develop between them that seemed to work well in their practical daily lives. The girl also began to show signs of emotional attachment to the supervisor, showing joy when she visited her, and distress when she left. Gradually, her facial expression also changed, becoming more lively and expressive and it was also possible to obtain eye contact with her. Slowly she began to reciprocate the facilitator's expressive initiatives with similar expressive utterances, such as smiles and bodily contact, for Example tickling. In time she was also able to focus her attention on one activity over a somewhat longer period of time.

When she was seen at a later point in time it was possible to establish eye contact and exchange mutual expressive utterances, smiles and sounds, in the same way as one would communicate with an infant. She could walk, albeit a little unsteadily, and she showed a particular trust in her brother and liked to sit on his lap. Evidently, there was a normalization and humanization process under way. This process started through sensitive communicative contact with another person, a facilitator, who managed to establish contact and communication with her through imitation of her *accessible* gestures and expressive utterances. This is where the development begins. At this level, one must begin where the child is, with the utterances and expressive initiative that are accessible.

Conditions that Impinge on Empathic Identification

On the basis of the Examples it should now be possible to summarize the conditions that may promote empathic identification with another person in need of human care (see Fig. 2):

1. In order for a caregiver to feel caring towards another, the other must be defined as a person and as a fellow human being with the same needs and rights as himself or herself. This makes it possible to co-experience and empathically identify with the other.
2. It is easier to identify empathically – to sense their state, feelings, and thoughts – when we relate to people with whom we already have a close and intimate relationship, such as our children and our family, friends, and relatives (Eisenberg, 1992). These are people who are experienced as being inside of our zone of intimacy. Psychological and social distance appears to be a crucial factor. The greater the social distance is, the smaller the chance for empathic identification is (Bauman, 1996; Vetlesen, 1998).
3. It is easier to identify empathically with the other when we can see and recognize the feelings and intentions of the other person (child). We do not identify with expressions that are outside of our own emotional repertoire for recognition. For this reason, people who have similar background also culturally will probably be more empathically responsive and sensitive because they recognize the feelings and responses of the other, than persons with different background.
4. It is easier to identify empathically with people with whom we have direct *face-to-face contact*. This makes it possible to exchange expressive and *imitative gestures* and expressions in a process of mutual affirmation and intimate confidences. This also applies to persons with whom we have intimate relations through *touching and physical contact* in an immediate and directly communicative and expressive interaction, as opposed to a more remote and abstract relationship (Trevarthen, 1988; Bråten, 1999)
5. The feelings that appear to elicit empathic caring are primarily the other's person's (victim's) feelings of pain, helplessness, and humiliation, combined with an appeal for help. In this way the first person is brought into a position of experienced responsibility.
6. It is easier to identify empathically with a person (a child) who is responsive, who accepts and responds to our expressive appeals for contact and fellowship, and who responds affirmatively to our caring actions.
7. Finally, it is easier to identify empathically with a person (a child) *when* our capacity for joining in with the child's initiatives and activities – for "sympathetic participation" – is not exhausted or engaged in other activities; in other words, when we have the time and opportunity and availability for participating in interaction and joint activities on the basis of the person's (child's) initiatives and interests, i.e. that we are not too stressed or engaged in other activities making us attentionally and emotionally unavailable.

A mother or father with a heavy work load and many children in a stressful family situation in which the struggle for survival prevails has little psychological space and motivation for active and empathic participation in their children's experiences and suffering at all times. These sufferings are beyond their relevance structure in their present situation – even though it may not be beyond their capacity in a different and more relaxed situation. For this reason Whiting and Edwards (1999) have shown that the mother's workload in a poor community is one of the best reversed indicators of the quality of care for their children: The higher the workload the lower the quality of care (ibid.).

Beyond the Primary Cycle of Care

It is important to be aware that there are more complex and subtle forms of human suffering that require human experience, insight and intelligence for the need for of caring to emerge, for Example suffering related to injustice, defeat, humiliation and insecurity, which people may experience in situations involving loss of face, honour, and self-respect. Under such conditions empathic identification requires human insight and experience to occur. In other words, there are conditions of human suffering that require more reflection and experience from a caregiver than what is required in what has been called the primary care cycle. This is associated with a more secondary and reflected form of caring and altruism (Berger & Luckman, 1966). In such a context, human experience and understanding of the more subtle and complex aspects of human humiliation and defeat become crucial for the emergence of empathic care (Lindner, 2000). It is interesting to note that for several of the leading moral personalities of our time, from Mandela to Levinas, experience with human suffering provided the background for their moral engagement and perspectives.

Natural Care as Opposed to Professional Help?

It is important to realize that professional helpers seldom have an immediate relationship with their clients, as described in relation to the primary care cycle and within the zone of intimacy. In fact, being a professional implies that one does *not* have such a close relationship. Rather, one is advised to avoid such relationships because they may burden the professional on a personal level so that he or she may more easily bring personal subjective and emotional issues to bear on the situation, issues that can obscure a balanced and fair understanding and treatment. This viewpoint may have much in its favour. Yet on the other hand, one must also acknowledge what may be lost in a professional diagnostic distancing: The professional may easily come to be experienced as a bureaucrat who sees the other as a case in an abstract diagnostic category. It is precisely this remote and abstracted relationship without closeness and mutuality that Levinas criticizes when he speaks of "the totalizing glance" of the bureaucrat, or perhaps one can say "the totalitarian view". In this context, the other person or the child is not recognized as a unique person, only as a case within a category or even just as a number. This is well known to be a pervasive danger in all bureaucracies and totalizing institutions (Bauman, 1999; Foucault, 1976). But this danger applies also to bureaucratic social work, whether in social security offices, childcare offices, political asylum offices, or medical institutions. The situation becomes even more serious when such attitudes are allowed to dominate the routine interaction with clients who are viewed as cases of diagnostic categories. The danger is that feelings of fellowship and compassion disappear altogether, and there is no emotional attunement and authentic communicative contact with the client. Thus the professional helper no longer serves as a fellow human being, rather the client experiences disappointment, alienation, and humiliation. The client's particular suffering and sorrow are not recognized as anything but a case history in a diagnostic category. The primary cycle of direct compassion and care is obstructed, or as Levinas may have expressed it, "seeing the appeal of the other person's face" has been blocked.

Conclusion: The Ethics of Closeness and the Primary Circle of Care as a Child Perspective Orientation

In this account an emphasis has been placed on what has been called the primary care cycle. This implies an assumption that caring has its roots in a pre-verbal and pre-theoretical disposition that is apparent in the infant immediately after birth. In more general terms, one can say with Trevarthen that there appears to be a "dynamic 'together-with-the-other-consciousness' that comes first and that is sustained throughout our lives in our deepest moral core". He further emphasizes this in the following quote:

> The human consciousness seems to emerge from a completely non-rational, non-verbal, concept-less and totally non-theoretical potential for participation and communication with other persons that one can see first in infants. (Trevarthen, 1998, p. 8)

This is a radical claim that goes against the traditional view that human consciousness (the mind) is formed as a result of linguistic socialization. According to the new perspective, it is rather the primary intersubjectivity that is formed before language that comprises the basis for how further socialization evolves. This viewpoint appears to accord with Levinas and his idea about the "first philosophy" in which ethical responsibility for the other through the appeal of the face itself comprises the basis for our subjectivity. In Levinas' words:

> When the other looks at me, I am responsible for him without expecting reciprocity on his part (...) responsibility for the other is the crucial, primary and fundamental structure of our subjectivity. (Bauman, 1989, s. 183)

Bauman further concludes with the claim: "Morality is not a product of society, rather it is the moral relation that is primary, something that society manipulates, edits and confuses" (quotes from Bauman, 1996, pp. 182–183). In a review of the relationship between the new communicative developmental psychology and the ethics of closeness, Vanderberg (1999) points out that the new findings in early communication appear to lend support to the basic perspective of the ethics of close-ness, as exemplified in views on the moral relation as "the first philosophy", on the appeal of the face and expressive closeness as fundamental to the development of responsibility for fellow human beings, on the dangers of distant relationships which deprive human beings of the direct experience of the other's face and thus the feel-ing of direct responsibility, on the dangers inherent in the abstracted and totalitarian gaze of the bureaucrat and the negative definitions that can legitimize dehumaniza-tion and infringement, freeing the perpetrator from the feeling of responsibility for fellow human beings. In accordance with this viewpoint, the care of others is not only something we do for others, but something we do in order to recreate our own human subjectivity – our deepest moral core.

Summing up, the two different pathways developed in Part II can be illustrated in this way:

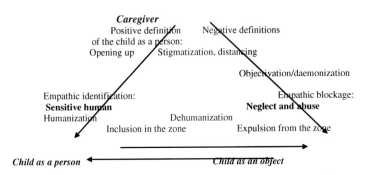

Fig. 3 The child as a person and the child as an object

So, what can be described as *a child perspective* is exactly this adult's realistic reading of the child "face" as reflective of his or her emotional and intentional state. When this empathic identification and participation is present, there is an authen-tic basis for compassion and care that is finely tuned in to the child's experience of need and suffering. This will, as we have seen, be in contrast to *a non-child-oriented perspective* that would be an attitude of non-participating alienation and distancing from the child's experienced needs, feelings, and intentions. As mentioned in this, this may easily arise when the abstractive diagnostics and categorizations prevail over direct human participation – seeing the child's face. Thus, empathic participa-tion with the child can be seen as a main criterion of a child-oriented perspective in line with the ethics of closeness (or proximity).

The Interpretive Approach to Children

As pointed out in this book, it is not easy to know a child's experience directly, or for that matter, Another's experience, except through sensitive observations of the Other's expressivity, behaviour, or utterances. Based on these utterances, we try, more or less sensitively, to reconstruct the other's experience along the lines of our own taken for granted and shared background, as constituted through language and socio-cultural practice (Berger & Luckman, 1966). This applies equally to children and adults; we do not have direct access to the Other's mind. In this respect, we are all observers and interpreters of the Other.

So what is then the difference between an adult-oriented perspective and a child-oriented perspective? A child perspective occurs when the adult makes an effort to adjust himself or herself in order to feel and understand what she or he assumes is the child's experience of a situation. This means that we, as mentioned previously, use our capacity for "empathic identification" or to use Bråten's word "altercentric participation" in order to reconstruct what we assume is the child's experience based on our own background experience (Bråten, 2007). In addition, a child perspective seems to have a humanistic participant intent in the sense that the child's experience could have been our own if we were in the same situation as him or her. This potential of seeing oneself in the child's position creates a positive and forgiving flavour similar to the way a defence lawyer in court tries to present his client – if we were in the same position, we might have acted similarly... Instead of judging him, we are requested to understand him empathically – it could have been any of us.

In a similar way, when a child behaves differently from the established social code of conduct, we are requested to understand the child's action in a way that take into account his or her particular background and position. As Smedslund (1997) points out, an interpretive point of view takes the child's rationality for granted. This means that we assume there is some consistency and sense/coherence in the child's actions; the problem is then, what were his background assumptions for the action. Or to put it simply, as Piaget did: "A child always answers correctly – his own question" (Piaget, 1972, s. 37). Our problem is then what were his or her questions? What is the child's underlying assumption – that is his way of understanding and feeling the situation and the world, so that we can understand his actions as consistent and coherent (rational) extensions from these assumptions? That is the problem

D. Sommer et al., *Child Perspectives and Children's Perspectives in Theory and Practice*, International Perspectives on Early Childhood Education and Development 2, DOI 10.1007/978-90-481-3316-1_7, © Springer Science+Business Media B.V. 2010

of interpretation, which is the core of a child perspective. As a research project, this implies that we try sensitively and empathically to reconstruct through indications from the child's expressivity, actions, and utterances, what might be his or her underlying assumptions – understanding and feeling of the world or the particular situation that is in focus of investigation.

But what is then an adult-oriented, or maybe better, "a non-child oriented perspective"? It may mean a rigid adult-fixated perspective without any attempt to adjust and tune in to the child experience. This means ignoring the child as a person, ignoring his or her subjectivity, and judging the child's actions from his own adult standards that may be alien and unknown to the child. Thus the child's deviance from the adult standard norms and codes is then interpreted as a deficit in the child; there is something wrong with the child. In other words, understanding the child's actions and expressivity is not considered a problem but is taken for granted. What is considered a problem is the child's rationality: How pathological, how unintelligent is this child? The child's deviance from accepted standards requires an individualized diagnosis of deficit that is located in the child. This is an example of a non-child oriented approach that is the opposite of an interpretive approach, where the child's rationality is taken for granted while understanding the child's expressivity is taken as the problem: How can we make sense of the child's actions and expressivity? How has this child understood the situation when we reacted like this? What does the quality of his voice and facial expression indicate regarding his state of feeling and intentions? We are, in other words, trying to *decode expressive signs of an underlying state of mind* that makes sense of his actions/reactions.

Now the question is whether this humanistic empathic attitude towards children that is indicated above – seeing the child empathically as a person with the same needs and rights as adults – is this part of wider social reorientations that can be described as historical and collective. This is what is assumed when child historians write about the emergence of "childhood" as a new category in history linked to industrialism and modern school systems (Aries, 1979; de Mause, 1976) and when sociologists and psychologists talk about the emergence of a "child-oriented perspective" linked to globalization, democratization, individualization, and postmodernism (Giddens, 1990; Lasch, 1994). In similar ways, we have, in this book, analyzed the emergence of a child-oriented and human rights oriented perspective in Scandinavian preschool curricula. This is a part of a similar understanding of a child perspective, not only as an individual person's perspective but as a collective historical and cultural meta-perspective as well representing a change from previous periods when this perspective was not as predominant or absent. Legal documents like children's rights or educational curricula and prescriptive manuals of child rearing, indicating a humanistic, individualized, and child-oriented attitude, have come more into the foreground in recent times – at least in public documents relating to the welfare of children (Cunningham, 1996; Rudberg; 1983). Looking back into history, we find indications that are individualization and adjustment to children as persons is not necessarily a modern "invention" as Aries expresses it. Here is a quote from Plato written 2,000 –3,000 years ago that indicates otherwise:

It would seem then that a study of individual character is the best way of making education perfect, then each child has a better chance of receiving the treatment that suits him. . . . (Ethics 10, Chapter 9)

The Interpretive Approach as Opposed to Competence Diagnostics

If an interpretative approach is attempted, one will discover that there is always a basis or background for a child's reply, and it is this interpretive basis that one tries to get at by an interpretive approach. Thus, instead of defining a child as deficient based on some external normative criteria reflecting the experimenter's or interviewer's conception of the question and the situation, an interpretive approach would start by exploring what would be the child's conception of the question and the situation, which produced this particular reply. In that case, one takes for granted that there is a plausible connection between how a child defines the situation and the task, one the one hand, and how the child responds and acts in the same situation, on the other.

This may appear obvious, but in reality it is rather seldom such an interpretive attitude is practiced. The opposite seems to be more usual; when a reply or an action that deviates from what we judge as normal is experienced, there is a tendency to attribute this deviance to the person explained as some negative personal characteristic like stupid, low intelligence, mad, or some psychiatric diagnosis. It is mostly in cases, particularly in relation to a person with whom we have a close personal relationship, that we spontaneously take an interpretive stance where we try to understand the person's actions in the light of his own conception of the situation and the problem. It is easier to attribute a normality deviance to a person as a deficient personal quality than to look into the person's interpretive world, his intentions, conception of the question, the situation, and in the last instance, the person's conception of his reality – and then finally to interpret the person's actions as a rational response given this background.

The two conceptions, called *normative-evaluative* versus *interpretive*, are not restricted to evaluation of children's responses in artificial experimental situations; they are to be found more generally in all fields where persons are to be understood and evaluated/judged – from law and legal institutions to education, art and psychiatry. Often these two attitudes or perspectives are in conflict, but both say something important about human beings. The normative evaluative locates each person in relation to the values and norms that are prevalent in the society – how adapted, how clever or intelligent, how rich he or she is in relation to others. This is useful knowledge placing each person on a scale comparing with others with regard to the values that are important in the local society or community. But this perspective has its limitation, it only says something about where a person is objectivated, located in relation to others.

But when it comes to the insight into human actions, one has to take on the biographer's interpretive perspective, where one, without judgment, tries to see the meaningful connections in a person's life: That Hans has got a low mark in maths tells something about his location within the class or at best in relation to other pupils at the same age level; this low mark does not say anything about why he has got this low mark. The why question can only be answered by getting to know and understand more about Hans' background, interests, and personal values and goals; his relationship (or commitment) to school and to teachers and other pupils; his personal history of maths experiences, situations of experienced maths failures; and last but not least, something about how he experiences the maths-testing situation. In other words, one has to inquire into his personal world and find out how relevant maths is in relation to his personal priorities of values (in his "relevance structure") and in his understanding and interpretive background (Hundeide, 1981). When this is known, then it is possible to say something about why he has got this low mark. This insight cannot be read from the mark itself. Still, despite this obvious fact, it is not unusual to find that assessments in particular subjects, like marks in school, or some competence diagnosis (like IQ), are reified and elevated as a casual explanation, the maths mark becomes "deficient mathematical competence" in general – as a personal stable trait – "deficient capacity" in particular. This goes far beyond the information contained in the child's relative positioning on a standardized scale. Also this reified diagnosis implies something fixed and unchangeable, almost biologically determined.[1] This implies furthermore that there is little one can do about it. Thus the diagnosis may easily become a negative sentence or stigma that closes further possibilities for development and improvement (see Mehan et al., 1996).

Despite this, Hans with his extremely low school achievements is the best chess player in his class and involved in complicated strategic data plays that he seems to master as long as they are relevant to the projects and activities in which he is involved and committed, projects that are central in his world. This is in fact the key to an interpretive approach: One should primarily judge a person's potential capacities in the fields or domains where he or she is maximally committed – fields that are relevant and central in his phenomenal world. This implies that the assessments typically practiced in school diagnostic contexts are badly suited to assess the potential capacities or competencies of problem-children, because assessments are usually carried out in contexts and domains that these children dislike and have withdrawn all interest and commitment. Instead they have invested their engagement in projects that are outside and beyond the school world. The same apply, even more, to persons with a different cultural background. In such contexts, it can be extremely misleading to apply tests or diagnostic tools standardized on a population with a different cultural background because cultural differences can then be misread as cognitive defects.

---

[1] We call this "biological reification". There is a lot of this in newer neuropsychological diagnostics (Newnes & Redcliffe, 2005).

Instead of using traditional diagnostic approaches which lock the investigator into fixed standardized test Procedures, there is an alternative approach where the objective is to uncover the personal and local meaning system that gives coherence and rationality to a person's actions – so to say from the inside. But in order to explore the inside meaning system, there must be *trust and confidence* between the investigator and the person (child) to be studied. This is a subtle process that requires sensitivity and patience. Sometimes it may be necessary to use insiders in the local community, someone who is trusted and who knows the local codes and rituals, who can speak the local dialect and genre, and who knows the rituals that opens up for confidence, intimacy, and access. When a contract of trust is established, it is possible to proceed further and direct the conversations towards topics that are relevant for the problems to be investigated.

Studies of schools' failures have shown that in informal and intimate interview situations, a child produces replies different from the replies produced in formal test-situations; they speak more fluently and with great imagination. Labov (1972) produced in one study improvized poems about heroes in their environment, and the children showed great tactical skills in solving problems that represented challenges in their everyday life. But there is evidence of how rigid test diagnostics have been applied on culturally deviant groups or ethnic minority groups with the result that children are diagnosed as mentally retarded. In others words, cultural difference are interpreted as mental deficiency through the implicit logic and options of the testing Procedures itself (Ginsburg, 1972; Mehan et al., 1996). This example illustrates the weakness of what has been called the normative evaluative approach as it appears in unreflective use of standardized tests on culturally deviant groups.

It may be objected that his is an unduly negative presentation of normative competence diagnostics, still, irrespective of sensitivity in which the test is implemented, only one perspective on the analysis of a child's situation is represented. It does not make us understand the inner connection between the child's understanding of the situation and the task and the child's reply, nor does it say anything about the connection between the child's way of life and the development of his or her mental capacities, the structure of his or her interests and commitment, and the structure of his or her mind. The normative evaluative perspective can say something about how a child is located in relation to a comparative group of children on the dimensions that are selected for measurement, but if these dimensions are not relevant or outside the child's experiential background, is it valid, then, to describe a child's performance on such scales in terms of inner competencies? The tendency to think in this simplistic way is not only limited to psychologists and pedagogues but has become common part of a widely held belief system – a reified part of commonsense culture. According to Woodhead (1999), this has lead to a one-dimensional and limited conception of childhood which may imply reduced tolerance for cultural diversity and possibly also discrimination both of children and of mental capacities and skills that deviate from the mainstream conception of how normal children should be and how a typical Western mind should operate according to the normative evaluative standards that dominate the Western world. If we wish to help children, we need

to know more than where a child is located in relation to the normative evaluative standards of the dominant reference group: We need to know the "child's life
world" and its "relevance structure". What are the content and the structure of the
child's experienced world (see Keen, 1975)? What are the topics that are central
and important within his world? Which activities are central? Which goals? Which
interpretive background and episode structure (narratives or scripts) constitutes the
basis for his or her understanding and definitions of new situations? In which situations does he or she perform well and succeed? In which situations does he or
she fail and feel insecure? How do key persons in his or her environment define
him or her? How does he or she define himself or herself? Which topics are central
in his or her conceptions of himself or herself, which form the basis for his or her
self-reliance and self-respect? Which human ideals, models and styles has he or she
tacitly appropriated and identified with?

More specifically, how does he or she interpret the interview situation? How is his
or her relationship to the interviewer? What are the child's expectations for what is
going to happen? How is the child positioned in the diagnostic situation? How does
he or she understand his or her role? What does he or her experience as difficult?
What is "the child's question" that he or she is trying to answer? Do interviewer and
child have the same conception of what is going on and what is the child's question
and task that he or she is going to solve? What is the child's definition of his or her
problem in the situation?

These are some questions that need to be answered and clarified when one adopts
an interpretive approach. By adopting this interpretive strategy, it will also be possible to answer the question of why a child fails on certain cognitive tests or tasks, not
as a consequence of deficient mental capacities but as a consequence of deficient
common understanding and intersubjectivity: The child may have answered another
question because he or she has defined the situation and the question differently or
because the question falls outside his or her field of engagement and relevance. A
researcher should try to focus where his or her subject is focusing. This means that
he or she should try to uncover what is the child's conception of the situation in
which he or she is situated and where the interaction is going to take place – in other
words, attempting to establish a child perspective. We will look closer at this in the
next section.

Reconstruction of How a Child Interprets the Situation

In order to understand how a child defines a situation, the author has invented a
reconstruction method, where the child – after the experiment – retell, demonstrate,
and dramatize his or her experience of what happened during the experiment or
event. Stepwise, the Procedure is as follows: First the child is brought into the experimental room or laboratory equipped with a video recorder that films what is going
on during the experiment. When the experiment is finished, the child is taken care
of by the preschool teacher who has brought the child to the experimental room.

She asks the child whether he or she has got the reward indicating how clever he or she was during the experiment. The child will answer negatively and she will be led back to the experimental room to fetch the reward. In the experimental room, all the material used in the experiment is still lying on the table as when the child left the room. Usually a small piece of chocolate functions as a reward. When the child has received the chocolate, the reconstruction Procedure starts:

1. While the child is eating the chocolate, the preschool teacher says, I have never participated in such an event before; maybe you could tell me what happened while you were here together with the man or woman? The child then gives a verbal description of what he or she experienced.
2. Then the preschool teacher goes further and comments: I see these bricks (from the Piagetian conservation experiment) are still lying there (pointing to the table), could you show me exactly what happened?
3. When that is finished, the preschool teacher says, Maybe we could try to play together what happened, you can be the man and I will be the child – ok?

In this way, the child's experience of what happened in the experimental room is reconstructed in three different ways: First through telling, then through demonstration, and finally through dramatization/role-playing with the child in the role of the experimenter/interviewer.

Let us now have a look at the outcome of such a reconstruction of a simple number conservation experiment in the Piagetian tradition: Five bricks are presented to the child in a row and the child is requested to place the same number of bricks underneath the first row, like this:

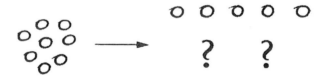

Fig. 1 Number conservation á la Piaget

After the child has placed the bricks (small wooden houses with windows) on the table, the child is asked whether he or she believes there is the same number in the two rows or whether there is more in one or the other. When the child has confirmed that the number is the same in the two rows of bricks – and this a precondition for the whole experiment – the bricks in the lowest row is spread out so that "it looks big...", and the child is asked the same question again whether there is the same amount or whether there are more in one or the other row of bricks. In accordance with Piaget, children at the preoperational stage (roughly preschool age) will tend to answer that there are more bricks in the row that is spread out because the child at this stage tend to be more focused on the appearance of things, how things look, and the child is supposed to lack the cognitive ability to deduct that that number must be the same irrespective of the fact that appearance may indicate the opposite (reversibility). But this is not the problem in this context. Our problem is to find out how the child has experienced the situation or the experiment that he or she has just participated in: What was the purpose of the event/experiment according to the child? How did the child experience and understand the question? What would be an appropriate reply to such a question? etc.

Instead of using bricks, we used small play houses with windows, which could be understood, as houses with flats (like the ones most of the children in the experiment lived in). Let us have a look at some typical Example of how some children reconstructed this situation:

Anne, 6 years: The experiment itself was carried out without any problem and she managed to solve the conservation question without counting. But after the lower row had been spread out, she formed it like a half circle and then commented, after having given the correct conservation reply, "this is a snake".

Fig. 2 The "small house experiment" ("Slange" = "Snake")

A small insignificant detail during the video experiment, that rows were spread out looked like a snake, becomes completely dominant in the reconstruction. In the reconstruction, with role-playing where Anne is playing the experimenter and the preschool teacher is playing child, this becomes even clearer:

Anne: "Can you count them all (the brick houses)?"
Preschool teacher: "1-2-3-4-5 and 1-2-3-4-5"

Anne spreads out the bricks in the lower row so that the row appears like a snake; she then asks the following question: "Is this a snake?"

Preschool teacher: "Whether it is a snake?"
Anne: "Yes, it is a snake!"
Preschool teacher: "Did he really ask you about that?"
Anne: "Yes."
Preschool teacher: "Why do you think he asked you this question?"
Anne: "I don't know."

Like many other children of her age, Anne seemed to move between two "realities" or interpretive frames: an adult and school oriented, where she is supposed to play clever girl and answer complicated logical and boring questions, and another, more fantasy- and play-oriented reality, which is far more attractive and becomes dominant when she is in a more familiar and informal play oriented situation with role-playing of what had happened.

But in order to answer correctly from the experimenter's point of view (position), the child has to know the appropriate interpretive frame or "discourse" that applies in the present situation. Her correct or incorrect reply appears therefore not to be so much a question of "operative competence" in the Piagetian sense, as a question of knowing which situational definition and interpretive frame is appropriate and applicable in which contexts – or, to formulate it differently, which script, "discourse" or "game" that is expected from the point of view of the experimenter in the present situation. If the child knows this interpretive frame and is sufficiently sensitive to take the hints from both the situation and the experiment about which frame/script would be relevant and appropriate in the present situation, then the child would be in a position to give the "correct reply" as expected by the experimenter. But, as pointed out in another context, this search for the appropriate interpretive frame and script, is just as much a *social-discursive and dramaturgical, as a purely cognitive capacity* (Hundeide, 2003c).

This interpretation is confirmed in further experiments on children's event reconstruction. For example, we used children in one experiment, children who had previous been involved in socio-dramatic play in the same experimental room or setting. These children arrived with *different expectations and interpretive framing* for what were supposed to take place in the experimental room compared to the experimenter. As a consequence, they gave quite different replies from what was expected as correct by the experimenter. This is a clear example of what in the definition part of this book was called a non-child perspective, because it does not live up to the "correspondence principle" (Bronfenbrenner, 1979). In other words, there is a lack of correspondence between the experimenter's and the child's understanding and meaning of the experiment. But when the children were interviewed afterwards and role-played the same situation, they indicated that they had been participating in a "guessing game" and that "they had answered all the questions correctly". Other children produced fantasy stories linked to the bricks in the number conservation experiment – stories about the families that lived there, about the mother who went out shopping to the other "block", etc. In line with the expectations from previous experiences and activities in the same room, the children believed this was a *free play fantasy situation and they behaved accordingly*. In other words, they introduced a different interpretive frame and a different script from the one that was presupposed (by the experimenter) in order to produce the "correct reply" in a formal testing session. Thus the children's fantasy replies were assessed as "preoperational" according to the Piagetian norms.

But do we know from this experiment whether a child diagnosed as preoperational is unable to play a different game or script that would invite a correct "operational" reply? The answer is negative. In the example above, the difficulty of the problem is primarily to determine which interpretive frame, which reality, which game or script is to be applied in this situation. When the interpretive frame is clear, the child's definition of the task/operation will naturally follow and so will the child's reply as a plausible extension of the way he or she has interpreted the situation and the task. Such an interpretive analysis can also give insight into "false positives" – how children may produce seemingly correct replies based on false premises: As mentioned above, the bricks used in the number conservation experiment were small wooden house blocks with many windows in each block. One of the children reconstructed the main question like this:

> Per: "He asked me whether there lived the same number of people in this house as in the other house" (pointing)
> Preschool teacher: "What did you answer then?"
> Per: "I answered that there lived just as many persons in both blocks because they were of the same size."

As Per focused on the number of persons in each block of houses, he was not disturbed by the fact that the blocks were spread out. He answered correctly, but on a different question than the one posed by the experimenter. The same did the children who interpreted the question to be whether there was the same number of windows in each block.

Another interesting feature that emerged during the reconstructions was that some young children were more focused on replicating as exactly as possible the *actions* that the experimenter did rather than what was said. In addition, some of the children were preoccupied with that the actions should take place at exactly the same spot where the experimenter had placed and spread out the bricks. Possibly this reflects the children's lack of a meta-cognitive framing of the situation, which prevents them from understanding the experimenter's intentions with the questions. For that reason, they cannot distinguish between what is relevant and irrelevant when they perform their reconstructions.

These examples reveal an important feature with an interpretive approach, namely that the same situation or event can be defined or understood differently and that the replies or the actions/responses that follows from the different definitions are rational and consistent if they are assessed from the point of view of the children's own interpretation or definitions of the situation and the task. In other words, children respond consistently in relation to their own definitions or assumptions. This is illustrated in Fig. 3.

What are called interpretive positions are the typical background assumptions that different persons bring to the situation that they are confronting. This may be a certain meta-cognitive expectation of the situation in a particular direction, for Example that this is a test of school competence or that it is a session of dramatization or free play. Such meta-communicative framings of the same situation will produce different replies to the same question.

In other words, different interpretive positions will invite different situational definitions, conceptions of the task, which again will have different action consequences, as Thomas stated in his famous postulate (Thomas & Thomas, 1928; Keen, 1975; Smedslund, 1983). Another way of formulating the same thing would be to say that *we are always perspectively bound to the position in which we stand.* This is an illustrative: a spatial metaphor that conveys that our utterances, points

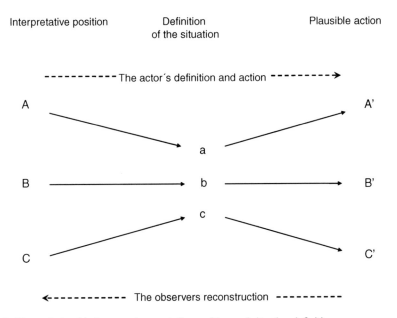

Fig. 3 Then relationship between interpretative position and situation definition

of view, attitudes, and understandings are always "situated"; we will always operate within, or from, a defined situation or a context, or to formulate in line with
Mannheim's (1936) famous saying: "Knowledge is always from a position" – we
are always in some way "positioned" within a space of multiple possibilities. This
implies furthermore that it is always possible to define and understand a situation
from different perspectives or positions – meaning is never fixated in an absolute
sense (Rommetveit, 1992). From this perspectivistic point of view, it follows that in
order to make sense of utterances or actions, it is necessary to localize from which
interpretive position the utterance was produced – how the actor producing the utterance was localized in a space of possible positions (Mannheim, 1936; Hundeide,
1985; Harre & van Langenhove, 1999).

This approach can also be used to diagnose misunderstandings and "deficient
intersubjectivity" between experimenter and experimental subject. Assuming the
experimenter defines the situation from interpretive position B, which means that
it is a test of school-related competence, while the child defines the situation from
interpretive position A, which means that it is a free socio-dramatic play that is
going to take place, this will create misunderstandings because the participants will
interpret the situation and the task differently and they will, as a consequence of
that, produce different replies in what appears as the same external situation. If we
take experimenter's interpretive position B as the normal taken for granted standard, all children in interpretive position B will give replies that will necessarily
be assessed as incorrect. When this state of misunderstanding, in addition, is mis-
interpreted as an inner mental deficit in the child, for example in conception of

numbers or maths, which often happens in diagnostic test situations, this becomes an unacceptable interpretation of children's performance in such situations.

It would be more appropriate to interpret deviance or failure as a misunderstanding or disagreement between child and experimenter on which interpretive positions and frames should apply, which questions should be replied, which game/script or play should be followed. In the case this is described as a deficit or failure, it must be a "definition deficit" – which means that the child has not been able to understand the situation and the task in the same way the experimenter intended. Whether this deficit should be attributed to the child, which is normally done, is more doubtful. After all, it is the experimenter who has posed the question – at best it is a joint definition failure – that can be described as deficient intersubjectivity.

In the situation described above, it is the experimenter who has the definition-control. It is he who decides what is the appropriate situational definition and thus also what will be assessed as a correct reply. Those children who are considered intelligent from this perspective will be the children who have sufficient knowledge and sensitivity to assess which interpretive frame, game, or script is appropriate in which situation, and flexible enough to adjust their replies accordingly. This competence is important because we live, after all, in a complex society where the mastering of certain joint competencies is necessary in order to cope within a collective and to sustain the functions of society. This will be a socio-cultural conception of intelligence (Resnick & Nelson-LeGall, 1997; Hundeide, 2003a).

In Fig. 3, there are two horizontal arrows: one from the interpretive position to action and the other the opposite way, from action to interpretive position. These two arrows describe the difference between an actor in the situation, in this case a child, and the interpreter or observer, who is going to create meaning in the actors actions through an interpretive approach. Let us have a closer look on these two opposite positions: *The actor* comes into the situation with a particular background with special expectations or "predefinitions" as to what is going to happen. This implies that he or she will define the situation, the game, his or her role, the task, and what are appropriate solutions or replies, in line with these expectations, and he or she will act plausibly from this interpretive position and situational definition, as the arrows indicate. *The interpreter* is in the opposite position; he starts with the actions and utterances of the actor. They are his "documents". He can of course apply a superficial normative interpretive scheme that gives an external determination of what is a correct or an incorrect reply from a given interpretive position as is done in intelligence testing, but this would not be an interpretive approach. An interpretive approach would be to take the child's replies as meaningful, intelligent, and competent utterances as a point of departure, given certain assumptions, and it is these assumptions that need to be uncovered by "interpreting backwards" by requesting which situational definitional and interpretive frame the child seems to have adopted when he or she acted in this way or arrived at this seemingly odd reply. The goal is to reconstruct how these actions or replies can be understood as meaningful utterances from the child's point of view. By disclosing how the child has understood the situation, the task, his own role, and what would be an appropriate reply given the total interpretive frame, it is possible to reconstruct the child's reply as a plausible extension of how he or she has defined the situation and the task.

But it is also possible to proceed further and ask why one child understands the situation in one way and why another child understands the same situation in a different way. We then precede one step further in the interpretive analysis and approach what above is described as interpretive positions; interpretive background and the scripts that children have learnt apply in different situations (Hundeide, 1985, 2002; Nelson, 1996). This can be a momentary expectation that is created before the child entered the situation, or it can be stable long-term expectations that are related to the child's socio-cultural background – expectations like school, play, meals, etc. If one applies the interpretive principle described above, that a child's replies, utterances, and actions in a situation are extensions or projections of how the child has defined the situation, then the disclosure of the child's definitions of the situation will be the key problem in interpretive analysis and in the efforts to understand the child's behaviour or conduct as "acts of meaning" (Palmer, 1969; Bruner, 1990).

In this section, children in typical experimental situations have been in focus. But these are just one kind of example. The same interpretive approach that is used in an experimental situation can also be applied in a traumatic family situation, or in a school situation with failure or a diagnostic interview situation. More generally this means that before one starts diagnosing a child's competence or pathology based on observation of behaviour in a given situation, one should first try to understand the child's conception and definition of the situation, the task, and what the child believes is appropriate behaviour in such situation, and not least, how central such situations are in the child's life world.

When Misunderstanding Becomes a Deficit

As we have seen in the previous section, a child constructs a context and a situation in which he or she places the question or task, and it is this construction or definition that regulates the child's reply. In this connection, it appears that the child's construction of the experimenter's or teacher's intention is essential: Where am I? What are his intentions? Why does he ask such questions? What is the objective of this event? What kind of reply does he expect? These are "meta-questions" – the questions beyond the question – that locates an utterance into a universe of meaning or that relates to how the child interprets the episode, the goal, his role, and his task within it. This becomes the interpretive frame for the question, as Rommetveit (1974) calls it "the why of the situation". If we go closer into this, we will see that we all, as adults, also construe meaningful contexts of the whole into which we interpret the present situation and the task. Without being aware of it, we tacitly locate the present situation or problem into familiar scenes with typical sequences of action that has its actors, roles, and interactive rituals. This is what Piaget would describe as "assimilation – the basic fact of psychology". Understanding requires that we interpret the task and the instruction in an experiment or interview, by locating ourselves ("positioning ourselves") into a role, a scene and into a project with interactive rituals, genres, roles, and tasks that serve as prototype for how we make meaning of the situation. As Piaget stated in his famous educational essay, "To understand is to invent" (Piaget, 1972).

However, as Wason and Johnson-Laird (1972) pointed out in their criticism of Piaget: It is not the Piagetian logical schemes that dominate our immediate interpretation of the world, but prototypical schemes from our everyday-world of repetitive routine experiences (Hundeide, 1985). It is within this interpretive background that we locate ourselves in certain interpretive positions. In other words, we understand by assimilating single utterances or actions into these prototypical scenes, action sequences, or episodes from our everyday life and from our dominant symbolic world of meaning. This approach is therefore not only interpretive but also dramatic, discursive, and constructivist, because we interpret single utterances as if they were responses in a dialogue with an actor in a role, in a plot, in a scene, in a play. This means that there will always be the possibility of multiple constructions of any utterance, action, or situation depending upon which total scene or project that serves as a basis for interpretation (Kelly, 1955; Rommetveit, 1998). Also this implies that we bring with us a resource of taken for granted background knowledge that can be used to "fill in" open spaces when an utterance or action is going to be located or assimilated into a dramaturgical whole. In these acts of meaning construction, we read in implications that are tacitly part of the dramaturgical whole into which the action or utterance is assimilated.[2] This happens quickly and involuntarily – we hear an utterance and immediately we project it into a scene that identifies a person and a project – for example, sitting on the tram on my way home from work, opposite to me are sitting two middle-aged women. One says to the other: "... She did not come home yesterday either...". Immediately I see in front of me a divorced woman with a teenage daughter with oppositional and behavioural problems – maybe drugs, maybe prostitution... Then she continues: "She is quite happy in college, I suppose ...". The scene changes and the picture does not look gloomy any longer.

At the same time as we hear utterances of this nature, we project them into scenes or into interpretive frames which provide a plausible meaning for the event – simultaneously as the utterance becomes meaningful, we create the interpretive frame, or it may be that we already have an interpretive frame in advance, and then construe a plausible meaning for the utterance that is adapted to the frame. In this way, we all the time interpret forwards (prolepsis) or backwards (ellipsis): In this dialectic, the whole and part are reciprocally depending upon each other; they create or constitute each other from what is given. We know that this is continually taking place in adults' interaction (see Goffman, 1974; Rommetveit, 1992), but what about children's interactions?

Let us have a look at the scenes children construe, for Example when they are going to learn about time. Pramling (1983) describes how a group of children in

---

[2]This is what in ethnomethodology is called the "etcetera principle " (Garfinkel, 1967).

preschool learn to read the clock. In this connection, they used paper and scissor to cut paper clocks/watches with pointers, etc. After having been through some learning sessions, the children were interviewed about their conceptions of what they had learnt. These interviews showed that children participating in the same learning sessions could have very different conceptions of what they had learnt and what were the intentions of the learning sessions. Some children simply told that they had learnt "to cut clocks or watches". These children had a purely external action-oriented conception of what they had been through and seemed to have no idea that the watches they had cut had any relationship to the concept of time. Some other children had grasped the idea of time, and they had a completely different conception of what had happened and why they had been through these learning sessions.

Despite the fact that these children had been through "the same learning sessions", they construed different scenes, action sequences (project), and goals. Thus the task itself turned out to have completely different meaning depending upon the context. In addition, when they afterwards described what they had been through, they described this as if they were completely different events. Thus they remembered and learnt differently, despite the fact that they had been exposed to the same physical event – because they in fact had experienced different "defined" meaningful event or situations. The essential point in this connection is the child's definition or construction of the present event, because, as Kelley (1955) puts it: it is the construction or the definition of the situation or person that canalizes the human psychological processes.

When the child construes the scene, the action, the goals, and the roles (positions) in line with the experimenter's or the teacher's conception, he or she will know what to look for, which interpretive position to take, and thus the problem-solving itself follows as a projection from being in this interpretive position. Or, as Marton (1981a) formulates it: "those who grasp the point (or idea), are those who are looking for it". To be "looking for it" is a meta-cognitive strategy we tend to take for granted, still this can be instilled into children and prepared by providing the correct interpretive frame or scene, so that the task will be understood both as relevant for the child and in line with the teacher's intentions. However, this is not always what happens: In another investigation by Pramling (1983) carried out in a Swedish preschool, she found a surprising lack of concordance between the teacher's expressed pedagogical objective and children's conception of what actually happened and what was the objective. For example most of the children believed that resting time in the middle of the day was for the sake of the teachers!

This is not a trivial problem because what can easily happen is that children, who have a different conception of the goal of learning, may come into a "private-perspective circle", where the situation is systematically defined in a different way than what the teacher has assumed; for example, "we are carving nice clocks, today". This means that their goal is to cut more and more beautiful clocks while other children are learning about conceptions of time. We see in this example how deficient joint understanding or intersubjectivity of the situation and the task may have the consequence that those who deviate from the teacher's definition may run the risk being labelled as "retarded".

From what has been concluded previously, it will be misguided to treat pupils' deficient school performance as only manifestations of more or less deficient intelligence or other individual personal traits. Such an approach would misinterpret the social interactive play and discourse that is taking place both in daycare and school classrooms. As an example some sociologists would insist, "what children learn at school, is learning to go to school". By this paradoxical statement they refer to the meta-communicative interactive "games" or discursive practices with its own codes and genres that children learn, through school attendance. These discursive practices also include a more or less tacit agenda about who they are, their social position in class, how they are supposed to relate to each other and to the teacher, how they are supposed to reply, in which style or genre, and how they are supposed to dress and present themselves. When children start attending school or preschool, they learn these codes and ways of being tacitly, as part of their participation in everyday discursive routines that provide clear guidance for what would be appropriate and correct conduct at school. This has been described as *socio-cultural micro-skills* (Hundeide, 2003c).

Different schools may have their own culture and discursive practice that emphasizes certain routines – like the British public school as an extreme example. In this context, certain routines may become so dominant the pupils' appearances or "habitus" that an outsider may recognize and identity the type of school the pupil has attended through his body language and ways of being. The main point in this connection is that attending school is more than learning specific subjects; it is also to learn socio-cultural micro-skills, participant structures, particular discursive practices, routines, ways of being, genres, and codes that are tacitly part of being a competent pupil or student. All this seems to be acquired tacitly through participation and practice.

For a child from a different culture or having a non-middleclass background, it may be difficult to uncover and understand the hidden code and for that reason they may easily become marginalized and end up as school failures. Despite the fact that these children competently speak the national language, for example Norwegian, they have not yet learned the more subtle aspects of the Norwegian "discourse" or the Norwegian "way of being" – the tacit codes are required in order to become popular, to appear as intelligent, or to appear as "cool", and to become an insider in a group of friends. To learn "the Norwegian way of being" in school is therefore far more than learning Norwegian language in a narrow sense (Edwards and Mercer 1988). When this topic is related to the process of reciprocal definitions and who owns "definition monopoly" to decide what is cool and appropriate genre or style (in the classroom), then we are in a position to understand more about the mechanisms that make some children feel included and accepted while others are excluded and expelled from the intimate collective of the classroom.

The Intersubjective Space

The intersubjective climate of a classroom is dependent not only upon the personal qualities of the teachers but also upon the reciprocal adaptation or negotiation between teacher and pupil. This adaptation creates a kind of frame or "meta-contract" of reciprocal expectations with regard to position and responsibility, intimacy/distance, which genre or way of speaking that is appropriate, plus which position, role, and rights pupils are supposed to have within the collective of the classroom. In other words, the participants arrive (through negotiation) at a tacit agreement and reciprocal definition (or metacontract) of which relationship they are going to have towards each other, and this definition guides and regulates what is appropriate behaviour within the classroom. This goes on within "the intersubjective space", a space that emerges between the participants and which silently regulates what is natural and plausible to express both from the position of the teacher and from the position of the pupils. It is like a silent conductor, which decides which type of interaction, can and should naturally take place within this interactive frame.

The British researchers Edwards and Mercer (1987) call this "the silent ground rules for communication". This resembles the implicit communication structure in the previous discussed concept of "intersubjective space". Maturana and Rwezepka (1998) are also touching upon similar ideas when they write: "...to create a relational space (between pupils and teacher) where children can develop as self-respecting individuals and socially conscious and responsible individuals with self-respect, is the major task of all education" (op. cit.).

The idea of the intersubjective space can be useful when we are going to analyse the silent and subtle bonds and regulations that emerge and are active when people meet. In particular, the regulations apply in the classroom because they create a new understanding of pupils and teachers' contributions and responsibilities. Seen from an intersubjective perspective, a response from a pupil is not only a reflection of his or her inner individual competence but, first and foremost, a reflection of his or her sensitivity and mastery of the codes for what is plausible and appropriate to express in the intersubjective space between him or her, the other pupils, and the teacher within a particular situation. A pupil's utterance has therefore two aspects: One, the utterance is adjusted to the teacher, or to the person that the pupil is talking to (addressivity). The other, that his speech is taking place within a genre or code that Bakthin called "social language" which again is linked to the socio-cultural group to which he or she belongs. The same applies to the teacher.

This perspective changes how we understand who is responsible for what is presented. Instead of attributing all responsibility for failure or incompetence to the pupil or student, it is more reasonable to raise the following questions: To what extent is what we describe as school competence or academic skills a question of acquiring and mastering the communicative code and genre applicable in the intersubjective space that prevail in the classroom? Like finding ones position and role, being able to adjust to the dominant genre and style and pleasing the teacher through exchange of nonverbal approving eye contact, nods, and gestures. To what extent does the code of the intersubjective space include some pupils and expel others? As an example, pupils with other ethnic and cultural background may easily fail because they do not know "the appropriate way of talking and answering" a teacher in the classroom. Since this is genre – a particular way of talking – not traditional school knowledge, this deficit may easily be overlooked. This is particularly important when it comes to children with another cultural background. To what extent are the failures of marginalized children a result of self-fulfilling definitions and exclusion for intersubjective space of the class (Rogers, 1995)?

This is not a theoretical problem, but very real problem in most classrooms. It refers to basic questions about commitment versus withdrawal, being active and creative versus being inactive, blocked and inhibited versus being included and accepted versus feeling depreciated, expelled and humiliated as a failure and outside the intersubjective space that is shared by the others. Most of us will know from our own experience how easy it is to exclude someone by choosing a subject for conversation that is unfamiliar for the other. Or more subtly choose a local genre of joking, style, or body language that includes someone and excludes others. These are all experiences not only from the classroom but also from any interactive situation of where people meet.

Successful emotional inclusion and confirmation of pupils into the collective of the class require a sensitivity towards the subtle aspects of communication: A dominating and child perspective insensitive teacher may impose his personal style or personal topics in such a dominating and inflexible way, that he, without being aware of it, expels most of his pupils from the intersubjective space of the classroom. In this way, he creates an emotional climate and atmosphere of anxiety and failure. Few feel at ease and motivated because there is no space for the pupils' natural expressivity and creativity, instead; an alienated communicative situation is created where neither pupils nor teachers feel at ease and safe. They are all brought into "false positions" in relation to each other (Hundeide, 2003). A good teacher, on the other hand, is a person who is able to create an intersubjective space where all pupils feel safe and where they can communicate in an easy and natural way.

In the Fig. 4 below the difference between an interpretive and a competence-oriented approach to children's utterances in diagnostic situations is summarized:

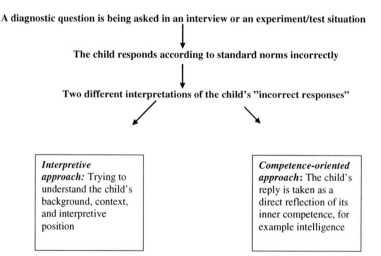

Fig. 4 Differences between the interpretive and the competence-oriented approach

The adult is responsible for avoiding the communicative mistakes that stem from different interpretations of a given situation that are turned into various child deficits. Using the interpretative approach, one will discover that there is always a basis or background for a child's reply and action, and it is this that is grasped by an interpretive approach. Thus, instead of defining a child as deficient based on some external normative criteria reflecting the experimenter's or interviewer's conception of "the situation", an interpretive approach would start by exploring what would be the child's conception of the question and the situation that produced this particular reply. This approach clearly is an Example of what, in the introductory part of this book, was defined as a genuine child perspective, i.e. the direction of adult's attention towards an understanding of children's perceptions, experiences, and actions in the world. The intention of the adult is not to "learn to think as a child", but to approximate children's experiences, perceptions, and understandings of their life world.

Part III
In Search of Child Perspectives and Children's Perspectives in Early Childhood Education

Introduction

In the third part of this book, we will turn our attention towards early childhood education and what it implies to educate the next generation for an unknown future. What do child perspectives and children's perspectives mean in the context of early schooling?[1] This topic will be developed and discussed mainly in relation to an approach to early childhood education called *developmental pedagogy* (Pramling Samuelsson & Asplund Carlsson, 2003). Developmental pedagogy is a research-based preschool pedagogy in which the teacher is expected to embrace a view and a knowledge that will create preconditions for challenging children's creation of meaning in different content dimensions. The preconditions created for making children's experiences visible also contribute to children developing their own understanding of different aspects of their world. Learning then becomes the same as developing and thereby being able to relate to and experience different phenomena in the surrounding world in a new way. This approach also implies that play and learning are integrated into a whole. Before we go into this pedagogical approach, however, we will look at preschool education and how it emerged historically. The questions we will try to answer in this part of the book are

- What roles have child perspectives and children's perspectives played in preschool education?
- What can we learn about child perspectives and children's perspectives from empirical research studies?
- What are the features of child perspectives and children's perspectives in developmental pedagogy?
- What does it mean to act in practice with children, based on children's perspectives?
- What are the preconditions for an early schooling built on children's perspectives?

---

[1] By early schooling, sometimes called preschool here, we mean all public and private learning environments where a group of children come together under the supervision of an educator, as in daycare, preschool, nursery classes, pre-primary and primary schools, etc.

Before we go into the different questions and the early childhood education context, let us talk about what childhood in Scandinavia was like 50 years ago compared with today.

In the 1950s, hardly anyone could read when they began school. Fifty years later, the vast majority of children can read by the time they start school, at least to some extent. How come so few could read 50 years ago while most can today? Although 50 years ago children were told bedtime stories, often fairy tales, and probably also had some books, they spent much of their time outdoors in the neighbourhood (Sandberg & Pramling Samuelsson, 2003). From the parents' perspective, a common view was that "children should be actively playing and not sit indoor and read books" (Johansson, 2000). Why should anyone choose to read books if all of one's friends were outdoors playing? In other words, many children had not discovered the joy of reading, but had discovered the joy of exploring nature and playing, instead. So, can we claim that there was a children's perspective 50 years ago? Yes and no! What it meant to read was defined from an adult perspective in the context of school – reading fluently. At the same time, one can claim that many parents accepted their children's choice of activities outside school – thereby appearing to take the children's perspective. On the other hand, this could have been a child perspective, as they thought this was best for their children.

Children today live in a different time. Some children have more books than a preschool. Many children have also been borrowing books from the book bus or library since they were really young. Many libraries have special story telling and play environments and allocated times for children's story telling. Further, TV and computers with a variety of programs have been available all through children's preschool time. Bedtime stories are read to most children, and books and texts are a natural part of their life – it is normal to read, write, and talk about books.

Society has changed in the past 50 years, and books have become everybody's property. Our way of thinking about children's ability to read and write has also changed. We have discovered that children are children of their time and respond in accordance to the activities in their surroundings. Let us describe a situation with two children, Hjalmar aged $3\frac{1}{2}$ and Albin aged $4\frac{1}{2}$, and a small episode of relevance to the written language.

> Both of them were visiting their aunt, and played in her house while she was working in the kitchen. The aunt happened to find one of Hjalmar's books and said to him: "Look Hjalmar, I found one of your books. You must have forgotten it here last time you visited me. I don't think Albin has heard this story, why don't you read it to him." She gives him the book and continues with her work. Suddenly she hears how Hjalmar "reads" to Albin in the next room! He is sitting on the floor besides Albin, turning pages and "talk-reading". Some of what he "reads" may be about "Bob the Builder" while other things are not in this particular book. Albin partly listens, partly looks at his own book and pretends to read himself, while Hjalmar recites beautifully.

Well, how does this reading situation differ from children's reading 50 years ago? We cannot, of course, know that for sure, but let us discuss it anyhow. According to many studies about reading and writing (Gustafsson & Mellgren, 2005; Hagtvet-Eriksen, 1997; Roos, 2004), early literacy, that is the basis for later becoming a fluent reader, is also perceived as a precondition for becoming literate. This means that Hjalmar considers himself a reader on his own merits – what he himself does when he acts as a reader – that is his perspective!

Furthermore, children *are* different today. Parents negotiate with their children, and the preschool teachers make children participants in projects where equality is the rule – they are given opportunities to express their own standpoints; they are listened to and have a chance to understand what is going on in different situations. Teachers are expected to listen to children and explain things that we earlier took for granted that children did not understand (Hundeide, 2006; Kjørholt, 2001).

Hjalmar, now a few months older, recently took part in a big party in connection with the defence of a doctoral dissertation. When everybody had been seated, the children were called in from the yard where they were playing so we could all have dinner together. Then Hjalmar said: "I don't want to sit here, I want to sit at the main table" (at the table of honour). And of course he could! After a while, when the doctoral candidate's supervisor held his speech and talked about the dissertation in his academic way Hjalmar asked loudly: "What is he saying?" and wrinkled his forehead. He could obviously not make sense of anything, and from his perspective the speech was a completely foreign language. We discovered that it was a totally unknown language to him through his actions, his words, and his body language. *Making sense of oral language comes before making sense of written language, as we know* (Nelson, 1996), and it was clear that Hjalmar was used to being able to make sense and when he could not, he let people know.

Yes, the world and the preconditions for becoming able to use the written language certainly look different today from half a century ago. Expectations have changed and our view of what counts as written language has changed as well – children are seen as competent learners right from their early years.

Parents as well as preschool teachers may be more focused on the written language today. Earlier they did not think of small children as readers and writers, but they were satisfied with children developing an understanding of the visual codes we are all surrounded by, gestures, facial expressions, voice level, body language, relations with the family and with friends, artefacts, and characteristics of the environment – features that are all part of becoming a literate individual – step by step (Kress, 2003).

With this short story, we want to draw attention to the fact that the notions of "the child perspective and the child's perspective" can be expressed differently at different times and in different contexts. When people in our generation grew up, nobody asked themselves what reading and writing were from the child's perspective, while today we are aware that this phenomenon is related to literacy (Hagtvet-Eriksen, 1997, 2004, 2006; Dahlgren & Olsson, 1985; Tolshinsky-Landsman & Levin, 1985; Dahlgren, Gustafsson, Mellgren, & Olsson, 2006). Björklund (2008) just published her thesis about how children under the age of 3 deal with and interest themselves in literacy in their everyday life in preschool. It is fascinating to see how they actually do communicate and take the initiative with regard to written texts. This also paves the way for perceiving literacy as multimodal (Kress, 1996). While it is true that half a century ago adults also listened, to a certain extent, to the children's perspectives in terms of their interests, we have since generated new knowledge about children from research, which has clearly revealed the child perspective. Maybe the child perspective held by adults creates opportunities for children's perspectives to appear?

Children and their opportunities to learn may not have changed in one sense, but they have in another. Most 2-year and 7-year olds still have different levels of skill or knowledge in general. However, since the influence of culture and knowledge formation within this are now better understood, children and their capabilities are now viewed in another way. Children live up to expectations in the culture surrounding them and develop individually, according to their respective experiences. It may also be the case that children's reasoning is less influenced by cultural experiences than by cultural features such as artifacts and scripts.

What then about child perspectives and children's perspectives in early childhood education through history?

In Search of the Role of Child Perspectives and Children's Perspectives in Early Childhood Education

In a large part of Europe, and particularly in the Scandinavian countries, Fredrich Froebel (1995[1863]) is considered to be the father of young children's preschool education. According to Johansson (2007), Froebel had worked unsuccessfully all his life to try to change schools until, at the age of 58, he began to take an interest in kindergarten. Against reforms in the area of education were the schools, the churches, Protestants as well as Catholics, and the state. His idea was that preschool education should be different from formal school education. Behind the backs of the establishment, he began to set up kindergartens with the support of parents' organizations and mothers. He also had the support of certain women in the Liberal and Conservative parties who had very liberal ideas concerning marriage and morals towards the end of the 19th century. Schools, however, never accepted theme work and play, which are central concepts in kindergarten, and did not want to see kindergarten as the first step in the compulsory school system. This is a conflict that remains unresolved to this day! The churches still want to have power over young children in many countries. Sweden and Denmark may be an exception here, but in Norway we can see that many daycare centres are run by the church. The church and the state have never accepted early childhood education, but have seen it as a threat for mother–child relations. Here France may be an exception, since it has had another educational system for a long time. Froebel's ideas may still be regarded as radical in many places in the world, since his approach was intended to foster freely thinking human beings and not state machines!

The reason for developing a new approach in kindergarten was that young children differ from older children in their capacities and sense making. Instead of imposing the structure and content of school on young children's lives, he centred the pedagogy on family activities, such as housekeeping, gardening, carpentry (Asplund Carlsson & Johansson, 2000). One can imagine that this was his way of coming closer to the children's perspectives, to *work on the topics that children knew from home.* Still another Example of Froebel's intention to come close to children's worlds is structuring education in terms of learning, working, and playing. Play was a phenomenon that had never been adapted to education earlier. Here, one can imagine how the concept of play came to be accepted as something of importance to young children – providing a means of taking the perspectives of children.

This was seen as the nature of children, the way they were, which was also evident in Froebel's ideas about kindergarten (children should be nurtured like plants in the garden).

We have to ask ourselves, however, whether it is the children's perspective that is taken in early childhood education or whether something else is dominant? If you just follow them "the way they are", does it mean that you are taking a child perspective or the children's perspective? Today, in contrast to 150 years ago, we believe that children's learning depends on their cultural background. Or is this a misconception of the past? Plants also need fertilizers to grow!

How then should education for young children be characterized? One suggestion was made by Bruce (1987), as we will see below, who described what she felt has been the ethos of early childhood education.

How Young Children Learn in Early Childhood Education

The *act of learning*, that is *how* children learn, has been very strong and thoroughly developed during the whole history of preschool. All the way the child and his or her integrity have been met with respect in theories or programmes of early years' education. There has been a certain consensus about the fact that children are different from adults, which is a kind of developmental perspective. Children are not driven by long-term goals like adults, but are interested in here-and-now questions, and the concrete rather than the abstract is always in the mind of the child. Therefore, concrete actions and the present become central features in all programmes; how to arouse children's interests and get them involved is fundamental for children's knowledge formation (Bruce, 1987). Maybe this basis in the thought of the child being active "by nature" has made all the early childhood education people concentrate on the act of learning – or the issue of *how* children learn (Pramling Samuelsson & Asplund Carlsson, 2003). This means that the central ideas used have been the child as a psychological individual and concepts such as play, wholeness, inner motivation, self-control, active child, starting where the child is. Consequently, the focus during the early years has been, and still is, on the act of learning – how learning comes about – as well as on children as persons. Furthermore, more general theories of learning, such as those of Piaget (1970[1929]) or Vygotsky (1972[1934]), also focus on the act of learning. By taking into consideration knowledge from the whole field of child development (Hwang et al., 2005) in pedagogy for young children, we have constructed a child who, by both nature and culture, is different from older people and who also learns in a different way from adults. We can also see this in modern ways of looking at early childhood education. For instance, when standards of quality are developed in the USA, the notion of "developmentally appropriate" practice is central (Bredenkamp & Copple, 1997). Certain ways of working with children are more appropriate than others, and that is when the pedagogy is adapted to the child's level of development. This is clearly a child's perspective – trying to do what one thinks is best for the child according to what we know about children.

There may be a reason why the focus on how children learn has been so strong throughout history (Bruce, 1987). Young children are different from schoolchildren, not just because they have not learned to be schoolchildren, which for many children means following instructions and waiting for their teacher to give response. Young children are active by "nature". They are constantly moving around, which studies of toddlers have shown us (Gonzales-Mena, 1986). This leads to certain demands on the teacher. These demands could be described as making children interested in specific learning tasks, but also capturing the child's interest. The teacher has to be able to *tune into the child's world* (Stern, 1985). Siraj-Blatchford et al. (2002) talk about "shared sustainable thinking" as one important quality factor in children's learning. This means that the teacher and the child/children share the same object for communication and thinking – something many studies have shown to be rare (Kärrby, 1985; Doverborg & Pramling Samuelsson, 2000a; Pramling, 1983). However, this demands teachers who are able to adjust their perspective or get children interested in order to see the same learning object as she does. This leads to the question of *what* children are supposed to learn in early childhood education.

Although the focus in preschool is on the act of learning, there has obviously always been a content area, that is, something the teacher has got children to work around. The content as such has, however, not been of great importance, except in the case of Froebel (1995), who had the intention to develop children's understanding of mathematics and morals. Curricula have long existed in schools, but a curriculum has also been drawn up for early childhood education today, and the objective of learning has become important again, as in the early days of preschool. This means that a content area is now clearly spelled out. In this respect, one can claim that the adults' perspectives on what children are supposed to learn come through. Here the preschool tradition, with its focus on the act of learning, encounters the school tradition where focussing on the learning object has been strong. Research has shown also how this is a problem for the active teachers since they often perceive conflicts between the traditional more child-centred preschool and the knowledge distributing school (Pramling Samuelsson & Pramling, 2008), and, not least, where they perceive a problem with the role of play in pedagogy. At the same time, it is still common today to consider play to be a necessary element in children's life in preschool.

The teacher's role is equally important in learning and play, something not always visible in practice where teachers often withdraw when children play. The teacher's role is important for giving support and inspiration, for challenging and encouraging the child's willingness and desire to continue the process of making sense of the world. Thus, the focus should be on the process of communication in play as well as in learning.

Early childhood education is not a place for children's general lives, but a specific arena where children learn and develop within a certain framework. Preschool is not home, even though many activities that often take place there have the home as a role model (Dahlberg & Lenz Taguchi, 1994). What takes place in preschool is different from what takes place at home, and both teachers and parents are aware of this.

There are always objectives and an *object of learning*, what the child is supposed to learn, something we will come back to.

Maybe we could say that knowledge about child development is a strong indicator of the pedagogical approach used in early childhood education. However, it is not only knowledge about children's development that is shaping practice but also a strong belief in children's natural development (Gesell & Ilg, 1961), something which could be destroyed if adults are insensitive to their needs, interests, intentions, own activities, etc. Is it the vulnerable child we still see in practice, although new theories talk about the competent and resilient child (Sommer, 2005a, 2005b)? Do children need to be protected? If so, from what?

We claim that many preschool teachers in Scandinavia, and also researchers (Olfman, 2003), think that children in preschool have to be protected from the school culture (Skolverket, 2004; Elkind, 1988), as children should not be forced into learning about the different school subjects, or have a day divided into lessons totally structured by the teacher. Whether we share their opinion or not, one might ask whether it is a sign of their taking the children's perspectives or just adopting a child perspective. Or what is behind this negative perspective of school from early childhood education teachers (Ackersjö, 2006)? Are the traditions of preschool and school still so different that they cannot meet? According to Karlsson, Melander, Pérez Prieto, and Sahlström (2006), there are sophisticated differences in the communication between teachers and children in preschool and in preschool classes (in Sweden and Denmark for 6-year-olds) and primary school. Open exploration and free expression are encouraged among the youngest children while activities among the older children are more teacher-led and the children are guided towards the right answers. Further, in the two interactive ways of having dialogues, it is obvious that younger children are allowed to express themselves, and thereby their perspectives, far more than schoolchildren. Fleer (1995), in her study about early science teaching in transition class and primary class, shows how two teachers, both using an interactive model, do this by focussing either on procedural orientation or on children's thinking about the conceptions used. Children had a far better chance to make meaning within science in the latter approach where interaction concerned central concepts for understanding the particular phenomena used. So children's understanding may be a question of the teacher's approach rather than of the age level of the children.

Child-Centredness

A principle that is widely followed in early childhood education is child-centredness. In the footsteps of Froebel, we talked about "centres of interest" for topics around which work and learning took place. This was supposed to be a way in which to organize the preschool day with a variety of activities that could be linked together to both create meaning and prevent children from losing interest and becoming bored. From a school perspective, it is said that young children have limited powers of concentration. At the same time we know that babies can concentrate for a long time if something catches their attention (Stern, 1991). At the centre of interest is the topic, which one attempts to comprehend as a whole. The child-centredness is shown in children's actions – that is, the active child – being allowed to touch, smell, manipulate, create, and talk about the topic he or she is learning about. In early childhood education we imagine a child who is allowed to act and take the initiative, although the teacher sets the frame. However, within the frame, room must be made for the children's perspectives and expressions.

Many people relate child perspectives in early education to child-centredness, which is something that becomes obvious when searching the databases for "children's perspectives" (Pramling Samuelsson & Sheridan, 2003). With the help of our observations of children's nature, early education is adapted to what we believe is natural for children – or what we as teachers, researchers, or administrators believe is best for children. But do we know, from this description of education for the youngest, if the child's perspective is ever taken into account in practice?

One approach in early childhood education, which has strong links to the origin of preschool education, is the pedagogy of Reggio Emilia. A main feature of this approach is that there is a great effort to throw light on the child's perspective. Listening to children can specifically provide teachers with an insight in children's world, for example by documenting their ways of talking and expressing themselves, verbally or in drawings (Åberg & Lenz Taguchi, 2005). With the help of skilled art teachers who can help children to express themselves in beautiful patterns or through fantasy and real objects in colours from the whole rainbow, children's own ideas have taken the early childhood education field by storm. It is fascinating and empowering to become aware of the child's perspective, and here Reggio Emilia is *one* of many sources for making this visible. As we have seen in the first part of this book, the Scandinavian countries and particularly the research there have contributed a great deal to making children's perspectives visible (see, e.g. Doverborg, Pramling & Samuelsson, 2000; Pramling, 1983, 1990, 1994; Johansson, 1999). On the other hand, there is a great deal of rhetoric about children's perspectives in early childhood education.

When we search for the role of children's perspectives in preschool education, we can establish that the intention is there, but also realize how it differs from formal education in compulsory school, which is one factor influencing our perspectives of the child and his or her world. It is when we contrast our perceptions of early childhood education with school learning that we think of preschool education as closer to the child's world and experience than school education, which is more focused on the intention of society, what is to be learnt. However, is not preschool education directed towards the intentions of society, to foster the next generation to become good citizens and acquaint them with the kind of behaviour and knowledge we want them to achieve? The idea of learning in terms of learning "from the outer to the inner" world of the child has been a guiding star since far back in the history of preschool education, a perspective that has grown with the theory of Vygotsky (1972) into modern times. That is, that children can act and express ideas in cooperation and interaction with others before they can do things or make sense by themselves. Does this mean that the child's perspective is that children need a teacher of some kind, whether the teacher is an adult or another child? Or does it mean that it is more likely that a child's perspective will come through if teachers adopt a pedagogical approach based on a child perspective?

Curriculum – A New Phenomenon in Early Childhood Education

In the middle of the 1990s curricula also began to appear in early childhood education in many places of the world, something that had long been common in compulsory school. Now, after about 10 years, many countries have developed their own specific curriculum for early years (see Oberheumer, 2005). The OECD (Organisation for Economic Co-operation and Development) has also taken an interest in curriculum questions for the youngest (www.SourceOECD.org). When the OECD arranged a seminar about curriculum and pedagogy in early childhood education in 2001, they chose the *Te Wāriki* (New Zeeland), *High/scope* (the USA), *Reggio Emilia* (Italy), *Experiential education* (Belgium), and *Lpfö* (Sweden) as Examples of high-quality preschool approaches (for a more exhaustive comparison, see Pramling Samuelsson, Sheridan, & Williams, 2006). What these preschool approaches have in common are the following: (1) the perspective of the active child, who initiates communication, who is interested in the surrounding world and who constructs knowledge in interaction with others. (2) The view of children's rights, communication, and interaction as a key factor in children's learning and development to become a citizen in a democratic society. It also started to make the child's rights visible in early childhood education. (3) Cooperation with parents has been recognized since Froebel's time and is emphasized in all curricula. (4) To visualize the child, as something the staff need to become better at doing, to understand each child better. This might be realized if we get more reflective teachers. Documentation is a key factor here. (5) Value orientation and teacher professionalism are evident in these curricula, and also an effort to develop more professional teachers, although they use different approaches for this. There is a strong belief of giving children a good start in life! However, the curricula differ in the following respects: The view of the child, the pedagogical approach, and the importance attached to the learning environment, and assessment and/or evaluation.

While there are similarities and differences between the curricula that are culturally specific, Pramling Samuelsson, Sheridan, and Williams (2006) claim that there are also elements that are more general, that is, children are perceived as subjects, and as different from older schoolchildren. One reason why these curricula have been chosen as Examples of good curricula may be that they have never fallen into the trap of making preschool into a traditional school, as is often the case today (Olfman, 2003). This is something that many researchers have fought against (see, e.g. Elkind, 1988, 2003) or others have proved to have no future (Klugman & Smilansky, 1990; Marcon, 2002). Another reason for success may be that the programmes are either research-based or driven by a strong ideology. Pramling Samuelsson, Sheridan, and Williams (2006, p. 26) say

The programmes' intentions for the pedagogical environment, activities and content in preschool, teachers' actions and interplay with the children are in symmetry.

It is, however, important to take into consideration one of the Results in *Eager to learn* (National Research Council, 2001), where it is clearly spelled out that there exists no single particular method or preschool programme which is the optimum choice and superior to all others. This is important to consider when people get fanatic about a specific pedagogy, which everybody then wants to be involved in as a guarantee of quality. This is, of course, a false belief, just as the NRC report states.

It is interesting to note here that the formal instructions for early childhood education come under different names, e.g. framework, guidelines, curriculum (Pramling Samuelsson & Fleer, 2008). These documents also differ enormously. For instance, in Germany alone, guidelines vary in length from 20 to more than 400 pages.

There may not have been legally binding national guidelines but, as Vallberg Roth (2002, 2006) states, various types of curricula have always existed in a broad sense, guiding the work in preschool in Scandinavia. The curricula have, however, changed in historic times, and she classifies them accordingly, for Example, Curriculum of God, around 1850–1890 (with a patriarchal code), curriculum of the Good Home, around 1890–1930/1940 (a sex-segregated code), curriculum of the Welfare State, around the 1950s to the middle of the 1980s (the gender-neutral equality code), and finally curriculum of the Situated World Child, from the late 1980s up to today (the pluralistic, sex/gender code).

In his book *The Power of Play*, Elkind (2007) talks about how spontaneous, imaginative activities lead to happier, healthier children. He believes that in early education play, work, and love should be intertwined into one whole. When these three entities are integrated, Elkind says that the child's actions are similar to Csikszentmihalyi's notion of flow. The following elements are present when people are experiencing truly enjoyable experiences: (1) there are clear goals, (2) there is immediate feedback on one's actions, (3) there is a balance between challenges and skills, (4) actions and awareness are merged, (5) distractions are excluded from consciousness, (6) there is no worry about the future, (7) self-consciousness disappears, (8) the sense of time becomes distorted, and (9) the activity becomes autotelic (an end in and of itself) (Elkind, 2007, p. 12). We understand Elkind to mean that the element of play and openness for feelings and communication carry children into a mode that could be compared with the notion of flow. Children are in charge and are allowed to use their imagination.

To sum up, early childhood education culture with child-centredness (child perspectives) differs from the school culture with mainly adult-centredness by tradition. The intention today, at least in the Scandinavian countries, is to merge the two cultures into a third more goal-directed one that is driven by adults but retains the child perspectives. A further aim is to direct early childhood education more towards children's participation and perspectives, something we will come back to. What can we then learn from research about child perspectives and children's perspectives?

What Can We Learn About Child Perspectives and Children's Perspectives from Empirical Research?

Research has changed tremendously in recent decades. The number of qualitative studies aiming to describe and analyse children's everyday life and experience has exploded in the Scandinavian countries. We will look at some of them here, to see what we can learn about child perspectives and children's perspectives. Maybe one should say that many of the researchers who work in this tradition have experience of preschool teaching themselves (Klerfelt, 2002), which means that, from the start, they have a kind of child perspective aiming to find out more about children as individuals. It is possible that there is some intention to use the findings in practice, although the studies as such may be purely analytical and basic research.

The focus of much of the research in all three countries is on quality questions, the history of preschool, the adults in preschool and their education, curriculum implications, etc., all topics that are more or less necessary to anyone trying to take a child perspective (Gilbrandsen, Johansson, & Dyblie Nilsen, 2002; Haug, 2003; Sheridan, 2007). Research is also used to a great extent in policy documents concerning children in the Scandinavian countries (Kunskapsdepartementet, 2006:227; SOU, 2000:3). We will here, however, only touch upon some studies dealing specifically with interaction between children and between teachers and children in preschool.

Raising Teachers' Awareness Through Development Studies

Working with young children has traditionally been closely related to personal relations. In this perspective it is interesting when a person specifically points out the professional commission of the teacher, which has to be separated from the personal individualized one. This view is emphasized in the official Swedish report *Jämställd förskola* ([Equal preschool], SOU, 2006:75) by pointing out that the commission of teachers to work with questions of equality in preschool is superior to their personal views. This is in no way an easy equation, how to ignore one's own values, but most certainly a question that has to be discussed – a question of great relevance to the Discussion about child perspectives and children's

D. Sommer et al., *Child Perspectives and Children's Perspectives in Theory and Practice*, International Perspectives on Early Childhood Education and Development 2, DOI 10.1007/978-90-481-3316-1_9, © Springer Science+Business Media B.V. 2010

perspectives. One can imagine that the possibility of separating one's own personal perspective and the one stated in the laws depends on the awareness of the teacher.

In the Scandinavian countries there is a tradition of doing research close to the teacher, which goes under the name praxis-orientated research or development studies. We will now present a few and see what one can learn from them in relation to child perspectives and children's perspectives.

Young children in daycare centres (Palmérus, Pramling & Lindahl, 1991) is a development study based on Pnina Klein's theory of early intervention (Klein & Hundeide, 1995). She uses five criteria for interaction and communication between children and their teachers for developing children's cognitive skills. These are intentionality and reciprocity, expanding and going beyond the immediate (transcendence), mediating meaning and excitement, mediating feelings of competence, and regulating behaviour by helping the child to plan before acting. The teachers in the study used these five categories but expanded them to distinguish between interaction and communication as initiated by the child (child's perspective), on the one hand, and by the teacher (adult's perspective), on the other hand.

Teachers and children were video recorded in their daily practice. Each month, over a period of $1\frac{1}{2}$ years, these films were analysed and discussed in the team of teachers together with the researcher. Teachers developed their skill to communicate and interact to a very large extent and become aware of their own actions, by using the child's perspective as a source. By the time the project was completed, the most skilful teachers were able to catch the child's initiation of communication during more than 50% of the observed time. By observing themselves in action, analysing what they did from a specific theoretical viewpoint, the teachers became aware of themselves as communicators as well as of children's skilfulness and creation of meaning in communication (Pramling, 1995).

The study *Caring, Guiding, Learning* (Lindahl, 2002) is a similar developmental project with preschool staff working with toddlers. They were video recorded in practice, and these video sequences were analysed continuously together with the researcher. The Results of the study show that a number of the project participants initially held an old-fashioned view of children, which formed the basis of their relations with them. Children are seen as immature, delicate creatures that do not think so much, but instead mainly hum while toddling around at preschool. Children are fragmental creatures who, on the one hand, cannot focus their interest for a long period of time but, on the other, can busy themselves and potter about forever. The teachers agree that infants need a lot of care, tending, and emotional involvement. However, the teachers feel that the children need orders and guidance in order to learn "appropriate" behaviour. The main emphasis at preschools is on security and calmness, while learning and development are not especially prioritized for these young children. Since children are not considered mature enough for certain phenomena, little demand is made on the adults' pedagogical knowledge. In fact, the children's intellectual immaturity leads to a decline in the adults' professional pedagogical ambitions. Accordingly, the majority of project participants are of the opinion that work with infants does not place large demands upon an adult's actions, but instead demands social and emotional involvement.

The study Results seen after the intervention show that the teachers have gained new insight. They have begun to think about the competency expected of them as preschool teachers. The children are now seen as competent creatures with their own ideas and intentions although they are very young. For the teachers, it is now a question of being able to interpret the children's actions, meet and respond to the children's initiatives in a manner that they feel furthers development and learning. Discovery of the children's cognitive abilities motivates the teachers' professional actions. Care and security are important, but development and learning are not over-looked. At the end of the project, the project participants regard care and learning as one entity. At the same time, the teachers' responsibility for making use of dif-ferent situations, both routines and miscellaneous everyday activities, is stressed. In this manner, the adults' contributions further the children's learning. The teach-ers have discovered that it is often small signs in interaction between children and adults that determine how the interaction continues and develops. The teachers now see competent infants who should be treated with respect and who need *challenging activities* so that their learning processes can be furthered. Therefore, the infants' actions demand that the teachers change their methods and create a favourable learning environment for young children. During their own learning process the teachers have become aware of children's capabilities and perspectives in terms of their actions.

This kind of basic research carried out with teachers in practice, and at the same time with the intention of influencing practice, may be specific to the University of Gothenburg. This means that one sets the stage with what one wants to study and follows the process.

Children's Expressions, A Question of Contexts

The purpose of the study *Young children's influence in preschool* by Anette Emilson (2007) was to investigate how very young children can influence their daily life in preschool, in relation to teacher control. The specific questions studied were as follows: What opportunities do the children have to make their own choices and take the initiative? How does teacher control manifest itself? What form do perma-nent structures, such as rules and routines, take? The Results show that the children do, in fact, make choices, mostly from several fixed alternatives, and that they do take the initiative, sometimes to express an opinion and even a right, sometimes to express what they want to do in circle time. It is also shown that the amount of influ-ence young children are able to exert varies with the amount of control the teacher exercises. It is evident that strong teacher control is maintained in different ways, that is, by directing communication, by using a playful voice, by being responsive, and by endeavouring to come close to the child's perspective. In communication directed by the teacher, explicit rules about conduct and manners appear. In such situations, the children are unable to exert any influence. When the teacher maintains control by coming close to the child's perspective, responding to them sensitively, and talking to them in a playful voice, the rules are implicit and no reprimands are necessary. In these situations, the children are freer to make choices and take the initiative. The Conclusion is that strong control does not necessarily limit children's influence; it depends on the *character of the control*. Children's influence increases when the teacher's control over the *what* and *how* aspects of communications is weak and is characterized by closeness to the child's life world and a communicative approach. In order to stimulate children's influence, it seems to be important to *develop teachers' powers of insight and mutual respect*, claims Emilson (ibid.).

In the study *Learning Encounters in Preschool* Eva Johansson (2003) focuses on the quality aspects of learning among toddlers in Swedish preschool. In the investigation, three main themes were found, which were significant with respect to the pedagogical encounters in preschool created by the teachers: *atmosphere, teacher's view of the child*, and *view of learning*. Each of the main themes was found to contain three sub-themes, which are brought together in her presentation. The Results indicate that an interactive atmosphere characterized by proximity to the child's life world is often accompanied by a view of the child as a fellow-being and confidence in the child's capacity to learn. When the atmosphere is unstable, the view of the child is characterized by a perspective from above and a view of learning based on maturity and the child's (in)competence. Finally, when the atmosphere is characterized by the teacher's need to exercise control, we can discern a view of the child as an irrational being together with a view of learning based on conditioning. The Conclusion is that children have the greatest opportunities to express themselves when the teacher sees the competent child and has trust in his or her learning.

In her thesis *Young children's ethics,* Eva Johansson (1999) has shown how children between 1 and 3 years of age fight for their rights in preschool. They fight for the right to objects and to sharing their worlds of experiences with other children. In preschool the objects, such as toys, are everybody's, something children perceive very soon when they begin there. What also seems to be a code in preschool is that the person who has something has the right to it, but conflicts arise when a child's right clashes with another child's right, e.g. when a child puts down a car or something, for a moment but still feels that it is his or hers, while someone else feels that no one has the car right now so I'm allowed to take it. How do teachers handle conflicts like this? Often they ask "Who had the car first?" – a value worth considering if one wants to distribute to children. Young children seem to have an intuitive feeling about justice. Personal objects seem to be perceived as an absolute right, e.g. the ownership right is superior to the user right. The norms applicable among young children are according to Johansson: (1) control, e.g. the one who is active with something has the right to it, (2) time, e.g. to be the first means to have the rights to the objects, (3) strength, e.g. if one has physical or psychological strength, then one asserts one's right. This means that the very youngest children's actions and cooperation with other children and teachers become the foundations for children's norms and values. Children's play in preschool is a question of existence in the form of rights and shared rights in a collective. It is in these encounters that the under-standing of values and norms is reinforced. That is when adults are needed, adults who have decided what values they think are most important and worth supporting in relation to societal goals in, e.g. curricula.

Elin Michélsen (2005) wrote her thesis about *Interplay in toddler groups*. Michélsen takes us right into Swedish preschools with toddler groups seething with life. Children meet, play, interplay, end up in conflicts, and "make up" peace among themselves. What happens between these toddlers and what kind of emo-tional climate is there? The author has observed 1- to 3-year-old children focusing on their interplay. The mutual creating, ingenuity, and understanding she sees as expressions of child culture, and she has studied how these children develop *a feeling of themselves as a peer*. She considers toddlers' interplay in preschool to be an expression of child culture. Typical of this culture is that toddlers invent play routines, which can be seen as culture. With engagement, interest, and joy, they interact with each other in movements, which they develop and change with delighted shouts and in agreement. This joint creativity includes traces of non-verbal consent. It also includes positive feelings and bodily communication, as typical fea-tures of child culture. With their own inventions they create their own space as a field of free action. Michélsen (ibid.) claims that it is easier to discover children's own inventions when they do something backwards or unexpectedly, but always bodily.

She says that children take each other's perspectives, which she believes is a way to socialize each other, something other researchers also express (see, e.g. Frønes, 1995). Also, the social strategies children develop for making them understood and for cooperating with peers are expressions of peer socialization. Michélsen (ibid., p. 129, our translation) says

> It happens sometimes that a third child educates two other children who are in conflict by physically creating justice and giving one of the quarrelling children the disputed toy. Children's arguments, e.g. in a conflict about a toy, are often both verbal and non-verbal about both partners expressing their perspectives "this toy is mine, and I am to have it". It is in these two conflicting perspectives the third child takes a positioning standpoint. Acting in conflicts between two other children in this way I see as a concrete situation where children practice taking another person's perspective.

Michélsen also discusses her empirical observations of toddlers' interplay in terms of the influence they have on each other's self-conceptions as peer self-conceptions. She also shows how concentrated and resilient interplay between young children can be in everyday settings. In momentary interplay children try to get into contact, which allows them to experience a kind of brief interpersonal meet-ing, which might just be a question of saying good morning and goodbye almost at the same time. In other sequences of interplay, where children spend a long time co-ordinating with each other around a joint project or toy, children gain experience of how one can keep the peer interest through, for Example, adopting each other's rhythm and tempo.

Marita Lindahl (1996) followed 10 children, aged 1–2 years, during their first 3 months in preschool to see what young children learn and experience there, that is, how and on what they spontaneously focus their attention. The study was inspired by phenomenography, and resulted in a number of qualitatively different categories in which children's learning could be described. Lindahl described how the result of learning (what) was shown in insights (being able to do something, showing knowledge about something) and understanding (creation of meaning), and in the way they focussed their attention and acted. The process of learning (how) in young children was characterized by their skill at mastering different activities, by focussing their attention and concentrating, by discerning and evaluating, and by discovering differences. In this study, too, the data were obtained by means of video recording, which made it possible to study the same sequence over and over again and while trying to follow each child's actions: with whom they communicated and how they handled different situations.

Løkken (2004) also showed how toddlers interact with each other and create their own culture by, e.g. just following each other, imitating each other, or interacting in their own ways. It looks as if it's just for fun, but they most probably also create meaning and in ways that adults do not think of as meaningful interaction. Løkken has a phenomenological approach in her studies, which means that she interprets all the things that young children tend to express with their bodies. She characterizes children's expressions in a very similar way to Michélsen, but also describes children's consent in joint projects as a question of confirming and expanding through reciprocity in the form of glances, smiles, and laughs. The intersubjectivity is obvious, and it is easy to see how children share feelings, attention, and intentions with each other.

Lindahl and Pramling Samuelsson (2002) describe the young children's learning process in preschool as both imitation and variation, that is, children not only imitate each other's behaviour but also use a conscious strategy with variation to learn something. This means that the imitation and variation are interwoven in their actions. An analysis of two case studies, one with a toddler trying to master a skill and the second with a group of children playing together, shows how the learning object varies. The little boy, Wataru (14 months), learns to master the idea of spinning objects, which presupposes objects with certain features. Wataru finds a variety of objects (rings of different sizes, a tray, a wooden piece from a toy) to practise the phenomenon of spinning, and he develops the skill quite remarkably for his age. The whole sequence of observations begins with Wataru observing and imitating the teacher who gets a ring to spin. He shows, however, that he can distinguish the round shape feasible for spinning from the other forms. He appears to understand that the spinning can be transferred from one object to another. Wataru develops the idea of spinning and the conditions of shape and manual activity required by sampling various objects.

In the second case study, a group of seven children aged 15–30 months both imitate and vary their behaviour while trying to master a piece of gross motor equipment, a slide. This entails ensuring that the object in the observation is constant. It is the children who introduce variety in their actions on the slide. The children sometimes imitate one other, but many times they try to develop new ways of sliding which differ from other children's methods of sliding.

In the first case study, the child kept the act of spinning constant or at most imitated or repeated it, varying the objects spun. This enabled the child to acquire the skill of spinning (a general phenomenon). In the second case study, a group of children focused their attention on the same phenomenon, sliding, which in this case is the part that is imitated or varied. Here the children use their bodies to create variation. The authors claim that imitation and variation go hand in hand in young children's learning.

One of the most recent studies is called *How do children involve teachers in their play and learning?* (Johansson & Pramling Samuelsson, 2006). In this qualitative descriptive study, five different categories of ways how children try to get their teachers involved in their world could be traced. The data are derived from video observations of times when an individual or a small group of children approach a teacher. The conversations between the teachers and children have been transcribed verbatim. The Results in the form of categories show that children involve teachers because they want support and help in play and learning, want to be seen, make the teacher aware that someone is breaking the conventions, want to know how things are, or want the teacher to participate in their play. The youngest children also invite teachers to join in their play by offering make-believe coffee or a cake, while the older children tend to do this verbally and humourously. In general, one can see that children handle numerous tasks and situations in preschool without turning to an adult. When children need help, they first of all turn to a peer. There is a lot of communication and support going on among children. When children want to get teachers involved, they have strategies for this. It may be culture-specific with coffee drinking in Scandinavia, since this behaviour has been noted in other Swedish studies (Tullgren, 2004).

Liv Gjems (2006) has written a thesis about *What children learn when they narrate*. The children she observed were between 3 and 5 years of age. She claims that children's narratives in the family are quite different from those in preschool. In the family, the listeners have usually taken part in the situations the child is talking about. This is not the case in preschool, which puts demands on the children to be more specific in their telling. First of all she was surprised that there were so few narratives in the communication between teachers and children. She was specifically looking at telling in the form of "as if" and if children purposefully take the adult with them into the story by introducing background information about the situation or the people they are talking about. If children do so, Gjems interprets this as an indication that children are able to take others' perspectives. The reason why children tell stories about their experiences could be sharing, making sense, exploring. Already at this age level children use words for mental activity, for Example, think, know, guess, remember, forget, want to, believe, decide, and mean. The skill of expressing oneself in a way that others can understand is said to affect the writing process. What she also saw was that the teachers who told the children most stories were the ones who got most stories from the children.

Elin Ødegaard Eriksen (2007) also focuses on children's constructions of narratives in toddler groups in her thesis. She shows how the narratives differ in content and action depending on whether the dialogue is initiated by a teacher or by a child. Children's narratives are often about their culture, while the adults' narratives deal with more pedagogical and fostering topics. Aukrust Grøver (1992) has also studied learning, language, and communication in everyday life in preschool, and how early language is mediated by the culture in preschool (Aukrust Grøvre & Snow, 1998). Children's play and playfulness are other themes in research. Humour has been described by Søbstad (1990) and construction play by Trageton (2005). Haugen, Løkken, and Röthle (2005) are the editors of a book on pedagogy for young children based on phenomenology, focussing on dialogue, play and aesthetics research.

Children's Participation as a Democratic Value

Working towards the goal of developing children as democratic individuals has not been spelled out so obviously until today. This is, however, closely related to the perspective of the child. Williams, Sheridan, and Pramling Samuelsson (2000) have shown in an analysis of official documents in Sweden how the idea of participation has changed during the last 30 years. At the end of the 1960s children's cooperation and participation were expected to lead to the development of social competence for living in a democratic society in adulthood. The dialogue between children is expected to strengthen their feeling of togetherness, that is, cooperation is to be perceived as a working method for children's well-being and turning them into becoming democratic members of a society.

In the beginning of the 1970s a state commission presented a report on the content and methods for work in preschool (SOU, 1992:72). It was suggested there that children of different ages should be mixed in the same group (sibling groups), mainly to give them the opportunity to learn from each other and communicate. This approach to pedagogy was actually called "dialogue pedagogy" for some time (Schyl-Bjurman & Strömberg-Lind, 1976), to show the emphasis on cooperation and everybody's role in children's learning and also to give children models for solving conflicts in communication. The teachers became psychologists who should listen and communicate with children but not influence them!

In the 1980s the authorities stated that children's cooperation should be with the society surrounding them in order to develop as democratic individuals. It was also stated again that young children need each other and find joy together. However, it was asserted that adults could never be replaced by peers with regard to children's possibilities of developing as equals, which is one important aspect of democracy (Socialstyrelsen, 1987:3).

When we reach the curriculum of today the perspective has changed from just talking about democracy as a question of cooperation and joy to also seeing children's influence on everyday life. Communication and dialogues are also perceived as necessary conditions for learning, not simply for well-being (Skolverket, 2006a, 2006b). What we can see here is that the view of children and their learning and, consequently, of what it means to develop as a democratic individual has changed.

We believe it is fair to say that today democracy is perceived both as a way of being involved (participating) and as a content to become aware of (Doverborg & Pramling, 1995).

Although the right of participation is clearly stated in official texts, it cannot be claimed that all children are active and equal participants in early childhood education. Some children may be, others not, depending on their position in the group. However, being an active participant depends on whether this opportunity is given to children or not, says Eva Johansson (2005). She also points out that it is a question of respecting children's integrity. Sometimes children's needs are separated from their rights, but as Colwyn Trevarthen (1998) says, the human infant's most fundamental need is to become part of a culture.

Marita Lindahl (2005, p. 35) refers to Askland and Satagøen (2003), who talk about a negotiating family where children can grow as individuals.

> In the family both humanization processes, being heard and seen, are especially important, being unique, and having specified needs are focused. In the democratization process, the focus is the fact that rules can change, that individuals are self-determining, they have the ability to experience self-determination, and the desire to engage in society, to demand to be seen and heard as a person, and may experience a weakened faith in authority.

The above quotation can be seen as an Example of democracy both as a way of being and as an understanding of how humans can change things. We can also see how democracy, as a phenomenon, turns towards what we have talked about earlier, that is, both to live democracy and to create knowledge about it! We have to realize, however, that children in preschool are tremendously aware of what they can have opinions about and what they cannot (Alvestad, 2001). Sheridan and Pramling Samuelsson (2001) also showed in an interview study of 5-year-old children how they experience their own participation and possibilities of making decisions in preschool. The different categories of conception that emerged in the analysis of what they perceived as decision making were as follows: to do what one wants to, to invent and fantasize, to exercise power, to do what most children want to do, to allow or forbid. Children felt they could decide in play together with other children. They also expressed the feeling of being equal in decision making when they played a game together with the teacher. In all other cases the teacher was seen as the one who decided.

A topic not often associated with toddlers is mathematics. Camilla Björklund (2007) has, however, taken up this theme in her thesis about young children's experiences and how they take form in everyday life in preschool as notions and problems that could be related to basic mathematics. She calls what the child chooses to focus his or her attention on as "holding points", which are aspects of basic mathematics from an adult perspective. Her own definition is (ibid., p. 135, our translation)

> Holding points are critical conditions for children's experiences and learning in the world around them, since these holding points give support to children focussing on different aspects of specific phenomena. A holding point is what it distinguished and focussed and could be an object that new objects are related to or are compared with. Earlier experiences can also be holding points which children expressly relate their new experiences to.

Children spontaneously compare, categorize, make patterns, put things together (wholeness) and take them apart (in parts), make reasonable judgments, use number words, etc., and very much of their behaviour is related to their own bodies. Björklund convinces the reader that children are interested in and try to make sense of notions and phenomena that we consider to be basic mathematics. She also shows how variation is a central tool for children in their creation of meaning.

Bae (2004) has studied acknowledgement by teachers in relations between them and children. The aim was to understand how confirmation was mediated and in which way this creates opportunities for learning and development processes. This question also throws light on children's possibilities of exerting power and control. She finds two patterns of interaction and communication, which may be characterized as a narrow and an open attitude in the relationship. The open interaction and communication naturally allow children more space, and here they are also more confirmed as individuals.

We can also see from other studies how teachers spend more time in contact with boys than girls (Andersen, 1995). Randi Dyblie Nilsen (2000) asks in her study how we can understand and describe the process of socialization starting from the dimensions adaptation and resistance. Among other things she shows how girls and boys encounter a pedagogy characterized by female culture in terms of encounters between children's "life and movement" and adults' organization in terms of "peace and calmness", and also their creation of territorial control.

What Can We Learn from These Studies?

When it comes to *children,* we find that they are much more skilled than we believed 20 years ago. They are competent and intentional in communication and interaction both with peers and adults (Sommer, 2005). What we can learn about *teachers* is that they are often surprised about the competences and skills of toddlers, and this has been confirmed by a recent study (Pramling Samuelsson & Fleer, 2008). We can also see that the adults' ways of thinking about children's capabilities, and what learning means for this age group, affect their behaviour and interaction with children. However, we can also learn from some of the above-described studies that video observations of teachers' own settings and interactions with children greatly influence their knowledge formation, and many teachers become skilled in taking children's perspectives – a vital prerequisite for understanding how children make sense and meaning (Pramling Samuelsson & Asplund Carlsson, 2003). Discovering each child's world of experience and trusting their willingness to learn are key factors in the work with toddlers as well as preschoolers.

To sum up, research which focuses on children's perspectives tells us that even very young children have their own culture and are competent and skilful in many ways. Research also tells us how the surroundings and the context influence children's possibilities of making their perspectives visible. From praxis-orientated research we can learn how teachers' discovery of children's perspectives or creation of meaning changes their own perceptions and, consequently, their behaviour as teachers.

The research studies presented above all look for the children's expressions and perspectives as far as it is possible for an adult to grasp them. In some respects, children express themselves verbally and in others bodily, so evidently it all becomes a question of the researcher's skill in putting herself or himself in the children's position. In this much help is to be gained from the new technology with video recordings as it enables us to study children's actions over and over again and also discuss them with other researchers to reach a consensus on how things can be interpreted. In the first studies we could see how teachers were influenced by viewing themselves in action with children, and no doubt researchers are also influenced by spending their lives capturing the children's experiences and realizing how capable they are. It all has to do with children's own participation in the research settings. In the same way, we can state that children's own role and participation are becoming more and more obvious in the official curricula. The UN Convention of the Right of the Child, and particularly its paragraph about listening to children, has become a guiding principle in our time.

To become aware of young children's capabilities, where their perspectives may be traced, adults must look for them – believe they exist! This means that a child perspective is a prerequisite for seeing the child's perspective or, in other words, children's perspectives cannot be analysed and described if we do not bear the child perspective in mind.

Let us now turn our attention to a pedagogy based on children's perspectives and their active involvement.

In Search of the Features of Child Perspectives and Children's Perspectives in Developmental Pedagogy

The Research Background

Developmental pedagogy[1] (Pramling, 1990, 1994; Pramling Samuelsson & Asplund Carlsson, 2003) is a research-based approach developed and used in early childhood education. The research base is double in that it first of all sprang out of a methodological approach (phenomenography) to discovering the subjective world of the participants in different research studies (Marton, 1981a). Second, a didactical[2] approach has been tried out in practice and evidence that it has helped to develop children's understanding of different aspects of the world around them has been shown (Pramling, 1996).

The phenomenographic approach has clear links to and roots in the phenomenological perspective described in Part I. The main difference is that phenomenology is a philosophy focussing on the essence of meaning, while phenomenography is a research methodology aiming at finding the variation in the understanding of different phenomena.

When phenomenography was developed in the 1970s it was focused on capturing how a specific phenomenon in texts was interpreted by a group of students, that is, how it appeared to them (Marton, 1981b). The reason was not to see who understood a certain text and who did not, but to find out in what way they made sense of the text and later also how this was related to their ways of thinking about their own learning (Säljö, 1982). It was in other words a question of making the subjective world of the participants, which in itself is both subjective and objective at the same time, visible as a relation between the students and the world around them, in this case as a text.

Learning in this approach became a question of an internal relationship between the child and his or her world (Marton & Booth, 1997). The doctoral thesis of

---

[1] The name developmental pedagogy stands for a pedagogical approach aiming at a development of children's values, skills, and understanding as knowledge formation.

[2] Didactics here does not mean instruction, but the way the teacher can create opportunities or an environment for children to learn and make sense of the world around them.

D. Sommer et al., *Child Perspectives and Children's Perspectives in Theory and Practice*, International Perspectives on Early Childhood Education and Development 2, DOI 10.1007/978-90-481-3316-1_10, © Springer Science+Business Media B.V. 2010

Pramling (1983) about children's conceptions of their own learning is an example of what constitutes the core of phenomenography. This includes first of all finding out how children create meaning about a specific phenomenon (learning); second, finding out the qualitatively different ways in which this phenomenon can be distinguished by children; and third, describing the various ways children think and express themselves in terms of critical features characterizing each category of conceptions.

The results of Pramling's study can be summarized in terms of *what* children (3–8 years) experience that they learn to do, to know, and to understand and *how* children experience that they learn in terms of doing, growing older, and experiencing or creating meaning of something. These categories emerged from the data collected, that is, children's expressions and statements about specific things they learnt and how they went about learning it. The categories are abstractions of children's expressions. When children say, for example, that they have learnt to ride a bike, to wash their hands before lunch, these expressions have a common feature from the child's perspective – doing something! Examples of the category of knowing are when children say they know that bus 58 goes to grandmother or that this flower is called tulip. The category learning as understanding can be exemplified by a child saying "When I was 3, I knew what a car was, but I did not know what traffic was." In this case the child relates changes in her or his perceptions to learning.

Central Features of Developmental Pedagogy

To obtain the relevant Results that can be generated within phenomenography, it is necessary to apply methods for data collection where, *first* of all, the children are supposed to think, reflect, and, in different ways, share their world of experience. This is the most important component now when the research approach phenomenography has developed in the direction of a theory of awareness (Marton & Booth, 1997) or – as we call it when we talk about young children – a developmental pedagogy (Pramling, 1994), a pedagogy aiming at developing certain values, abilities, and meanings.

The second important component is the teacher's attitude. It may be assumed that there are manifold ways for children to express an eagerness to communicate their ways of experiencing something. Teachers' ways of relating themselves to children are, however, not endless, but above all a permissive and interesting attitude and a willingness to learn about each child's creation of meaning are crucial for being able to challenge children's learning. Children must be able to express themselves and make free associations and feel that this is what counts and not the production of "right" answers as defined by the adult. Here preschool has traditionally had a more permissive way of working with children and also a greater trust in children's capacity to make sense of their world than compulsory school has – a question discussed earlier (Pramling Samuelsson, 2006).

The third important element in phenomenography, which we mentioned above, is the description of the variation in ways of thinking. For the teacher the task is obviously something else than for the researcher. As a teacher one cannot describe and characterize the whole variation in ways of thinking in a group of children, but try to see the various ways children think and give children preconditions for becoming aware of the various ways they think about something (Doverborg & Pramling, 1995; Doverborg & Pramling Samuelsson, 1999c, 2000a). In this way, teaching will focus on children's own ways of communication and thinking. Since the variation in ways of thinking is expressed, children are challenged to relate their own ways of thinking to other children's ways of thinking. In this way each child's taken-for-granted way of thinking is challenged. But once again children's understanding of different aspects of the world around them takes place in the encounter with objects and people.

In phenomenographical research, people's subjective world and their ways of creating meaning about the world around them are in focus. This means that the ontological base is non-dualistic, i.e. the subject (the child) and the object (the world around) are perceived as being included in an internal relation, making one whole between the child's understanding and his or her context. In developmental pedagogy creating meaning is also in focus; children are given the opportunity to act out their experiences, thereby making them visible, both to themselves and to others. In phenomenographical studies, deep interviews are common, giving participants a chance to think and reflect. Similarly, being skilled in interviewing children, that is, communicating, giving them the opportunity to express themselves in different ways, is of central importance to teachers working within the framework of developmental pedagogy (Doverborg & Pramling Samuelsson, 2000b).

Using interviews as a tool requires not only skill in asking open questions or getting children to talk and narrate but also the skill to analyse and make sense of children's experiences. Language must be trusted as an opportunity for people to participate in each other's life worlds, including children's. There are, naturally, other ways of getting access to children's worlds, such as drawings (Pramling, Asplund Carlsson, & Klerfelt, 1993; Doverborg & Anstett, 2003) and making video recordings of their actions (Pramling Samuelsson & Lindahl, 1999). The analysis of the data obtained by any of these methods is all about trying to see what the child sees or experiences.

The result of a phenomenographic research study is the variations in ways of thinking[3] and experiencing something in the world around the child, that is, the variation of meanings expressed by the group studied. It is this variation of ways of understanding which is used as a content in communication by teachers who apply developmental pedagogy. Before children's ways of thinking can be used as content, their ideas must be made visible in one way or another and the next step is being able

---

[3] In the perspective of phenomenography one does not separate thoughts and verbal expressions. What is thought about or understood can be verbalized, and the verbal language is not separated from "real" thinking.

to reflect on them. The two principles of developmental pedagogy which emanate from phenomenography are as follows (Pramling Samuelsson & Mårdsjö Olsson, 2007):

- Noticing and taking advantage of situations around which children can think, reflect, and express their ideas, verbally and in other ways.
- Using the variation of ways of thinking expressed by children as a content.[4]

The creation of meaning by very young children also varies according to their experiences and how they perceive a particular situation or task. In Pramling Samuelsson's and Doverborg's paper (2007), we can, for example, see how toddlers in preschool solve the task of putting four teddy bears to sleep in two boxes in four different ways. The bears come in two different colours and two different sizes. The analysis of the video recordings shows four categories of how children solve the task: (1) all bears in one box, (2) dividing the bears between the two boxes without taking notice of colour or size, (3) putting red bears in one box and green bears in the other, (4) putting the large bears in one box and the small bears in the other. This means that the way each child experiences the task and the bears as such makes them act in various ways. At the same time, there is an age trend showing that more of the youngest children put all the bears in one box and, the opposite, more of the oldest categorize the bears according to either colour or size. It is also obvious that one can find all the categories throughout the age range (1–3 years).

With this example we simply wish to show how it is possible to trace the very youngest children's perspectives, acted out bodily by them. This is something Johansson (1999) has shown with regard to children's creation of meaning in relation to ethics, that is, how children under the age of 3 act bodily to express ethical standpoints about what they find to be right or wrong in preschool (see previous chapters for more examples).

Children's creation of meaning is seen in their actions, in their bodily expressions, as well as their verbal ones.

Traditional Views of Playing and Learning

In early childhood education it is generally agreed that play is an implemented aspect of young children's lives. At the same time, however, preschool differentiates between play and learning in everyday practice.

In play children are the ones taking the initiative. This might be a way to let the child's perspective come through. Play is also considered to be joyful, light-hearted, and driven by children's interest. Play is viewed as process-orientated and children are active physically, emotionally, and intellectually. The child sets the goals, goals

---

[4] For an Overview of research on metacognition in learning, see NSIN Research Matters (2001).

that may be changed whenever the child wishes. Adults generally think of play from the child's perspective and respect their freedom to choose.

Learning, on the other hand, is often planned by the teacher and is goal-orientated as well as product-orientated (by the teacher or the curriculum). The child's cognitive development is the main objective, and the teachers are active and control what is going on (Pramling Samuelsson & Asplund Carlsson, 2003). Although we always claim that children learn when they play, we do not want them to play when they are supposed to work on a specific task decided by the teacher. Does this mean that we think of play as the child's world, and that we adults need to keep in control by planning learning situations for the benefit of their growth?

The National Research Council in the USA asked 20 of the most distinguished researchers in the field of early childhood education to come to a consensus on what we know today about young children's learning. In the book *Eager to Learn* (2001) the Conclusions are as follows:

- Young children are capable of understanding and actively building knowledge.
- Development is dependent on and responsive to experience.
- Education and care in early years are two sides of the same coin.
- Cognitive, social–emotional, and physical development are complementary, mutually supportive areas of growth all requiring active attention in the preschool years.
- Responsive interpersonal relationships with teachers nurture young children's disposition to learn and their emerging abilities.
- No single curriculum or pedagogical approach can be identified as best.
- Children who attend well-planned, high-quality early childhood programmes in which curriculum aims are specified and integrated across domains tend to learn more and are better prepared for mastering the complex demands of formal schooling.

This is an interesting summary of what we know today about young children as attendees of early childhood programmes, and we can agree with it. However, in the whole book of 420 pages there are two sentences about play. This means that we researchers also separate play and learning.

On the other hand, the document shows signs of not working with traditional subjects (school subjects) in early childhood education but focuses more on centres of interest, themes, or projects, whatever they should be called, where *the object of learning is put into a meaningful context*. The Reggio Emilia approach might be one Example of this more integrated early childhood pedagogy, where children have a lot of freedom and can make choices although the object of learning is invisible here (Rinaldi, 2001). Choices, however, have been a main factor in early childhood education ever since Froebel's time. In children's choices there is room for their perspectives and preferences.

Today we also know that the quality aspect is decisive for children's learning. Here the qualification of the teachers, cooperation with parents, the objects and acts of the program, and structural aspects, such as the number of children in the group, play important roles (Asplund Carlsson, Kärrby, & Pramling Samuelsson, 2001; Gustavsson & Myhrberg, 2002).

Play seems to be an aspect of young children's learning that is taken for granted and about which there is a great deal of rhetoric. Play often seems to be the ultimate good in preschool, although we know from research that rivalry for power and excluding mechanisms are common. Play and learning are still kept apart and not problematized in curricula for early years (Karlsson-Lohmander & Pramling Samuelsson, 2003).

Play is difficult to define – and should not be, according to Wittgenstein (1971). He believes that play is not an intertwined wholeness – but a variety of meanings where all definitions together constitute a larger wholeness.

There are, however, two contradictory discourses in the perspective of play today. On the one hand, play has gained acceptance within certain areas. For example, play is mentioned in the curriculum for primary school in some countries, but ICT has also brought play into older children's lives. Kick-off meetings in companies are often days of play, even if they are called something else, such as creativity or similar labels.

On the other hand, there are also signs that early childhood education is becoming more school-orientated and less play-orientated. Reading and writing have become the main focus in many American kindergartens (Olfman, 2003). In Sweden we can see how the preschool classes have adopted the time structure of primary school and also introduced many more school subjects, such as literacy (Pramling Samuelsson, 2006). Murphy (2004) describes how the curriculum in Ireland is very much child- and play-centred, but praxis is orientated towards distribution of knowledge by the teacher. This means that there are two contradicting discourses on the arena, and the question is the following: Which of them will become most dominant and, consequently, be in a position to form future early childhood programmes? Or can play be considered in another way than the traditional one in early childhood education?

The Outcome of Recent Play Research

Play researchers today mainly see play as an area for learning (de Jonghe, 2001). They also claim that children are in control when they play, something that is also important in learning (Hadley, 2002).

Social, emotional, and cognitive aspects are involved simultaneously in children's play. This also means that children develop in all these areas as a result of their play experiences (Johnson, Christie, & Yawkey, 1999). The field of theory of mind claims that children learn to understand others in play (Astington, 1998). Marzano (1998) also claims that metacognition is the "engine" in learning. All interaction and negotiation between children, whether we call it play or learning, will raise their awareness of themselves and of their peers.

When children play, they have to keep a lot in their minds. A child may act in a certain role, but also keep in mind what the roles of the others are, or what different objects represent. This means that there are a variety of demands to focus on simultaneously in play – a theoretical aspect that has also been shown to be important in learning (Runesson, 1999; Marton & Tsui, 2004).

Another interesting research finding is that "play creates on-the-spot collective improvisations" (Sawyer, 1997). Compared to earlier ways of perceiving play as work in which earlier experiences are processed, Sawyer says that the group of children together create new experiences in interaction with each other. This means that something new is created – and that this is not a question of cultivating earlier experiences. Sawyer seems to think about play in the same way as we think about learning – the emergence of a new understanding. This also relates to the notion of "communities of learners" (Lave & Wenger, 1991) or "learning from each other" (Williams, 2001). Children not only communicate in play but also take part in meta-communication about their play, as a kind of direction of play (Knutsdotter-Olofsson, 1993). This also includes a dimension of metapragmatism, which is what children use for communicating in play (Sawyer, 1997).

Flow is yet another notion that has come up in play research, meaning when children are engaged, involved, or absorbed in the play situation as such (Laevers, 1993). This idea is connected with Csikszentmihayli's (1992) notion of flow in the adult world. But, in what way should we interpret the child's engagement and devotion to something (see Chapter 10, page 189)?

The notion of lifelong learning is widespread, but now researchers, like Sutton Smith (1997), are beginning to talk about play as a lifelong project. To sum up, one can state that the notion of play has been widened and is about making discoveries and being innovative or exceeding boundaries in different ways – a perspective very well in line with theories of, or perspectives on, young children's learning (Pramling Samuelsson & Asplund Carlsson, 2003).

Since research has revealed that play and learning have certain features in common, perhaps they should be seen as two dimensions of one whole in preschool pedagogy.

The Playing Learning Child – In Developmental Pedagogy

If we as adults try to take the child's perspective, which is a hard thing to do and always related to our adult skills and knowledge, we will not see a child playing for some part of the day and learning during another. We will see *a playing learning child*. Let us look at Hjalmar, 16 months old.

> Hjalmar is opening a large drawer in the kitchen, exploring all the objects there are, pushing all the buttons on the oven. He then takes out a lot of kitchen tools. All the plastic bowls are sorted according to size. He tries out, changes his mind a few times. He then begins to put back all the kitchen tools and bowls into the drawer. Suddenly he bends down and lifts up a plastic bowl with both his hands, pretending that it is heavy by groaning "oh, oh!" He does this twice.

Hjalmar himself initiates the whole project, and he makes his own decisions and seems to enjoy it. He approaches this drawer for the first time. He explores, and we can see basic mathematics when he compares sizes. But at the same time we can see that he pretends that a bowl is heavy. So what we can see here, in our opinion, is a child who plays and learns simultaneously. When Hjalmar plays he has an object in his mind, just as we claim that children must have in learning. Children's play is always focused on something, an objective (what they want to play). There is an enacted aspect, when they arrange and negotiate in the process. Finally, a lived object, which might be the result (what they end up with), which can be seen in how they experience something – as "a touchdown in time". We will come back to the object of learning.

A playing learning child creates meaning, communicates and interacts on two levels, and uses variation as the source of playing learning. Knowledge is then an internal relation between the child and his or her world. This means that the context, experience, situation, familiarity, relations to others, etc. mean a lot, influencing how children make sense of the world around them (Hundeide, 2003a). This is not an argument for a post-modern perspective. Instead children are perceived as being part of an internal psychological process – but environment and experiences in the culture have an impact on every situation.

Here the creation of meaning as a playing learning child is related to taking the child's perspective, whether or not the child or the teacher initiates something. This means that the child has to contribute by expressing himself or herself verbally or bodily in order to create meaning. In other words, this is achieved through partic-ipating in the creation of meaning (Pramling Samuelsson & Sheridan, 2003). This puts demands on the teacher. First of all the teacher must have knowledge of chil-dren in general (child development) *and* about the particular child in focus (family, daily experiences, interests, etc.). The teacher must also make an effort to listen to and observe children and be willing to see what the child sees and to interpret that. There must also be a respect for each child's experiences, knowledge, and competence. This might be what Dahlberg (2006) is talking about as pedagogy of hospitality and welcoming built on listening. The pedagogy in Reggio Emila is used as an example of this kind of approach.

Communication and interaction on two levels mean that both play and the specific pedagogical approach, labelled "development pedagogy", are based on two levels of communication (Pramling Samuelsson & Asplund Carlsson, 2008). When children play they *spontaneously* use both communication and meta-communication, as described earlier in this chapter. The *equivalence* in the learning approach is that, *assisted by the teacher,* children's interest is focussed on thinking and reflecting about something. When children have expressed their ideas verbally, in drawings or other ways, the teacher then focuses children's attention on how they think about something, that is the meta-cognitive aspect of learning (for example, see, Pramling, 1996). This means that the teacher's task is to try *to make the invisi-ble visible for children.* The third similarity between play and learning is *variation* as the source of both play and learning – variation that could be used spontaneously by children or as a tool and strategy for challenging children's learning (Pramling Samuelsson et al., 2008; Pramling Samuelsson & Pramling, 2008).

Variation Is the Source of Play and Learning

Sutton Smith, in his book *The Ambiguity of Play* (1997), first of all refers to biological evolution as a model for human development, where *flexibility* rather than precision is important. Evolution is characterized by *flourishing change* and *latent possibilities* – both play and learning could be described in this way.

His second principle of variation refers to *abundance*, that is, the body's skill at overproducing synopsis. Similarly, play and learning are an endless reproduction of many different possibilities. Flexibility is here the keyword for the biological world – without great flexibility neither play nor learning is possible!

All of a sudden I saw in this piece of information another useful metaphor with which to understand the role of play. We could say that just as the brain begins in a state of high potentiality, so does play. The brain has these connections, but unless they are actualized in behavior, most of them will die off. Likewise in play, even when novel connections are actualized, they are still not, at first, the same as everyday reality. Actions do not become everyday reality until there is a rhetoric or practice that accounts for their use and value. Play's function in the early stages of development, therefore, may be to assist the actualization of brain potential without as yet any larger commitment to reality. In this case, its function would be to save, in both brain and behaviour, more of the variability that is potentially there than would otherwise be saved if there were no play. Piaget's theory of play is, of course, the very reverse. He says that it is only after connections are established by real-life accommodation that they are consolidated in play. The present thesis would hold that another play function, perhaps the most important one, might be the actualization of novel connections, and therefore the extension of childhood's potential variability. (Sutton Smith, 1997, pp. 225–226)

One form of variation in *play* is the oscillation between the *fantasy and reality* – in *learning* the *concrete situation and how the thoughts exceed towards an understanding* (something which is seldom concrete). Both play and learning have a temporal and a spatial variation.

Sutton Smith also talks about play as a neonatal biological process, as cultural variation (music, dance, song, etc.). He also claims that there is transference of "play skills" to everyday skills and that children create a repertoire of ways of acting in play. However, from our point of view, there is also another perspective that means that variation creates a basis for differentiating, which is as important in play as in learning.

Let us consider the variation. Both similarity and variation are fundamental to several critical aspects of cognitive development in childhood, including the ability to distinguish one learning object or phenomenon from another, which, in turn, is fundamental to the categorization process. For example, for a young child to be able to understand the concept of flowers, rather than simply naming a single flower a flower, it is necessary for the child to experience a variety of flowers in order to distinguish the essential features that constitute what we call a flower. However, it is not sufficient simply to let the child experience a variety of flowers. He or she also needs to experience that the flower differs from other plants, such as trees, shrubs, and grass. Gradually the child will become able to understand the concept of a type of flower, distinguishing the critical features of the rose from other flowers. Even if young children can recognize a rose as a flower before they have understood the concept of flowers, they probably do not understand what constitutes a rose.

Certainly this case applies to other dimensions of content. To be able to learn an important rule in an early childhood programme or at elementary school, the rule has to have personal meaning, which can be induced by using it in different situations (the rule being constant). It also has to be clear that this rule can have various meanings (variation). Finally, this rule must have critical features that make it discernible from other rules. There can be a rule of "every child's right to equality". This has to make sense to each child, but it also needs to be discussed in many different contexts and negotiated in a variety of situations before this rule of value will have a deeper meaning for children.

The kind of variation we advocate defines learning as the *variety of ways* in which *one child* produces variation, a group of children produce variations (Lindahl & Pramling Samuelsson, 2002), the *variety of ways* in which *a group of children* think about one and the same phenomenon, the same problem, or concept. The variety of ways in which a child thinks about a single phenomenon, problem, or content is itself the content of the teaching process. In other words, the teacher uses variation as a strategy to make particular knowledge, skills, ideas, or phenomena visible to a child. As the child thinks in various ways about a topic or phenomenon, she or he becomes able to recognize variations within the topic or phenomenon, different meanings which may be derived from it.

People who agree about actions, persons, objects, and situations constitute play as well as learning in a society, time, motives for play or learning. So what we have tried to advocate within education for young children is seeing play and learning as equal dimensions with many similarities. We believe this will give the child room to act, react, and express his or her perspective.

Play Is Not the Same as Learning

We are not arguing for perceiving play as learning or vice versa, but there are play dimensions in learning and learning dimensions in play which are important to work with in young children's learning and development.

These dimensions are *creativity*, here viewed as the source of all learning objects. This means that all learning is a question of creating something new for the individual – that is, experiencing something in a new or slightly different way (Next Generation Forum, 2000). *As if* is another notion often related to play – but this notion is as important in learning as in play (Vaihinger, 2001[1924]). This means that learning tasks must also contain the aspect of "as if" for children, in order to be able to exceed and challenge their own thinking.

Ellen Langer's (1997) notion *mindfulness* is another dimension of play as well as learning. By mindfulness she means, to be aware of, perceive, or be attentive towards something. Being responsive and interested is as important in play as in learning.

The last notion we will bring up is Anna Craft's (2003) notion, *possibility thinking*. In play children deal with possibilities all the time, but this way of relating oneself to the surrounding world is just as important in learning.

Taking these notions seriously means relating play and learning to a great extent. Often it is a question of the teacher seeing the possibilities in all activities in early childhood education.

Experience of action research with teachers involved in the kind of thinking presented here is that they can say "I have always been thinking about play as something children learn from – but I have never seen the play aspect of learning." Another teacher claims that today she has fewer planned activities for the whole group since communication and interaction is hard to use in large groups (Johansson & Pramling Samuelsson, 2006). What the teachers say is that they must make room for improvisation, interaction, and listening to the children, whether the situation is labelled play or learning from an adult perspective.

The link between learning and play is the communication and attitudes shown by the adults, which get children to contribute their ideas. Elkind says (2007, p. 202)

> When children have a say in their learning, they are much more excited and involved than when they do not. The respect their teachers show them is reciprocated and is the basis for bonds of affection. Under these circumstances children learn the skills and knowledge about the world in a way that is enjoyable and has a lasting impact.

So play and learning can enrich each other when teachers allow them to do so!

Being Goal-Orientated Towards a Learning Object

Different early childhood curricula have different ways of presenting goals for very young children. Oberheumer (2005) claims that the most common way to perceive goals is to state what knowledge or skills children are supposed to acquire before they leave the early childhood setting. The Swedish curriculum for early childhood (Skolverket, 2006a) is different since it only states *goals to strive for*.

As we have stated earlier, early childhood education, by tradition, was not good at focussing on the goals in terms of *what* we wanted children to learn, but focussed instead on the *how* aspect, that is, critical features of preschool pedagogy (Bruce, 1987).

Froebel (1995), however, had a very clear intention about the objects of learning, which were mathematics and morals. His perspective of the act of learning was play, work, and learn – three dimensions of early childhood practice which we will come back to.

Early childhood education, apart from Froebel's time, has focused on the act of learning – *how* children learn, while elementary school has focused on the object of learning – what children are expected to learn. But the object of learning is evidently related to the act of learning and vice versa.

Countries all over the world are now in the process of developing curricula for learning in the earliest years (Karlsson-Lohmander & Pramling Samuelsson, 2003). This raises interesting questions: What will the objects of learning be in those curricula? Will they represent a traditional view of school subjects for preschoolers or will it be something else?

The perspective we will argue for here could be illustrated in terms of

- the intended learning object
- the enacted learning
- the lived learning object

The latter results in "a touchdown in time" (Pramling Samuelsson & Pramling, 2009). An example could be when the teacher and the curriculum have an intention to develop children's understanding of signs as a cultural conception for communication (intended objectives). For this purpose, children are activated in a lot of activities and engaged in certain experiences in which they meet and relate to signs and texts. The teacher has a great impact on this process, which here is the enacted learning object. The result as "a touchdown in time" is what a specific child can express at a certain moment when the child's competence is documented (lived). The result can be different 3 days later when the conditions are changed. This means that the learning object includes the wholeness, since each aspect is dependent on the others.

Let us look at an example from a preschool that is part of a development study with 5- and 6-year-old children. One goal of the Swedish curriculum is to develop children's understanding of their own culture. The teacher's goal is then to make children aware of culture as a phenomenon. So the goal is both intended by the curriculum and made alive by the teacher's interpretation of it. The teacher then plans and organizes a lot of activities where children experience things that could raise their awareness. Children's experiences, in the process of enacted learning, were visiting museums, reading books, looking at films, giving children tasks to solve, etc. One task the children were given after they had read a book about people living in caves was to make a drawing of how people lived together in earlier times. On the second card they had to make a drawing of their own houses, how they lived today. Then the teacher said "But have human beings moved from caves into these houses we live in today? You can actually take as many cards as you want to and make drawings of what you think people have lived in during different times." As we can see below, the children came up with different ideas – a cave, an igloo, a shelter made of branches, a straw house, and usual modern houses (Fig. 1).

This means that the enacted learning is both a question of arranging situations and experiences where children have to think and express their thinking over and over again, to give them a chance to create meaning about the learning object, in this case understanding the phenomenon of culture.

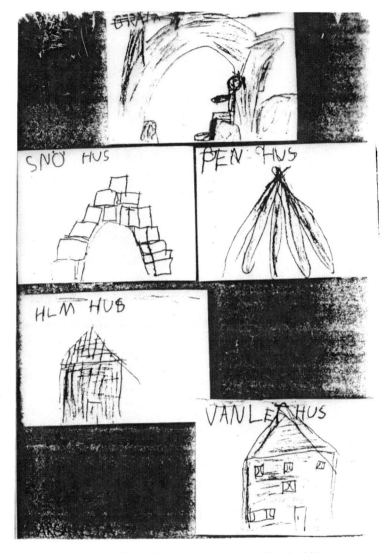

Fig. 1 Drawings of children's ideas of how houses have changed during history

The lived object of learning in this particular example was that the teacher arranged a situation where she talked to the children one by one, showing them two pairs of pictures, with, e.g. a kitchen in earlier times, a modern kitchen or a city environment from earlier times, and a modern city today. She asked each child to tell her about the different pictures, and in this way it became obvious how children talked about them and gave the pictures meaning. It was then quite easy to see which children had grasped the idea of human beings creating culture and which had not –

or rather what other ideas they had (for a more detailed description of children's understanding, see Pramling, 1996).

The goals for early childhood education are defined in the curriculum and in the teacher's mind. This means that the way he or she constructs the environment and what kinds of experiences are provided are decisive for children's learning and possibilities of making sense of the world around them. The curriculum must be internalized and lived by the teacher. This means that he or she must see the possibilities everywhere in the child's environment. The teacher must also contribute to a challenging and rich environment (Siraj-Blatchford, 1999). This includes using her or his own knowledge to create situations, tasks, play milieus.

One of the main features of the approach we advocate is how the teacher can direct children's awareness towards the learning objects. At one level the objects of learning in early childhood education are related to values and norms, skills and capabilities, and an understanding of different aspects of the surrounding world. This means that the learning objects are the same throughout the education system, but at different levels of complexity from a teacher's perspective.

From the child's perspective it can be as complex to grasp number concepts as to understand multiplication later in school. They are all dimensions of the same learning object at different levels of learning. This does not mean that preschool should be subject-orientated, but the basic dimensions of, for example, reading and writing, mathematics, science, culture must be there. This also applies to the more general dimensions, such as democracy, gender questions, and social, emotional, and cognitive competence.

The object of learning or dimensions of learning objects are thus similar throughout the school system. The act of learning, however, is different! Can the child's perspective be used when the curriculum and the teacher decide the object of learning? Yes, let us at least try to give one more example where children's perspectives are counted on in practice.

This example is when children worked in a group with the question of good and bad weather. They were given a paper divided into two halves and where requested to make one drawing about nice weather and one about bad weather. All of them did so, and then the teacher put all the drawings up and the Discussion began about what was bad and good weather. It became obvious to the children that what was good weather for one person could be very bad for someone else. The flowers were happy when the rain came, but children who were supposed to go to the beach to swim were sad, or the child was happy when the snow came down while a mother found it hard to pull the pram with the baby through the snow, etc. This was a way to get children to become aware of the subject perspectives and that the same situation could be interpreted in different ways (Pramling Samuelsson & Mårdsjö Olsson, 2007).

In Search of a Practice with Children Based on Their Perspectives

Communication, Relations, and Content

What constitutes the difference between the developmental pedagogy that we are arguing for here and the child-centred pedagogy that preschool has always protected? In our view, the difference lies in the fact that developmental pedagogy contains a conscious ambition to develop specific values and norms, abilities, and an understanding of certain aspects of the surrounding world, that is, the *direction* is central. There are simply clear goals to strive towards, and these goals are to develop a way of seeing and experiencing or a way of understanding values and norms to develop abilities and knowledge you should learn already in preschool: not as a final and finished product, rather as the beginning of a *journey within different content dimensions*, which will continue throughout the whole education system, even, perhaps throughout life.

In a child-centred pedagogy the children's individual experience completely steers play as well as learning (Kärrby, 1985). The adult answers and meets the child in the content and the thoughts the child expresses. You could probably say that it partly gives the child responsibility for his or her own learning, or formulated more positively, you trust the child to be able to discover what is important in the culture he or she lives – and many children are also able to do that. Naturally there has to be room for children's own spontaneous interests in the context of preschool, and we know that all children do not learn the same things even though they are present in the same setting.

However, we do think that the picture of reality might be a bit romantic if we believe that everybody develops and learns optimally if he or she is allowed to do exactly what he or she likes. Preschool is a collective arena (Carlsson, 1993; Williams, 2001), and in the communication and the interplay that take place there both the teacher and other children are involved (Sheridan & Williams, 2007). Does that mean that we can ignore communication with all individuals and let the "strongest" or the most status-filled or the most creative child steer the direction and thereby capture all the other children's attention? As a teacher you can and certainly should let each child express his or her own experiences and thoughts, something we believe to be the special contribution of preschool pedagogy to young children's education, but then *deciding about the content is the contribution of the teacher.* It is all about *leading and challenging* the children to think and talk about the kinds of learning object and content that our curriculum contains. This is first and foremost a pedagogical task, where the teacher creates opportunities for the child to experience critical features of what to learn. Another task could be to let children talk about things that they are "filled" with, for social, psychological, and sometimes pedagogical reasons. Both aspects could be important for each individual child but are different in relation to the pedagogical commission of preschool. In this book, we are focusing on the educational aspects of communication.

Language not only expresses our thinking, which we can easily believe when we look at the way we use metaphors such as "to let thoughts be expressed" or "to clothe our thoughts in words", but the use of language is crucial for thinking (Pramling, 2006). When the teacher asks the children in the group about their thoughts, they are given an opportunity not only to think and reflect but also to express themselves verbally or visually. The view of language we stand for means that we make use of the possibilities of the extended language of gestures, speech, and pictures. The thinking is not something that *precedes* the expression, but the thinking *originates* from or *is constituted* in the expression. Therefore we do not believe that children sit quietly with their thoughts, thoughts that nobody asks about. Rather, the inquiry, the situation, and the communication give birth to the thinking and problematize that which is taken for granted and intuitively anticipated by children.

Consequently, the proponents of developmental pedagogy adopt a special attitude, but this is far from enough – the content of the learning is an inseparable part of the attitude. As different contents call for different forms of understanding, there cannot, according to Marton (1992), be any teaching method or any way of acting that guarantees that everybody can learn everything. However, by being interested in and finding out how children react to different specific phenomena, through research as well as pedagogical practice, we will become better equipped to give children the prerequisites for learning about these phenomena.

Let us look at one of the preschool goals as an Example, where it is stated that preschool should strive towards each child developing an understanding of his or her own participation in the ecology of nature and *of simple natural scientific phenomena*, as well as a knowledge of plants and animals (Skolverket, 2006a, p. 10, our italics).

A small part of this goal refers to simple natural scientific phenomena. One such phenomenon could be that some objects float in water while others sink, something that even the infant can experience in his or her daily bath. Young children have therefore experienced that objects float or sink. But most children have probably never thought about why, since that is knowledge traditionally acquired in secondary school. So how can preschool give children the prerequisites for starting to understand this phenomenon? Step one must be that the teacher gives children the opportunity to focus on the phenomenon, that is, *directs children's attention* towards the fact that certain objects float while others sink.

Pramling and Pramling Samuelsson (2001) have analysed a video observation where the teacher is carrying out an experiment together with Jonas (3 years and

3 months) about objects that float or sink. Before Jonas starts to test each object, the teacher asks if the object will float or sink and why. He is so interested and curious that the teacher sometimes has to stop him from starting to test the objects by gently holding back his hand for a while. She just wants him to stop and think, to come up with a reason why objects might float or sink. She has chosen a large variety of objects. Jonas acts and reflects in communication with the teacher.

From the teacher's questions Jonas understands that she wants him to find a reason why an object floats or why it sinks, that is, to put forward a hypothesis, which he will then test. He gets the message and looks for critical aspects of the objects (what he thinks is the reason why they will float or sink). Many of the objects happen to have a hole in somewhere (a screw nut, a metallic ring). Jonas takes this as a starting point and says that it is the hole that makes the object sink. But later on during the experiment one object with a hole in it happens to float, and he then changes his mind and says that it is because of the hole that the object can float. For Jonas existing holes and imagined holes (e.g. in a pine cone, a wooden button) explain how the objects behave in the water. During the dialogue it becomes clear that he has not mastered the concepts floating and sinking, neither is he sure about the difference between heavy and light, conceptions he confuses a couple of times. After a period of experimenting, Jonas loses interest and the desire to play and fantasize takes over, and he says, "Now we pretend that the water is the sea" and dips his hand into the water.

Here the teacher has created a situation about which she and Jonas can communicate together. At the same time the child has a chance to act and reflect. The teacher makes use of the variation of objects and the child gets the message – to find and state a reason. Even though the conceptions were not clear to Jonas, we can see that he tried to find critical aspects of the objects that could contribute to an explanation. He is using an inductive method to create a theory for floating objects. We can see also that, even though Jonas' explanations are far from the established scientific explanation, he has started to think about the principle of cause and effect. Hopefully, it has aroused his interest in experimenting on his own and further reflecting in other situations.

Peter's First Encounter with Teacher-Planned Mathematics

Let us here follow a teacher trying to find out Peter's experiences of basic mathematical notions, and how she challenges him. He is $3\frac{1}{2}$ years old on the first occasion and 3 month older on the second.

The interplay starts with the teacher asking him to tell her how old he is. "Three years," he says. "Can you show on your fingers how many years you are?" "Why?" asks Peter. Being asked how old you are is something children are used to, but being asked to show this on his fingers seems strange to Peter. Then she gives him two tigers. He knows what they are and, without hesitation, can tell which one is *big* and which one is *small*. The next pair of conceptions the teacher wants to test is *first* and *last*. They play with the tigers and pretend that they run to get some food. To decide which one is first and which one is last when the animals are running appears to be difficult, but when the teacher instead puts four animals in a line there is no hesitation – Peter knows which is first and which is last in the line.

The next exercise is to *pair* raisins with cards with dots on them, up to 4 dots. To pair and put one raisin on each dot goes like clockwork up to 3 dots, even if he has to count and point to each dot. Then he was given 10 raisins. When he gets the card with 4 dots he says, "Then you may take all!" He takes them all, but when he starts putting raisins on the dots he says, "No, you have to put some of them [the raisins] back." So he is counting here, too, and stops when he reaches 4 as that is the *last number he says* when he points to the dots.

Next the teacher puts pieces of Lego and small balls in a row making a *pattern* and asks Peter to continue to put the Lego pieces and the balls in the same way, making a long row. "What did you say?" asks Peter. Once again the teacher asks him to continue to put the pieces and the balls in a row in the same way as the teacher. But he puts his arms on the table and his head on top of his arms and says, "I want to do something else!" The teacher does not seem to be able to mediate to Peter what she wants him to do, and when he does not understand he loses interest.

The teacher continues with the dot cards and Peter seems to think it is okay again. After a while he gets a piece of paper and the teacher places two tigers on it. "Can you draw or write on the paper how many tigers there are?" she asks. "I can't draw the ears of the tiger," he says. "That doesn't matter," says the teacher. "I can't draw the mouth either," continues Peter. "But perhaps you can find out some other way to write how many tigers you have?" He then takes the pencil and draws *one long and one short line* and looks very pleased. He places the big tiger on the long line and the small one on the short.

Here we can see that when Peter is given the task of representing the number of tigers; he does not understand what to do and thinks he has to draw the tigers. But in the dialogue with the teacher something happens; he realizes that he can draw a line for each animal. *The size of the lines, however, links the symbol with the real object*, and he underlines this by placing the animals on the lines.

Three months later the teacher gives Peter the tasks once again, extending them in different ways. Now Peter does not have to point to the dots and the raisins; *he can see how many there are* and, without hesitation, he puts the right number of raisins on each card. When he is asked to represent 3 on a piece of paper he immediately says, "Should I write a figure?" "Yes, if you wish," she says. He draws a slightly bent line (you can guess that it is a 3), but to make it really clear he draws three bent lines. "Twos are so difficult," he says when the teacher changes to two animals and wants him to represent them on the piece of paper.

This time the teacher adds an exercise. She hides some ducks in a Box after they have counted them together. Peter finds this exciting, but guesses even though the teacher tries to make him think about how many ducks they had. However, he is not there quite yet, i.e. *keeping both the whole and the parts* in mind simultaneously, even if he manages to guess "right" now and then. However, he does find hiding the ducks very exciting. We suggest that this is an Example of where the teacher's and the child's perspectives meet, since the teacher tries to understand the child's mind (perspective) and also challenges it.

So, what does this have to do with children's perspectives? First we notice that the teacher has chosen a number of conceptions that she and researchers often emphasize as basic mathematics (Schwartz, 2005; Doverborg & Emanuelsson, 2006; Emanuelsson & Doverborg, 2006). We can also see how these conceptions appear from Peter's point of view. His expressions clearly indicate that large and small, first and last, and numbers up to 4 all are in his experienced world. On the first occasion he did have to point and count to make raisins and dots correspond, but on the second occasion there was no hesitation whatsoever. He perceives the correct number to match the number of dots.

We can also see a situation where the child's and the teacher's perspectives are so far apart that the child gives up. Seeing patterns is one part of basic mathematics, but here the teacher failed. Perhaps she used unsuitable material, or she made a pattern on which Peter could not find any meaning. He is probably used to doing other things with Lego pieces and balls, and therefore the question was incomprehensible to him.

When it comes to the representation situation, the child's perspective is obvious when he draws a picture of the object. Later, after the teacher has challenged his experience, his perspective changes and he represents each object by a line. Finally, 3 months later numbers are represented by figures.

The teacher's intention is to *create situations* in which the child should be able to think and ponder, without demanding a "right" answer. For even if children often solve problems with mathematical dimensions spontaneously in play and everyday situations, the teacher needs to verbalize the question and give children the opportunity to "clothe their thoughts in words", in order to firmly establish learning about specific contents – here mathematical conceptions.

We would also like to point to something very delicate in the Scandinavian countries, from the Ministry level (Korpi, 2006) to public authorities (Skolverket, 2004, 2005) and teaching practice (Kvistad & Søbstad, 2005), that is, the problem of evaluating young children's learning. At all levels it is emphasized that the *practice, not the children,* should be evaluated in preschool (Oberheumer, 2005). But what is a practice without children? Children are certainly a part of the practice and obviously the most important part. The central question is, how do we perceive this kind of practice? If one can see the child's perspective change (he learns), we believe it is an excellent situation.

Looking at the situation with Peter, structured by the adult, you can see that it constitutes an opportunity for the teacher to see how the child experiences the mathematical conceptions introduced, but, *at the same time,* the situation also works as an opportunity for Peter to be challenged and to develop his own understanding. Using this knowledge as a foundation, the teacher can now create new situations, both in order to see how his understanding has developed and to give him new challenges. This is a kind of "evaluation", "a touchdown in time" (Pramling Samuelsson & Asplund Carlsson, 2003) that shows children's, as well as teachers', abilities and perspectives. Seeing how these are related is something we must dare to see in preschool as well! When the teacher works towards making the child's perspective visible, children will live up to his or her expectations and express themselves in the ways they can.

Working with a Theme with a Group of Children

The theme presented here is from an earlier published study about "The Bee and colony of bees" (Doverborg & Pramling, 1988). The intended object of learning was to get children to experience (1) the colony's structure and function and (2) the relation between bees and plants. The theme work began with interviewing the children and having a Discussion with them to trace their world of experience as a starting point. The children made drawings of what they knew about the topic and talked with the teacher about their drawings. Let us just look at a few dialogues between the teacher and children.

> Kalle: A bee is striped with a sting, it can fly, and it lives in a small house.
> Teacher: What do they do in the small house?
> Kalle: They eat honey and sleep there.
> Teacher: Do people like bees?
> Kalle: No, they just sting you with their sting.
> Teacher: But don't we have any use for them?
> Kalle: Yes, we get their honey.
> Lisa: A bee is one who flies around and has a sting in the back. They live in round things hanging in the trees.
> Teacher: Where do the round things come from that they live in?
> Lisa: They grow in particular trees.
> Teacher: What are the bees doing in the round things?
> Lisa: There are cleaning bees and a queen. She decides everything.

When listening to all the children it became obvious that they all knew that bees can sting people. They also knew that bees are related to honey and that there are a number of different bees having different functions. They also knew that they live together, whatever they call their beehive. The teacher also asked question about the relation between bees and nature.

> Cecilia: They eat nectar from flowers (when they are out flying).
> Teacher: What is nectar?
> Cecilia: It is honey that is yellow.
> Sebastian: They fly around and suck nectar.

> Teacher: Nectar?
> Sebastian: Yes, a sort of honey.
> Teacher: Where does it come from?
> Sebastian: The flowers of course, they have it in the middle.
> Teacher: What do the bees do with the nectar?

Sebastian: They give it to their children.
Teacher: Do the flowers like the bees taking the nectar away?
Sebastian: No, I don't think they do!

We could see that almost all the children had an idea about some kind of relationship between flowers and bees, although it was a very superficial understanding. Children took the perspective of the bee and saw that it could have a use for the flowers, but hardly anyone had an idea about the use of bees to the flowers.

After the interview and Discussion, the teacher now had to review her intended learning objects and decide what she could leave behind and what to focus on in their work with this theme. They were then exposed to many kinds of experiences (the enacted object of learning), like visiting beehives, playing with costumes of bee-growers, reading books, studying bees with a magnifying glass, making drawings of bees. Sometimes the children were given individual tasks in the first step and then shared experiences later; other times they worked with tasks in small groups. Children were asked to tell each other about what they were doing all the time. The teacher also created experiences where it was possible to discover a certain structure, e.g. the relation between plants and bees. The teacher showed children a film, and after which they were asked to make a book of the message it contained, and evaluate the lived object of learning. She also communicated and discussed continuously with them. The lived object of learning documented here was just "a touchdown in time" since the children then continued to work and expand the theme to include other animals as well as the dimension of the environment.

This approach in a group of children means that every child has to express his or her thinking about the phenomenon at hand. They get inspiration from the teacher as well as from other children. The dynamic in the group makes them eager to express their ideas, since they all know that they do not have to express any "right" answers but that all ideas are welcome. In other words, the focus is not on the product as such, the final knowledge, but on the children's creation of meaning in connection with specific skills or knowledge objects.

Categories of Interaction Between Teachers and Children

As we maintained earlier in this book, children are playing learning individuals and should be allowed to behave as such in the educational settings. This does not imply that learning and play are the same phenomenon!

Play and learning should not be regarded as synonymous terms, but the dimensions of play should be made visible in learning and the dimensions of learning should be made visible in play – and influence each other. The prerequisites for integrating play and learning should be carefully examined, which primarily means accepting the child as a playing learning individual although early childhood education has goals to strive towards, according to the curriculum (Ministry of Education and Science in Sweden, 1998a).

In a recent research project, eight teams of teachers in early childhood education were followed in their classes for children ranging from 1 to 9 years, using video observations. When the interaction between teachers and children was analysed, three distinct categories were found in which play and learning were being integrated as well as kept separate (Johansson & Pramling Samuelsson, 2006).

The concepts guiding the analysis were creativity, reality and fantasy, control and choice, positioning and power. This means that the researchers looked for situations where not only the distinction between reality and fantasy was transcended but also where and how something new was created in interaction. Control relates to who is in control, the children or the teacher, or do they both give and take? What positions do the participants involved in the video sequences hold? a question closely related to, Who has the power to take the initiative?

The three categories of interaction that were found are labelled: (1) explorative interactions, (2) narrative interactions, and (3) interactions bound to form. In the first two, play and learning were clearly integrated. There was openness in the situation, which meant that the children as well as the teacher could contribute. It was about reality, but there was also room for fantasy. The teacher and the children contributed on equal terms (although the teacher kept in mind what she wanted the children to focus their attention on). Unexpected things happened, and she could deal with these. There were minor differences between these two categories too, as indicated by their names; exploration tends to involve challenging, innovation, and creativity in a more open arena, while narratives tend to be built up in a joint effort between the teacher and the children. In the first category (explorative) the teacher began with a clear learning object in her mind, but in the second (narrative) the learning object was negotiated and created between the children and the teacher.

In the third category, where interaction is bound to a form, there is no interaction or integration between play and learning. The teacher is too focused on reality, the "right" answer or the "correct" way to do things, so there is little room for the children's own contributions. She does not take the role of partner in a dialogue but mimics the traditional schoolteacher, teacher or instructor, a strategy which other research has also found in everyday interaction in preschool (see, e.g., Johansson, 2003; Palludan, 2005). She can also choose to let children just play by themselves, which is not unusual in preschool either, in Sweden or in other countries (Pramling Samuelsson & Fleer, 2008). Old traditions impose a heavy burden, where learning is what the teacher plans to teach the children, while play is the child's own initiative and world.

If children are given room to take the initiative and contribute to activities with their own experience, we will get a preschool pedagogy where play and learning are integrated – the playing learning child will appear! This, of course, challenges the teacher – he or she has to be able to take the children's perspectives and keep the objectives of her teaching in mind simultaneously.

Once again, our contention is not that play and learning should be regarded as one and the same, but we are saying that there are dimensions of play in learning and dimensions of learning in play, and that if we utilize this openness, we will be able to challenge the preschool field and work towards a new approach to preschool education!

Teaching children a specific value, ability, or understanding means working towards the unknown future! But guiding children towards what is unknown to them demands teachers who can get hold of children's experiences and challenge them. There is an English expression, "hands on and minds on", which is central to young children's learning (Pramling Samuelsson & Kaga, 2008).

Summing up, we have in this chapter seen that practice with children, built on developmental pedagogy, needs to bring children's experience into the learning object, that is, what children's attention is directed towards, as well as into the act of learning, that is, to the way we believe children learn. This is where interaction and communication are vital assets for any teacher concerned with the playing learning child!

In Search of Theoretical Preconditions for an Early Childhood Education Built on Children's Perspectives

The preconditions for an early childhood education built on children's perspectives, or the ways they experience different phenomena, are set by their teachers' skills and knowledge. What we have argued for is that this theoretical approach has to be made by the teachers in person, bodily so to speak, and put into practice with children in their everyday life in preschool. Elkind (2007) talks about the Montessori approach in a similar way. He says, "Teachers learn to create their own curricula, which free them from the domination of textbooks" (Elkind, p. 203). The theoretical approach should be seen as a "framework", indicating that the theory or approach is still under development (Pramling Samuelsson et al., 2006). Here we will develop some points one by one, even though in practice they become closely related and integrated. It is also important to bear in mind that the whole approach to learning is subjective since both the aims and means are the children's perspectives – that is their experience and how they make sense of something. The starting point is children's experience of the object of learning, and the end is also the children's experiences of the same learning object, which if they have learnt anything have changed.

Some of the central ideas inherent in this framework are the following:

- What we can do, what we can know, springs from what we can "see", what we can experience or perceive.
- More and less powerful ways of acting and knowing originate from more and less powerful ways of "seeing", perceiving, or experiencing something.
- Ways of seeing and experiencing a certain phenomenon can be defined in terms of the aspects of the phenomenon discerned by learners and focused on simultaneously.
- In order to discern a certain aspect of a certain phenomenon, the learner has to experience variation in the dimension of that aspect.
- A certain pattern of variation and invariance is necessary for the learner to experience variation in the dimension of a critical aspect (it must vary while other dimensions are invariant).
- In order to help the learners to discern and focus on critical aspects of a certain phenomenon, the teacher has to contribute to creating the necessary pattern of variation and invariance.

D. Sommer et al., *Child Perspectives and Children's Perspectives in Theory and Practice*, International Perspectives on Early Childhood Education and Development 2, DOI 10.1007/978-90-481-3316-1_12, © Springer Science+Business Media B.V. 2010

What We Can Do, What We Can Know, Springs from What We Can "See", What We Can Experience

This means that what children do not perceive and experience does not make any sense to them. Before children understand what a symbol means it is a waste of time to try to teach them the alphabet. Or, before children have any conception of number, it is a waste of time to teach them counting Procedures.

Let us follow Vilgot's way towards becoming literate, and see how his experiences are mirrored in his actions in relation to books.

> Step 1: (1.2 years). Vilgot finds a small book among his toys. He opens the book, turns the pages, and begins to "read" (vocalize).

He shows in this way that he relates talking to turning pages in a book. This is all that books mean to him. He experiences reading a book as turning pages and talking.

> Step 2: (1.10 years). An adult asks Vilgot if they should read a book together. "Yes," shouts Vilgot happily and he runs to the bookshelf. He chooses a novel. The adult sits on the floor with him, turning the pages and telling him a story that has nothing to do with the actual book. Vilgot listens, looks at the pages sometimes, and is totally satisfied to listen to the story.

Now Vilgot relates the book as such with the narration of a story. This is the meaning of a book for him right now!

> Step 3: (2.2 years). Vilgot asks the adult to read a book to him. This time it is Alfie Atkins, one of his own books. He gives it to the adult, but since the adult does not have her glasses near at hand she starts telling the story in the book as she remembers it. Very soon Vilgot says, "No, read what it says in the book properly."

Vilgot has now understood that the book has a text, a content, which has to be read the same way every time. His world of experience has widened and he has become aware that the text is something exact without understanding the meaning of text as such.

> Step 4: (2.6 years). Vilgot chooses an old children's book and gives it to the adult. She asks, "Do you want me to read it for you?" Vilgot takes the book back and turn the pages forward and back for a while. Then he goes back to the bookshelf and replaces the book saying, "No, there is too much text in it!"

Vilgot has now grasped that the black pattern on the pages is called text. No one has taught him about this, but anyway he seems to have picked that up in a conversation and uses it now himself. He also evaluates the book, i.e. "too much text", which combined with too few pictures might mean that the book will be boring. So he takes a value standpoint.

> Step 5: (2.10 years). Vilgot is now playing with small plastic letters. He asks the adult to "write" the names of all family members and pets with the letters. Although he cannot write himself, not even his name, he recognizes certain letters. He shouts excitingly, "That one is in Vilgot" every time the adult chooses a word that includes any letter in his name.

Vilgot's awareness is now directed towards letters in the written world. He has discerned the letters in the words, that is, distinguished single letters from whole words.

In the observations above, we can see Vilgot's actions, both bodily and verbal, and how he develops qualitatively, step by step, in his ways of experiencing books, reading and writing, that is, he experiences the literate world around him in different ways.

Every little qualitative change, here described as a "step", indicates that Vilgot's perspective has changed – he "sees" features he did not perceive in the previous step. After the above observations he takes new steps by beginning to read words, and later, of course, also learns to read and make sense of the words. And this is not the end of being a skilled reader and writer; new steps will be taken even if nobody has yet described how the ability to handle the written language changes qualitatively.

In all education, for all human beings, there are basic grounds, which are often taken for granted or go unnoticed; this is a never-ending story. No matter how much knowledge you have as a teacher, surprises constantly occur. One day an adult was surprised when one of her children, sitting at the kitchen table, was labelling and talking about letters of the alphabet on the tablemat. After a while the adult said, "Now you will soon know all the letters. Then you can read the newspaper (pointing to the daily paper on the table)." The child, however, started to laugh and said, "No, there are so many letters!" And, of course, the child's perspective is just right. He may experience that a newspaper contains an enormous number of letters, while the adult knows that there are only 28 letters in the (Swedish) alphabet and that they are just combined in many different ways. It certainly does not help to tell him this; he must experience and make sense of this himself one day – either by chance or by an interaction in a teaching situation where it appears to him.

So a child can never learn to ride a bike before he or she has experienced what it means to do so. Or, a child can never label different birds if he or she has not experienced these birds in one way or other. To experience is to see, perceive, make sense – learn!

More and Less Powerful Ways of Doing Things

There are many ways of "seeing" or experiencing something. But if we look at particular problems or tasks, there might be ways that are better when it comes to solving them more correctly or efficiently.

Let us look at a study by Doverborg and Pramling Samuelsson (1999a) where preschool children were given the question: "You have 10 buns which should be shared among 3 children – can you draw a picture and tell me how you will solve this problem?" Children expressed a variety of ways to solve the problem in terms of sharing equally or unequally. If unequally, this could mean that they related to reality and said that some children can eat more than others, or that one can save some buns for later, etc. Children who tried to solve the problem through equality did that by giving three children three buns each and dividing the last one into three parts, giving one part to each of the three children. And someone divided all ten buns into three parts. All ways to solve the problem are correct if we take the individual child's perspective, since they all had an explanation which made sense in reality. On the other hand, if this had been a mathematical task, some of the children would have been more successful than others.

Dahlgren and Olsson (1985) described perceptions of the function of reading among 5- and 6-year-olds and found that some of them did not have any idea about why they should learn to read. Other children connected reading with something they had to do in school, or something you need to be able to do when you are an adult, that is putting the aim in the future. Finally, there was a group who saw the purpose of learning to read to be related to their everyday life as children, that is, they saw the communicative aspect of reading. It is obvious that there is a stronger motivation for learning to read if a child has a way of experiencing reading as something that gives him or her a meaning here and now.

If a child has not considered tidying or cleaning his or her room to be something of importance (or understood the consequences of), why should he or she bother with doing so when mother tells him or her? Doing something because someone says so is not particularly motivating for anybody. Motivation can be seen as a psychological aspect of learning (Giota, 2000), but an integral part of seeing or experiencing a task is that it gives children a meaning, which points to a pedagogical aspect. There are probably many paths to solving problems of different kinds. Therefore, one should not say that one way of seeing or experiencing is better than any other, but one should recognize that on certain occasions or in certain situations there are ways that are more effective than others – ways of seeing and experiencing that lead children onto the right track for becoming skilled in an area or understanding something better.

Elkind (2007) claims that children build their concept of numbers by understanding numbers at three different levels of meaning. First numbers can be understood just in a nominal sense, as names. Second, they have to be understood in an ordinal way, i.e. you have to identify their position in a series. Third, children have to understand the level of interval numbers, which is that numbers represent equal units and can be operated on arithmetically. These three levels of meaning lead to different interpretations and, consequently, can be used by children in different ways.

Ways of Seeing, Experiencing

The way something is discerned by the child defines his or her possibility of understanding or making sense of a situation or task. If the child perceives the task above, about dividing buns, as a moral question of dividing equally or as a mathematical problem, his or her attention is directed in different ways.

Wyndhamn (1993) has described a problem given to school children; they had to choose the correct amount of stamps for an envelope of a certain weight by using a table of costs according to weight. When the problem was presented in a maths lesson, the children solved it in one way. When the same problem was presented in the civics class, they solved it differently. In other words, the context framed the children's ways of solving the problem. And how did the teacher focus the children's attention on the object of learning she intended to develop by this activity?

How, for Example, do younger children discern the problem of laying a table in preschool? Is it a social activity to help the teachers prepare for lunch, or is it a problem-solving task? Children most probably act differently according to *how they discern the problem*. Teachers often believe that they give children a task for a particular purpose, but children grasp it as something else. Pramling (1983) showed how the teacher worked with teaching 5- and 6-year-old children to tell the time by making clocks. When children were asked later what they had learnt during the theme with clocks, most of them said, "to make clocks". The reason behind their understanding might be that the teachers organized concrete acting and doing and never asked children to reflect on the things they did. Another reason may be that the children's idea about learning was learning to do something. These two aspects, the children's understanding of what learning is all about and the teacher's way of thinking about children's learning in terms of doing, lead the children to grasp the work with clocks as a question of making clocks.

In Lindahl's study (1996), we can see how very young children use different strategies for making sense of and solving different problems. One little boy wants a toy car which is standing on a shelf, out of his reach, but cannot catch the teacher's attention to get it down for him. He then turns around and finds a small chair that he drags over the floor in order to be able to take down the car himself. This means that this child saw the problem as a question of reaching up to a certain height. Another child might have given up when ignored by the teacher.

Children always make sense in their own way and from their own perspectives and experiences. This means that different experiences lead to different ways of discerning. Making sense, however, is not only a question of discernment, but also of keeping things in mind simultaneously, or becoming aware of them.

When children of a certain age spontaneously occupy themselves with certain patterns or categories, such as round objects (balls, round flat objects, etc.), vertical patterns (up and down), straight lines (similarities in length, height, or symmetry), putting objects into or taking them out of something, or closing and opening, etc., this represents the first stage towards scientific thinking, according to Athey (1990) and Nutbrown (1994). However, according to our understanding, this behaviour also shows that children work on those patterns over and over and with different objects and in different situations and keep the variation of the same object in mind simultaneously. So how children see or experience something is a question not only of how the experiences have influenced each child's ways of discerning, but also of how they can connect earlier experiences with the one at hand.

The teacher, then, must be able to see what the child experiences – that is, take his or her perspective to be able to support or challenge the child. The reason is that one cannot help a child to expand his or her awareness or understanding of something if one does not know his or her present level of understanding.

In Order to Discern a Certain Aspect of a Certain Phenomenon

Going back to the studies by Athey (1990) and Nutbrown (1994), we see that children spontaneously try out these patterns in various situations and with a variety of objects. This means that the idea of roundness is invariant while the object representing roundness varies. Opening or closing something is an idea kept invariant by the children, while they open and close various objects (cupboards, Boxes, drawers, etc.).

In an earlier study by Pramling (1994), children were taught about symbols as conventions of society by letting all the children invent their own symbols for different kinds of weather (sunshine, rain, snow, storm, etc.). All their suggestions were then displayed and compared with the symbols used in the weather report on TV. The variation of ways, one and the same weather symbol was constructed, created conditions for children to discern certain features for a creating meaning, by realizing that symbols are societal conventions that can be constructed in many different ways. They also discerned the meaning of symbols as joint constructions for making the things they represent understandable for all in communication.

Children always discern something, and how they discern it leads to different meanings. On the other hand, if, as is the case in early childhood education, children should discern stated and particular learning objects, the teacher has to direct children's attention to them. This could be done by preparing the environment, by giving children certain experiences or events, or by asking questions or telling children about something. Let us look at one example where the teacher acts in order to make the child think about and reflect on symbols and knowledge.

Let us see how a teacher creates conditions for children to be able to discern certain aspects of their learning, built on a perspective of goal orientation related to play and learning. This situation challenges the teachers to be child-centred and directed towards objects of learning simultaneously. It also challenges the children to maintain their right of self-determination and to pay attention to the object of learning simultaneously. One Example of this is how a teacher can focus a child's attention on something she wants the child to explore his or her own thinking about (Fig. 1, see below).

A teacher and some children are working on a theme about mushrooms. This particular mushroom is called "Flugsvamp" (Fly agaric) in Swedish, which the child has illustrated to the left as a mushroom by the two crossing lines and flies above. The girl begins by stating that toadstools are poisonous. The teacher has the curriculum objectives in her mind – symbols – learning and knowledge. She asks the girl, "How can you let other children know that this is a poisonous mushroom?" (symbol). Her answer is, "Write a note!" "Can young children read?" asks the teacher. She then makes a drawing of the mushroom and puts a cross over it to symbolize that it is dangerous. The teacher then continues to challenge her by asking, "Are there more ways to *know* (learn) about poisonous or edible mushrooms?" The girl draws and talks about a specific book her mother has about mushrooms. The teacher continues the dialogue, "Are there more ways to find out?" The girl says, "If you instead learn to recognize specific good mushrooms (Karl Johan mushroom and Bolete) you will focus your attention on finding them and not see the toadstools."

Fig. 1 A 5-year-old girl talking about mushrooms

What your attention is focused on – that is what you create a meaning (learn) about, whether it is play or learning from an adult perspective. This is one of the main features of developmental pedagogy, i.e. that one of the teachers' roles is to focus children's attention on the learning objects they want children to develop an understanding about, whether this takes place in play or learning situations. Integrating play and learning in a goal-orientated preschool means not only seeing the playing learning child and thereby making room for children's creativity, choices, initiatives, reflections, etc., but also being aware of the objects of learning and utilizing the whole day and all activities to develop the child's understanding of different aspects of the surrounding world.

A Certain Pattern of Variation and Invariance

As already mentioned above, certain features must vary while others are invariant for a child to realize the meaning of something. There is a tradition in early childhood education to use variation as a way of organizing children's learning. This means that they work on, e.g. the farm as a theme and within this they read about the farm, dramatize events from the farm, sing songs about the farm, prepare food from the farm, etc. This variation goes back to the idea that children learn with all their senses and need variation in the tasks so as not to lose interest. However, this is not the kind of variation we are talking about here. Here we are referring to a specific learning object and how certain aspects need to vary and other have to be invariant.

When teachers apply the theory of variation or development pedagogy that they have learned, they often vary the object of learning too much. Excessive variation does not bring about any improvement. To be able to see what ought to vary and what has to be invariant, the teacher must be clear about what the object of learning is. If a teacher wants to help children to discriminate between different sizes, it may be better to do that with material that does not vary in other ways too. Using blocks of various colours makes it difficult for the child to see what the teacher wants him or her to see.

In a study by Pramling Samuelsson et al. (2008), the teachers worked on developing children's abilities in and knowledge of aesthetics (music, poetry, and movement). In the beginning it was very difficult for the teachers to find objects of learning within aesthetics, since in preschool aesthetics is perceived by tradition as something to do with relaxation and pleasure and not something to learn about. The study data clearly showed that the teachers varied their material too much to make the learning objects visible to the children. When a teacher wanted the children to become aware of rhythms, she let them listen to many pieces of music (some of which had vocal lyrics). After a while the teachers realized that only two contrasting pieces of music with the same instrument and without lyrics enabled the children to begin their discernment of rhythms.

Gerrbo (2008) describes a teacher who had a boy in his classroom who had problems with distinguishing between d and g. The teacher and a special language pedagogue carefully planned a programme, carried it out, and made an analysis. They repeated it until the boy grasped the difference between d and g. They found out that critical aspects were that the sound d was placed (pronounced) at the front of the mouth behind the teeth and the sound g in the back of the mouth. They arranged a sequence of tasks that were alternatively auditory or visual. They also used tasks with both similar and different sounds. In the end the boy was able to distinguish between d and g. The author has many possible explanations why the boy did succeed in the end, but the most important one is that it all became a question of how the boy became aware of how he experienced (made) the sounds.

In Order to Help Learners to Discern

If learning is to perceive, see, or experience, the teacher has a central role in making it possible for children to experience the values, abilities, and knowledge she and society, through curricula and societal discourses, want children to develop. As mentioned earlier, this puts two kinds of demands on the teachers. First of all they have to be clear about and aware of what the learning objects are for each preschool group, and then for each child within the group. If, for Example, the teacher and society want to foster equality between boys and girls, the teacher must have an idea about what it means to the age group she works with. He or she must be able to observe and react immediately when gender questions appear on the arena, and she must already have an idea of how to make the intended gender equality visible to children. What are the features she wants to foster and how can variation be used to make these features obvious?

If the teacher wants young children to develop a sense of what "sustainable development" means (Björneloo, 2007; Pramling Samuelsson & Kaga, 2008), she must have an idea about this herself and then find or create opportunities to vary the meaning she wants to make visible and keep the background invariant.

To work in line with the approach developed here, the teacher needs first of all to be able to decide what the learning object should be, towards which she intends to direct children's experience. Second, she must be acquainted with the framework of variation theory in a way that it is bodily sustainable so that she can adopt it whenever she finds situations in which she can challenge children's understanding of different aspects of the world around them. This means that the learning object and the act of learning are closely related and dependent on each other.

Let us look at a study by Wallerstedt and Pramling (manuscript) where they follow children learning to listen by discerning musical form. The children are 6–8 years of age. The lessons are planned according to the theoretical framework of variation. Children listen to the music and paint what they hear. They then have a dialogue about the different paintings they have done. The lesson is repeated a few times and video-recorded. What the Results describe is the process of learning musical form that children give expression to. In order to help children to discern this specific aspect of the music, the teacher needs to vary the form by using different pieces of music. The researchers claim:

> A first step in developing children's understanding of music is to choose a piece of music in which a particular aspect varies, for Example, tempo, volume, or instrumentation. A second step would then be to choose other pieces varying in other aspects. In the particular case used in this study (*Die Moldau*), the piece of music varied in, for Example, rhythmic patterns and instrumentation. Another piece may instead vary in metre. A third piece may not be dividable into separate sections at all. (Wallerstedt & Pramling, p. 31)

Helping children become aware of or experience specific aspects of the world around them presupposes that the teacher can arrange the learning situation in a way that ensures that the learning object varies and the background for learning is invariant.

Children's Perspectives and Participation in Practice

When the focus is on children's experience, children's perspectives are necessary. If the teacher does not grasp the child's perspective, there is no way of continuing the learning process. At the same time, we can claim that interaction between teachers and children is necessary but not sufficient to influence children's lives in terms of values, abilities, or knowledge. Unfortunately, most teachers think that they know how children think, but there is a real difference between having an idea about children's thinking in general and perceiving it in everyday work all the time. That is why we believe it is an absolutely necessary condition for young children's learning that the teacher asks open questions and gets children to express themselves. Furthermore, as we have pointed out earlier, the teacher must be able to interpret both children's bodily and verbal expressions. To be able to adopt this angle of approach, the teachers must develop special skills.

When the teachers meet the children and listened to them in order to determine where they are in their understanding and sense making, children are willing to share their ideas and explore new domains. Unfortunately, teachers have so many obstacles to their own thinking, seeing, and experiences, that *seeing the child's world* – which is a must if they are to get them involved and become real participants – becomes a great challenge.

Thulin (2006) has shown in her study about science teaching in preschool that teachers have great problems with keeping the children's attention on specific objects of learning. The theme worked on was "life in a stump". Even though they have planned and know what they want children to learn, they communicate and interact but do not challenge or support specific ideas. Instead, the teaching situation is a moment of pleasure, where the children explore and communicate. The object of learning disappears, and Thulin finds that the teacher introduces anthropomorphistic ways of dealing with science instead, an approach used more by the teachers than by the children (see also Pramling, 2006, and Thulin & Pramling, under review). Teachers may think that they come closer to the child's world in this way, but they are adopting a child perspective based on Piaget's (1976[1929]) earlier description of children as users of the anthropomorphistic approach, that is, humanizing objects that are not human. If this approach is adopted, the children will be prevented from participating fully and being respected as knowledgeable partners. The teacher probably has good intentions, but if she had listened to children and understood what they were concerned about she could have met them and challenged their experiences.

Thulin also shows that, in the communication between the teacher and the children, children sometimes use more proper science notions than the teacher does. It is also quite confusing for children to make a "tree stump" out of chicken wire and papier-mâché when focusing on the life in a real "stump". It is obvious that here there is no "shared sustainable thinking" as found in the good quality preschools in the EPPE-project (Effective Provision in Preschool Education, Sylva et al., 2004). We have seen this in many studies before, that the teachers' perception of what is going on differs from children's. Klein (1989) shows in her communication model how the reciprocity between the teacher and the child is necessary for the whole communication process and how it proceeds. This is what Stern called to "tune in" to the child's experience, which one has to do to get children to participate.

Thulin (2006) claims that her Results show a conflict between two different traditions and discourses, one concerning the education, the other the development of a person. This conflict prevents teachers from talking properly about science since they believe it is too serious for young children and not a question of play, as expected in preschool. The teachers believe that the two perspectives are impossible to integrate. However, we believe they are!

When we work with teachers, we realize that it is as if teachers believe that there will be no room for children if they have a clear learning object and work towards that. However, it is precisely here, at the crossroads between the teacher's intentions and children's participation, that the skills of the teacher are manifested. It is also here that children develop an understanding of themselves and their capabilities and get a sense of what democracy means.

Part IV
Child Perspectives and Children's Perspectives in Theory and Practice: Summary, Discussion, and Conclusion

Part IV contains summaries of the previous parts of this book and our conclusions about child perspectives and children's perspectives for a broader context than Scandinavia and Western culture. First we summarize the introduction and each of the book's three parts. Then the question is discussed, whether a Scandinavian welfare value approach to children has a meaningful voice in a global context. After that the present and future status of the ECE is evaluated. Next some major problems and dilemmas in the globalization of a child perspective are discussed, especially in relation to cultural differences and panhuman similarities. The book is closed with a final conclusion.

Summary of Introduction: Child Perspectives and Children's Perspectives – The Scandinavian Context

The concepts of child perspectives and children's perspectives have become increasingly essential in relation to children's rights in general, to research, and to various child-related professions, which is reflected internationally in a growing number of publications. This may give the impression that by now these concepts are theoretically and methodically well established; nevertheless, as documented this is far from the case. The child perspectives concept appears to be steeped in ideological, ethical, and moral values, and we are far from having reached a shared overall conceptual understanding, theoretically and empirically.

Behind man-made theory lies complex fundamental culture-specific values of historical origin, and the world of today consists of considerably different cultures, particularly when it comes to childhood perspectives. This book is to a considerable degree rooted in a late modernity context in Scandinavia. Scandinavia forms part of both the Western and the global world, and it shares fundamental values with many countries, despite this important differences do exist. The introductory part of this book describes a selected number of consequences of relatively rapid changes in the developmental ecology of children, mainly when it comes to the revolution in maternal employment and the day-care-for-all situation. Furthermore, it gives a brief presentation of the Scandinavian welfare model, which has its roots in a fundamental acceptance of a shared society–family responsibility as to the caring and protection of the next generation. This leads to a Discussion of the importance of the humanization and individualization processes in contemporary society, the acceptance of children as equal citizens, and distinct ideologies and values of child-centredness – important factors that manifestly or latently contribute to the growing interest in child perspectives and children's perspectives. Moreover, it is demonstrated and argued how child perspectives are embedded in Scandinavian curricula of early childhood education. The final part of the introduction offers specific definitions of the interrelated, but conceptual difference regarding child perspectives and children's perspectives. *Child perspectives* direct adult's attention towards an understanding of children's perceptions, experiences, and actions in the world. Despite child perspectives attempt to get as close as possible to children's experiential world they will always represent adult's objectification of children. By contrast *children's perspectives* represent children's own perceptions, experiences, and understanding of their life-world. In contrast to child perspectives the focus is on the child as a subject in his or her experienced life-world.

Summary of Part I – In Search of Child Perspectives and Children's Perspectives in Childhood Sociology and Developmental Psychology

The sociology of childhood has frequently been *used* as synonymous with a child perspective (e.g. Lewis & Linsay, 2000; Ottesen, 2002; Eide & Winge, 2003; Halldén, 2003), but with surprisingly little argumentation. Also architects of childhood sociology have specifically used the concepts child perspectives and children's perspectives and related them to their work (Norwegian Centre for Child Research, 2003). Others argue that a child perspective may be seen in recent developmental psychology, more specifically the contextual–relational approach. But is that a given fact? To answer that, child perspectives and children's perspectives are searched for within prospective parts of the so-called *new view/perspective of children* or *the new child paradigm*, occurring from the separate fields of childhood sociology and contextual–relational developmental psychology. The search for key conceptual and theoretical formulations of possible child perspectives and children's perspectives has been guided by the following key questions:

- *Are child perspectives apparent in certain aspects of childhood sociology?*
  If yes, how are children conceptualized in ways that enhance adults' recognition and awareness of children's perceptions and life-experiences?
- *Are child perspectives apparent in certain aspects of contextual–relational developmental psychology?*
  If yes, how are children conceptualized in ways that enhance adults' recognition and awareness of children's perceptions of life-experiences?

- *Do children's own perspectives take a central position within these bodies of theories?*
  If yes, how do the respective disciplines show and present children's own perceptions and life experiences?
- *Are common conceptual platforms for a future integration identifiable?*
  Which concepts are particularly imperative to an interdisciplinary integration of concepts from childhood sociology and contextual–relational developmental psychology?

This search, however, is not an easy task as sociological and developmental theories, originally developed to address completely different adult relevant topics. Despite that they have habitually been used as representatives of genuine child perspectives. For instance, feminist theory has been used as a perspective on children stating that children are socially suppressed in the same way as women (Alanen, 1988; Alanen & Mayall, 2001). Another Example is James et al.'s (1998) use of a Foucaulian inspired general sociological discourse about societal time regulation and discipline in order to study "real children" and the "experience of being a child". What about recent developmental psychology, then? The answer to this is a bit gloomy. A review of leading "state-of-the-art" international textbooks and handbooks within developmental psychology (for Example Berk, 2006; Harwood, Miller, & Vasta, 2007) reveals that although children's minds, feelings, and social relationships are extensively dealt with, theories and empirical studies specifically representing a child perspective are absent. Consequently, these have to be derived by means of analysis. Scrutinizing potentially promising concepts stemming from recent contextual–relational developmental psychology carry this out. Promising future integration of the sociological and psychological positions building a common conceptual platform may start with the shared understanding of children as experiencing, meaning making actors in their life-worlds. Furthermore the groundbreaking research within the realm of early intersubjectivity stemming from psychology holds integrative potentials (Bråten, 2007). The promises in using such a perspective are elaborated in Part II.

Summary of Part II – A Humanistic and Interpretative Approach

Part II argues that a child perspective approach is not something fixed, once and for all defined by some historical and professional authority, but is rooted in a humanistic and interpretative orientation to children that can be specified in different ways. This position is strongly influenced by a humanistic, cultural-dialogical, and interpretative theoretical orientation, building on several of the fundamental child perspective beliefs dealt with in the other parts of the book. A few examples: the ethos of humanization, children as citizens, child-centredness and child orientation, the child as a meaning making and active person as vital paradigmatic cornerstones. In addition the humanistic, interpretative orientation as a child perspective approach to a great extent holds common conceptual understandings with the contextual–relational developmental psychological paradigm presented and discussed in Part I.

The conditions that facilitate empathic care and identification with the child on the one hand and those that obstruct this care on the other hand are explicated. Care is not a one-sided contribution from the caregiver to the child, but a dialogical product between two active partners. The concept of a "zone of intimacy" is a space into which a child can be included and cared for through empathic identification and sensitive availability of the caregiver to the child's needs. But a child can, relatively easy in problematic developmental contexts, be expelled from the zone of intimacy with subsequent blockage of empathic identification, affective withdrawal leading to neglect, and possibly abuse. Some particular conditions were discussed that impinges on empathic care. This was summarized and related to the newly emerging field of "ethics of closeness" and Levinas' idea of the "appeal of the face" (Bauman, 1996). A model summed up and visualized the positive versus a negative developmental pathway that can emerge in the caregiver–child relationship. After that Part II introduced and discussed the interpretive position as a genuine child perspective approach. This perspective was counter positioned the so-called normative test and diagnostic "culture" argued being far from a child perspective orientation. The "deficit" model and its negative consequences were discussed. Then the implicit communication rules within the so-called intersubjective space were explained and illustrated by using everyday examples from a school classroom context. Part II ended by illustrating the vast differences between using an interpretive, child-oriented approach versus using a normative, testing, diagnostic approach.

Summary of Part III – Early Childhood Education

When we search for child perspectives and children's perspectives in early childhood education, we can establish that child perspectives in terms of a child-centredness have always been a platform for the education of young children. The difference between them and schoolchildren has meant that teachers/carers have been deeply sensitive to their needs, care, and development. At the same time, recent research on young children in the context of ECE (see pp. 115–126) has shown us how skilful and competent children can be if they are provided with the right opportunities. The child is as competent as the physical and psychological milieu allows. If we do not give children the best start in life it feels like a wasted opportunity. However, this is a tricky question. On the one hand, one can claim that children growing up in a warm atmosphere together with people who respect and accept them as they are gain a rich variety of experiences related to the surrounding culture and will acquire all the necessary equipment for success later on in school. On the other hand, in our modern society children spend most of their everyday life in early childhood education from an early age, which means children's experiences there have to be as rich as possible in order to realize all their potential – and this also applies to children who grow up in "poor" (problematic) families.

Given the above perspective of children and of knowledge as an internal relation between the child and his or her world, children's learning can and should
be influenced in the preschool settings. This is brought out in many of the curricula developed in different countries. It is also a question of the children's right to
develop the foundations of knowledge in early years. It is during this time that the
foundations for "doing sums", becoming literate, understanding basic science, etc.
are built.

We argue here for a pedagogical approach labelled *developmental pedagogy*,
which has emerged from many years of empirical research and cooperation with
preschool teachers. Almost all researchers in the research group behind this
approach have a background as preschool teachers, which is why one can claim
that developmental pedagogy is formulated by the early childhood education field
itself – in a combination of theory and praxis.

Developmental pedagogy brings the act of learning together with the object of
learning. The object of learning is children's creation of meaning. This is where
children's perspectives are both the beginnings of learning something and an end in
themselves – this is how children experience something, or how something appears
to them, from their perspective.

The theory of learning and teaching, which links the teachers' actions with children's experiences – the encounter and interaction between them, is the theory of
variation. This means that children's learning (seeing or experiencing) can be influenced by using variation and invariance to make what we want them to learn visible
to them, in order to develop their perspectives (see p. 153).

There is no particular material, no specific sessions, but the teachers have to live
the theory, that is, to understand the ideas of the theory and the approach to be able
to utilize situations appearing in everyday life. Of course, he or she can plan and
organize situations, tasks, etc. to put the object of learning on the stage. But it is
children's subjective experience – their perspectives as they express them in their
actions (verbally or bodily), which is shown in the playing learning child, that has
to be met on his or her own terms, but who wants to and has to be challenged by the
pedagogical setting, other children, and his or her teachers.

Since education is always normative, based on the intentions of the curriculum
or the teacher's ideas, one can say that child perspectives are respected in all early
childhood education of good quality, while we who advocate development pedagogy
also try to let the children's subjective worlds come through – that is children's
perspectives.

The Scandinavian Approach: Does the Logic of the Welfare State Have an Important Voice in a Global Society?

In the book *Nordic Childhoods and Early Education,* Kristjansson (2006) makes an analysis of the Scandinavian welfare systems. His basic assumption is that the present is born in the past, which is why it is important to consider the historical roots of the Nordic countries' welfare systems to be able to understand what child perspectives and children's perspectives mean in this book.

The aspects he brings up are (1) Nordic child-centredness, which manifests itself in child-related issues in the social and political discourse (Therborn, 1993). One Example of this is the Ombudsman for Children system.

> The Ombudsman for Children is a commissioner with statutory rights and duties to promote and protect the rights and interests of children and young people, first and foremost at the national level, but also internationally, as these rights are expressed in legislation and international conventions such as the UN Convention on the Rights of the Child. (Kristjansson, 2006, p. 13)

(2) Nordic welfare state model, and the family policy that is based on democratic values and efforts. He claims, "among its distinguishing features is the vision of an egalitarian (!) society, where all citizens enjoy equally high standards of living, as well as social and personal well-being" (Kristjansson, 2006, p. 14). "In the family policy this is manifested in enhancing gender equality within the family and between parents. According to a recent United Nations report (2004) these measures have earned the Scandinavian societies the distinction of being recognized as the world's most equal, economically and between the genders" (Kristjansson, 2006, p. 14). We have also seen a lot of Examples of the question of equality in the first section of this book, where it is obvious that women's fight for their right both to have a career outside the family and to have and be able to foster children has changed the structure of welfare in Scandinavia.

Kristjansson (2006) states that childhood in the Nordic countries may be valued on the basis of two loosely related perspectives. The first he calls proposed value. This focuses on the significance of childhood for its future value to society, both as a means of the future society and also for each individual child, particularly in the Third World, as a future asset for the family and security for aging parents. The second perspective on the value of childhood is the idea of here and now. "Its universality rests on the assumption that positive sentiments towards children for their own sake – ranging from love and affection to enjoyment and amusement over children – are ingrained in healthy human nature" (Kristjansson, 2006, p. 21). This perspective is closely related to notions like playfulness, fantasy, and childish naivety, in positive terms. This implies that all child-centred activities, such as all forms of children's play, are considered to be naturally healthy and conducive to optimal development. The implications are then that adults should give children ample time and space. This may be expressed, from a child perspective, as adults giving children time and space to express their own perspectives. This value can be seen as a luxury for children living in rich countries, but it may also be seen as isolation from the adult world in many countries where every child's contribution to the family's living is needed (Hundeide, 1991). However, it has to be viewed in a Nordic perspective as a positive appraisal of childhood in its own right. This can also be seen in the relatively late entry to formal, compulsory education in Nordic countries in comparison with most other countries. It is also shown in research that Scandinavian children live in a negotiation culture in the family, where parents and children discuss and negotiate about small as well as large things every day (Dencik, 1989). In all the Scandinavian countries, there is an almost full coverage of preschool places for all children. This has to be seen both as a provision of a place where children can feel safe and secure and enjoy life while their parents work and as a question of the children's right to be together with peers in a stimulating pedagogical environment. This model of both giving parents the right to work and children the right to develop in a child-centred environment was advocated in Sweden by Gunnar and Alva Myrdal (1934) more than 70 years ago.[1]

Myrdal's model could be seen as a feminist project, in which she fought for women's right to be part of the social and economic life in the society, and not only as mothers. But it was also a question of developing the modern society towards a welfare state. The role of women and their possibilities in education in a society are clearly linked to children, why women play a strong role in letting the child's perspective to come through. Vittachi (in Hundeide, 1991, p. 24) says, "Educate a boy and you will educate a person. Educate a girl and you will educate a nation."

On a global level, we can also see how the role of women in the survival and education of children is recognized in the UN Millennium Development Goals (www.un.org/millenniumgoals). The Millennium goals state that the world should fight to eradicate extreme poverty and hunger; achieve universal primary education; promote gender equality and empower women; reduce child mortality; improve maternal health; combat HIV/AIDS, malaria, and other diseases; ensure *environmental sustainability*; and develop a global partnership for development. When one looks at these goals, it is easy to see how privileged children in the Nordic countries are. But a much more central question is where do we state our goals in the global society? If all

---

[1] Alva Myrdal was one of the founders of the first global and professional early childhood education organization OMEP (Organisation Mondiale pour l'Education Préscholaire, see www.omep-ong.net) grounded in Prague 1948.

children's voices could be heard, they do not only want to survive or be free to develop knowledge and be able to actively participate in a democratic world.

Four of the goals in the EFA (Education For All) report (2008) are, however, also closely related to the questions dealt with in this book.

(1) *Care and education for young children.* Here the report emphasizes that most countries still do not take the necessary political decisions for providing care and education for children below 3 years of age. Even though the number of preschool places has increased for children over 3 years, it is still unsatisfactory in African and Arab countries. It is also clear that the care and education of young children seldom reaches the poor children who would benefit most when it comes to nutrition, health, and cognitive development. In this respect, there is a total lack of taking children's perspectives.

(2) *Reading and writing skills among adults.* There are still 774 million adults in the world who are illiterate, although the number has decreased during the last 10 years. About 64% of these are women – a factor that we know has a strong impact on children's survival and education. To take the child's perspective, it means to make all children members of the "writers club", and by this the children both gain knowledge and become an active citizen.

(3) *Gender equality between men and women is still far away.* In many countries, sexual harassment, unsafe school environments, and lack of sanitary engineering to a disproportionately high degree affect girls' self-esteem, participation, and school experiences. Textbooks, curricula, and the teachers' attitudes continue to maintain stereotype gender roles in many countries. This may mean that the girl's perspectives are less listened to than the boys' perspectives.

(4) *Quality.* The number of children passing through the whole school system has increased, but many children have a relatively small and uneven knowledge of languages (first and second) and mathematics. Many classrooms are overcrowded and tumbledown, and in many counties those who teach the children have had no teacher training, which may have a negative influence on the quality. Children cannot influence the quality of the school system, but they will feel with their whole body if they are in a school where there is interaction, communication, and *respect for each individual child* – so their voices can be heard.

Siraj-Blachford & Manni (2008) talks about doing what is most beneficial to all as an appropriate way of improving the circumstances for all. Changes in the world will not come from a similar quality or way of living, but from making the best of whatever is available. Just like each child's education has to begin where the child's experiences are, each country must begin their development from where they are. This also means that there are many paths to go!

Democracy is evidently not a simple and unambiguous notion, which is why different countries considered to be democratic may also have different systems of support for parents and children. Further, it is important for us to state that we are not telling the world that the Scandinavian model is the solution, but we have tried to analyse and express the ideas behind this system – also as an explanation for the preschool system and pedagogy.

Sometimes we have met people in the world who think that the Scandinavian countries have "kind" governments, since we have state support for parents and preschool provision. But as all educated people know, the societies' provision of their children is not a question of kindness, but a long-time commitment and political efforts. Experiences like this, however, raises questions like how do you tell someone who does not know what democracy is, that childhood in these societies are based on a long democracy process. How children are treated in a society is related not only to financial question but also to values and the mission of each society. Are all children treated as individuals with human rights? And as we have shown earlier in this book, this is not always the case.

This brings us to the question of what the future holds in store for the children of today, it is so uncertain, and what experiences in early years will benefit them most.

Where Are We Today in ECE and What About the Future?

Let us go back to the arena of early childhood education related to child perspectives and children's perspectives. Without saying anything about what is good or bad for children, we have shown that Scandinavian childhood and early childhood education are different from those to be found in most (maybe all) other countries in the world, that is, both when it comes to child-centredness and the welfare status. But as Kristjansson (2006, p. 38) says

> ... the Nordic childhoods are relatively well and thriving. We must keep in mind, however, that Nordic childhoods, both in the present and in the future, exist as mental categories rather than a concrete object.

Kristjansson (2002) also refers to a study of his own with 87 5-year-old children, where he states that it is worth noting that the adult instructions about Nordicness as a national cultural phenomenon generally took place in children's preschool settings rather than at home. One reason for this may be that Nordic democracy is lived and taken for granted in everyday life, but to make it visible for children it has to be focussed on and talked about – this is one of the main goals of the curricula in Scandinavia.

In this book we have described one approach to early childhood education developed in the Scandinavian context and research, developmental pedagogy, and it must be seen in this perspective. However, we still think that other people in other countries can learn and apply it in their context, based on their conditions, even though we understand that it cannot easily be transferred to cultures where individuals do not have rights but are always perceived to be a part of the whole family or community. Let us come back to this later.

As we have seen in the summary (see p. 236), the main idea in developmental pedagogy is to use a theory of variation. This has to be lived and enacted by the teacher in order to create opportunities as well as taking advantage of them to draw children's attention to the values, skills, or understanding of different phenomena in the world around them. Play and learning should be integrated to meet each child's experience as a playing learning child. This means that children have to create meaning with regard to certain values, skills, or knowledge that are of importance to the local as well as the global society. The education effort must, however, go far beyond the local society. We live in a world where children, early in life, have to be exposed to questions about sustainable development, and not least be educated for a sustainable society, which includes ecological, social, and economic questions, as well as a long-term perspective (UNESCO, 2008). Wherever children grow up, they still have to be treated as citizens with rights and responsibilities according to their age and experience.

In her opening speech at the OMEP conference (1948), Alva Myrdal said, "We have to educate children for a world that dwindles, a world coming closer and a world we know is different from ours." This does not mean that we should leave children to educate themselves, but that we should notice what key notions, ideas, skills, or knowledge the next generation possibly needs to be familiar with.

The perspective we advocate here may be seen both as a contrast to and similar to the Reggio Emilia approach as is presented in the book *Beyond Quality in Early Childhood Education and Care* by Dahlberg, Moss, and Pence (1999).

The political background in the province of Reggio Emilia in Italy, with a social democratic tradition and a strong emphasis on family policy and children's right to a preschool of high quality, is the same as in Scandinavia. In both approaches, there is child-centredness endeavouring to make children's experiences, hypotheses, and ideas visible in preschool. Value questions, such as democracy and children's active participation, are central in Reggio Emilia as well as in Scandinavian preschools. In Reggio Emilia, the pedagogy is sometimes called "the pedagogy of listening" (Rinaldi, 2001). For more than 20 years, a key competence for teachers in Sweden has been to listen to and have dialogues with children and to analyse what children say in terms of their perspectives or creation of meaning (Doverborg & Pramling Samuelsson, 2000).

The main difference between the two approaches is in the underlying theoretical perspective, which also affects praxis. According to Dahlberg et al. (1999), the Reggio Emilia pedagogy is based on a post-modern perspective in which power, uncertainty, complexity, and relativity are central notions.

> From a post-modern perspective there is no absolute knowledge, no absolute reality waiting "out there" to be discovered. There is no external position of certainty, no universal understanding that exists outside history or society that can provide foundations for truth, knowledge and ethics. Instead, the world and our knowledge of it is seen as socially constructed and all of us, as human beings, are active participants in the process (Berger & Luckman, 1996), engaged in relationships with others in meaning making rather than truth finding: the facts of knowledge are "textual and social constructed by us in our efforts to understand our situations". (Dahlberg et al., p. 22)

This leads to the question of the direction of the learning process or what we should call the object of learning. In Reggio Emilia, there are no curricula since they believe it would hinder the teacher from listening to and following what comes up in children's minds. As far as we can understand, this entitles every child to his or her truth. So maybe one could say that the ideal approach in Reggio Emilia is total devotion to the children's perspectives.

We do not at all share the post-modern perspective, but build our approach on humanization and a socio-cultural experience-oriented perspective. This means that education has to begin with children's experiences as these appear as a "touch down in time". The end of the learning, the meaning created by each child, can also be viewed as a "touch down" in time. As adults we also know a great deal about values, skills, and knowledge that children need to develop, in whatever society they live. They need to develop not only as persons, but also to begin to make sense of different aspects of the world around them.

We also have a modern child development base, which means that we recognize that children have different possibilities and preconditions for learning about specific phenomena at different times of life. We also think that the portrait painted of developmental psychology is too scurrilous – as if we should view children's possibilities of growing and learning with horror! As in all other disciplines, the theories and research move the field (see, e.g. Sommer, 2005a; Hundeide, 2006).

A child is not only a construction but also a human being with body and mind, growing up in a certain culture, which may or may not support the children's perspectives. We think, however, that there exists a kind of curriculum in all preschool settings, whether or not it is spelled out. Our view is that it is important to make the curriculum visible (in each preschool or on a national level) so that we are able to evaluate what we are trying to develop children's understanding about. A curriculum can never be objective, but it can be based on research as well as cultural values (Pramling Samuelsson, Sheridan, & Williams, 2006).

Cultural Differences and Panhuman Similarities? – Problems and Dilemmas in the Globalization of a Child Perspective

In this section some critical reflections and discussions will be dealt with about some serious problems inherent in the globalization of children's perspectives emanated in a specific (Scandinavian) culture. We are moving into deep water here and do not think we can solve this matter once and for all. But in highlighting and dealing with some important issues, we hope that others will carry on, sharpening our sensitivity to what children's beliefs that may be inferred from possibly shared panhuman universals and what beliefs that may be constructed from culturally produced differences (and similarities).

As stated previously, we do not embrace some recent constructivist post-modern theorizing that every notion about the child is a local-consensus construction, whereby any "truth" becomes an illusion. Such an approach leads to the conclusion (illusion) that any cultural definition and belief about the child is nothing but a "local truth", with little generalization potential. Not least disturbing is that research as such becomes just one example of particular, local discourse – a voice in a quire of several voices (Kvale, 1992). Some world phenomena are constructions and relative to interpretation, indeed, but others are not. For example, the fact that natural science matters as the existence of gravity on this earth has penetrating effects on all matter, or the truth that it is against the law of nature that an object (a toy car) drives through a solid wall with no openings. Groundbreaking research shows that human infants either are born with "core knowledge", i.e. knowing about fundamental aspects and functions of the physical world, or at least are endowed with some "highly constrained learning mechanisms", competencies that direct the child's interest towards specific qualities about the physical world and that explain human's surprisingly learning capacity very early in ontogenesis (Baillargeon, 1994). As we will discuss later, some aspects of the phylogenetic approach is to some extent based on types of evidence that may be open to interpretations, but not to any type of discourse. Another example is children's "embodied cognition", where psyche (mental activity) is inseparable from soma (body and brain). So, not being too stubborn, we hold a "both-and approach" to the constructivist approach. This opens for a discussion of whether some panhuman universals may be a potential foundation under a child perspective approach that to some extent goes beyond contemporary Westernized beliefs in humanization, individualization, democratization, and child-centredness.

But let's start with the Westernized context – more specifically Scandinavia: Sommer (2010) illustrates how the prototypic adult–child relationship in Scandinavia in a short historical period has moved from a strict authoritarian one in the 1930s towards the present egalitarian, child-centred relationship, building on widely shared cultural beliefs in humanization, democratization, and individualization (Fig. 1).

As described in the introductory part of this book this time–space context opens for the historically relatively new child-centredness in society, in daycare, and in family that to a great extent has paved the way for the recent emphasis on the importance of taking a child's perspective and that children are not small adults in the making, but have fundamental needs and unique ways to perceive and understand their worlds. The figure illustrates how major widely shared cultural and societal perceptions are influencing adult's child-centredness as well as children's experience and beliefs. The theoretical understanding behind that is based on the so-called time–space functionalist paradigm (Sommer, 2010). That means that (in complex and reciprocal ways) cultural and societal, time-bound beliefs are intertwined and in accordance with caring and learning practices. So, as illustrated in Fig. 1, it will not

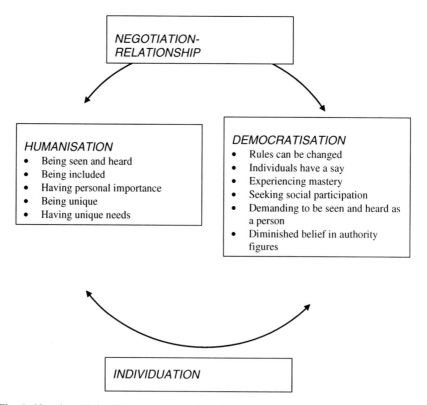

Fig. 1 Negation relationships as pertinent Scandinavian democratic values (*Source:* Sommer, 2010)

be in concordance with "normality" if a Scandinavian father is a strict authoritarian, giving top-down orders to be obeyed by his child – an adult not having any contact with the feelings and understandings of his child. In fact studies of Danish fathers and mothers confirm the functional approach that parents typically are involved in "negotiation relationships" with their children (Sommer, 2008a).

But arguing for the usefulness of a Scandinavian welfare approach to children's perspectives in a globalized world is filled with serious problems and dilemmas: How can we know what are meaningful child-related conceptualizations and belief systems in cultures very different from ours? Human mind and behaviour is just too rich to be "captured" by studies and theory that are conducted in only a single culture. As stated previously behind man-made research lie complex fundamental culture-specific values of historical origin, and the world of today consists of considerably different cultures, not least when it comes to the understanding of the child. Talking specifically about child perspectives in theory and practice, the authors of this book agree to a large extent that culture is a main factor in children's development of ways of behaving, thinking, feeling, and communicating. This raises some fundamental questions, problems, and dilemmas about any intention to "export" an idea of the benefits of ECE in general and the appraisal of children's perspective in particular. Furthermore the various childhood sociological theories evaluated in Part I was developed during the 1990s in Europe (Qvortrup, James, Jenks, & Prout) and the USA (Corsaro). Their perspective of the child may be seen as implicit cultural time-bound constructions, wrapped into programmatic statements as "the new child paradigm". Despite the fact that a micro-analytic, everyday cultural-constructionist approach is very prominent in childhood sociology – with Qvortrup as an exemption – there is remarkably little reflection on the time–space limitations of concepts like "agency", "inner self", "meaning making", "negotiated relationships", "cultural production", "co-construction", and "real child".

Experts and users of research in an independent culture intuitively accept such concepts, whereas they may not be meaningful, for example in Africa and some Asian countries, or at least have to be reformulated and adapted to interdependent cultures (Markus & Kitaymaya, 1991). (This important matter will be pursued later in this section.) The point here, however, is that everyday cultural discourse reflected in the new child paradigm takes place in specific Westernized contexts, for example Corsaro's analysis of daycare children in Italy–USA, and James, Jenks, and Prout's ethnographic-interpretative investigations of children in England. The same can be said about the in Part I presented contextual-developmental approach in psychology. This is seen in core concepts "intentionality", "intersubjectivity", phenomenological world". In other words, this is understandings implicitly derived from individualistic, self-autonomous, humanistic, democratic cultures. As Bewan (1991) pointed out in his harsh criticism of contemporary psychology, behind the worlds we construct, colouring both our logic and our rhetoric, are the ideologies that give our world views their dominant cast. They are like sand at a picnic – they get into everything. So, one should be careful – deliberately or un-deliberately – postulating universals about children, for example a child perspective. Because what we think is universal may be what we take for granted as cultural values, linked to our societal and cultural belief systems:

> Cultures in a sense are "invisible" (...). They are interpretative lenses that are taken for granted by the wearers. Like the air we breathe, in ordinary conditions, these value frameworks do not rise to conscious awareness. (Greenfield et al., 2006, p. 659)

In other words, there should be tolerance for variability of child values in line with the variability found in that society, and experts' recommendations have to operate inside that "space of acceptable variability". When this is said, *human beings are also biological beings with an evolutionary history* that sets limits to what is acceptable or possible in order to survive and develop in relation to other human beings and to prevent the development of non-adaptive functioning – that is pathology and psychological disturbance. There are certain basic needs in human beings like the need for food and nutrition, the need for movement, locomotion and physical activity, the need for love, attachment and inclusion with other human beings, the need for being guided into the skills, knowledge and values of a society, the need to explore and develop one's understanding and mastery of environment, the need to develop a self-respecting self and individuality (although as we soon will show, the cultural understanding of mastery, self, and individuality varies to a considerable degree; Rothbaum et al., 2000). The authors of this book share the following concerning species-like cultural similarity and individual specificity:

> All humans share a great deal of universal activity because of the biological and cultural heritage that we have in common as a species (e.g. two legs, communication through language, helpless infancy, organization in groups, and capacity to invent tools), and at the same time, each of us varies because of our differences in our physical and interpersonal circumstances. (e.g. visual acuity, strength, family constellation, means of making a living, familiarity with specific languages, Rogoff, 1990, p. 11)

Consequently it is essential to understand and take into consideration both the underlying cultural, ontogenetic, and evolutionary similarities and differences in discussing a child perspective in a global setting. There are a host of unsolved dilemmas and problems as well as potentials in this, which are far beyond the scope of this book to trace, but let us start by pointing out some basic premises for a discussion: some needs seem to be basic across nations in the sense that if they are not satisfied, either the person dies or the person develops physical or psychological pathologies in the sense that they become unable to adapt and cope within a culturally developed society. In other words, there are both biological and societal constraints and limits to human adaptability (they are in fact inseparable and intertwined – see Cole, 1996) and therefore, for example, child-centred recommendations have to build on these and stay within their limits. Some of these limits are codified as children's rights that are signed by several nations in the world, and they function as obligations (Unicef, 2008). In accordance with that working within a children's perspectives, i.e. society's and adult's belief that it is important and recommendable to practise a child perspective, this may be one factor in enhancing the well-being and mental health, not only of the particular child, but of the next generation.

As mentioned, everything may not be a question of cultural variability, differences, and solely environmental explanations. There is some rather promising research-based evidence for the existence of some panhuman similarities based on phylogenetic development that the argument of the benefit of taking a children's perspective may be founded upon. We do not intend to open a discussion about inheritance versus milieu. The importance of either inheritance/genes versus milieu, for example within developmental psychology, has caused a fierce controversy between two camps (e.g. Baumrind, 1993; Scarr, 1992, 1993). This theme is still in focus in research and assumingly is a never-ending debate among professionals in various disciplines. Promising newer progress within neuropsychological research, however, has shown that specific identifiable qualities of childcare (e.g. secure/insecure attachment) are not only intertwined with the development of brain structure, neurotransmitters, and chemicals as serotonin and adrenalin, but affect directly both the structural and physiological developments of the brain. Simultaneously brain structure and function highly influence emotional, cognitive, and social activities (Hart, 2006). This approach holds promises in breaking down the presuming stereotyped Descartesian dichotomy between mind versus body and nature versus nurture. The new "mirror-neuron" and "altero-centric" approaches to the human species as a fundamental and primary hypersocial being are other promising examples (Bråten, 2007). Furthermore recent approaches to children's learning link a phylogenetic and ontogenetic understanding of panhuman similarities: spontaneous activity, curiosity, and the child's constant search for meaning-making exploring both the physical and social world. Such human qualities can be observed and inferred from children's activities all over the world if the child is allowed to show them and the adult is able to see them.

This suggests the existence of some panhuman universals that are possible to identify, derived from growing research evidence. For example, every child's basic need for growing up in some "zone of intimacy" and being met with some type of "emphatic care", which appears to be necessary for any child's healthy development (Hundeide, 2007, see also Part II of this book). There is much cultural variability in this: The zone of intimacy may be a traditional nuclear family as in many cultures. In some cultures the mother will be the primary zone of intimacy and the effecter of emphatic care; in other cultures it may be the father, as well, siblings, the expanded family network, or the cultural subgroups. Weissner and Gallimore's (1977) anthropological investigation about caring practices in several industrialized and non-industrialized countries showed that the exclusive monotrophic mother–child relationship was prominent in only 5 out of more than 100 countries.

But if the baby's inherent and primary sociality and spontaneous interest in learning and discovering new matters has to be elaborated, competent cultural agents are necessary as developers. Despite cross-cultural plurality – in practices of care, upbringing and learning, the wide variations in normality – there seems to be limits that may not be obscured, otherwise mal adaptation will be the consequence. For example, child death or survival is caused by a complex array of causes. Mothers and families in parts of Africa are in a desperate situation where intimacy and emphatic care and the creating of a learning milieu are undermined (Unicef, 2008). Here we are faced with an extreme situation that goes far beyond the limits for emphatic care and fulfilling the child's need for a zone of intimacy. Some traditional cultural practices, for example the circumcision of young females, are an inhuman act, whether it is a tradition or not. Additionally, although infrequent, heavy spanking of the child is still occurring in Scandinavia despite legislation against it and society's wieldy held child-friendly beliefs. The point is that in any society or culture there will be evidence of beliefs and actions far from a child perspective, demonstrating little insight into children's perspectives. But the reasons behind that are multiple.

Hundeide's "zone of intimacy" and "emphatic care" as universals are promising concepts – two stepping stones in an argument for the importance of adults taking a children's perspective – "listening to", "feeling", "taking in" a child's understanding. Emphatic care is by definition a qualification of relationship that as a minimum requires an adult that more or less reflected takes the perspective of the other. This may be highly intuitive and embedded in cultural perceptions about what a child is. Bråten (2007), however, is highlighting some inborn human social capacities (i.e. capacity for empathy and perspective taking) – a promising conceptual prerequisite, arguing indirectly for children's perspectives, for example that children are phenomenological beings with their unique perspective on their world. This seemingly exists; the crucial thing is whether this is "seen" or not.

Until now cultural differences and variance have been discussed as important to consider when dealing with child perspectives in theory and practice. Specific cultural difference, however, has not been spelled out for real. So, let's take a closer look at some important major differences in cultures in a global world. We will do this presenting research made in *collectivistic and individualistic cultures*. What can be learned from this about what is culturally different and what are presumably panhuman similarities?

The idea that culture is completely decisive for development – that humans are born only having some spontaneous reflexes (i.e. sucking), but few or none innate, biological, or psychological features – is too unrealistic. Stern (1998) does not perceive culture as the only source:

> There are not an infinite number of variables through which any culture can be enacted early in life such that they will be perceivable by the infant. The repertoire comprises facial expressions, or the lack thereof; visual regards, or their avoidance; vocalizations, or silences; body orientations; physical distances; gestures; ways of being held; the rhythms, timing and duration of acts and activities; and so on. No other human alphabet for socio-cultural contextualisation exists. To continue the analogy: Different cultures can make different sentences with this same alphabet, but first we must examine how such an alphabet can (not must) work. (Stern, 1998, p. xxvii)

Thus, as seen here, there is a complex interaction between a universal "human alphabet" and the specific culture and era during which the child grows up. But what is the role of culture in relation to the self-other relationship, i.e. the relative importance of the child's inner phenomenological world vis-à-vis social partners? Understanding the nature of the self-other relationship is important for a child perspective and a child's perspective, because "the self" (at least in a Westernized culture) is assumed to contain the child's mental universe and hence idiosyncratic way of relating to the world. Let us start this, presenting a definition of self, derived from Berk (2006), an American "state-of-the-art" textbook of child development. (The book is globally exported and used in several parts of the world and hence in different cultures, for example Mexico City, London, Paris, Hong Kong, Singapore, Tokyo, Cape Town, and Sydney). Berk's (2006) definition of "the self" is as follows:

> ...self as knower and actor, includes the following realizations: self-awareness, that the self is separate from the surrounding world and has a private, inner life not accessible to others; self-continuity, that the self remains the same over time; self-coherence, that the self is a single, consistent, bounded entity; and self-agency, that the self controls it own thoughts and actions. (Berk, 2006, p. 438)

This is – perhaps unintended – a Westernized monopolization of a core child concept. Scrutinizing the above conceptualization reveals that it represents an individualistic ideology spelling out about the child's competent, bounded, feeling inner self, separated from the outer world and being in (self) control. Western culture is replete with beliefs in the inviolable self, which is in line with the features that previously were identified in the Scandinavian negotiation families, who go very far to accommodate children's independent opinions in everyday interactions. This reflects the parents' culturally affected developmental goals, which include the promotion of autonomy and independence. These families should not, however, be considered universal prototypes, whose lifestyle can be generalized out of context.

On the basis of what is by now a considerable body of cross-cultural research it can be concluded that people in different cultures have strikingly different constructions of self, of others and of their mutual relations (Kitayama & Markus, 1994; Rothbaum et al., 2000; Greenfield et al., 2006). This has important consequences for our discussion of the cultural vicissitudes in the understanding of a child perspective and the prominence of a children's perspective.

Let us illustrate this showing how variations in cultural practices have far-reaching consequences for self-development, right from birth. In Morelli and Rogoff's (1992) cross-cultural study of sleeping arrangements, they compared the ways that American middle-class families and Maya Indians handled bedtime routines from birth until the child was around 6 months old. None of the American babies slept in their mother's bed right from birth; instead they had their own, often in the parents' bedroom. Between the age of 3 and 6 months, most had moved to a room of their own. All the Mayan children, however, slept in their mother's bed until after they were 2 years old. The US mothers motivated their arrangements with a desire to foster personal independence in their children from the beginning of life; the Mayan mothers motivated their strategy with the importance of being close to the child. In order to ease the daily separation, the American infants used pacifiers and transition objects (soft toys), and at bedtime they were involved in transition routines to be able to fall asleep (walking around the room, holding hands, bedtime stories for the slightly older children, etc.). This was not the case for the Mayan children. Thus, from the beginning of life, the cultural requirement for self-development is expressed in different cultural belief systems and childrearing practices. Seeing this in the light of the cultural discussion of the relevance of a child perspective, there seem to be different routes here: It is difficult to argue that Mayan mothers are not taking a child perspective in the intimate caring in the domain of "being close". This goes for American mothers too, although within a very different caring practice: walking around with close body contact, holding hands, and reading for her child with the long-sighted goal of fostering "personal independence". (It may be argued, however, that the Westernized idea of fostering early independence is against human social nature, and hence not very child-centred at all.) What we try to communicate, using the study of Morelli and Rogoff's (1992) is that there's not a cultural ownership of a child perspective and the taking-in of the child's perspective, although it may seem much more "societal visual", reflected in contemporary Scandinavian humanistic beliefs and theorizing. Rather there exist various cultural beliefs and practices that are more or less in accordance with a child perspective within every culture.

Strong cross-cultural differences in development patterns are highlighted in Markus and Kitayama's (1991) review of Asian and Western research. Unlike Berk's (2006) ethnocentric definition, they approach the self as, respectively, the Asian *interdependent self* and the Western *independent self*. Independency was described above as a characteristic of Berk's (2006) autonomous self. This is not an adequate description of the interdependent self, as it changes with the changing social context. The Japanese word for "self" refers to "one's share of the common life space". The self is not considered a constant entity but as a pulsating entity with no sharp boundaries either between individuals or inside the individual; the self changes over time in reflection of different situations. This springs from the Japanese culture and its tradition for social relativism (Markus & Kitayama, 1991).

It seems that culture influences the self-other relationship in various ways right from birth by accenting certain adoption strategies more than others. The term "accenting" here implies that the process reflects differences in cultural *emphasis* rather than the complete absence or presence of certain features. Different *cultural lenses* affect the path of the species-specific attitude towards the social realm in cultural-specific ways. Cultures are like prisms that bend the light to produce different hues. This point of view is in accordance with Rothbaum et al. (2000). Their research review discusses the far-reaching implications of what is by now a substantial body of cross-cultural research into close human relationships. They (2000) illustrate their point with a model that represents different pathways in which the different lenses of the East and the West channel the biological panhuman substrate (exemplified by the USA and Japan, but this is observed among Latin Americans, Hawaiians, and Africans too (Greenfield et al., 2006)) (Fig. 2):

In the West (this includes Scandinavia), the species-specific panhuman biological substrate of relationships (proximity seeking; contact maintaining; separation protest; safe haven) is refracted through the *lens of individuation*. In the Scandinavian culture, children's relationships to their significant others are dominated by *generative tension*: Early in life, the child encounters strong demands

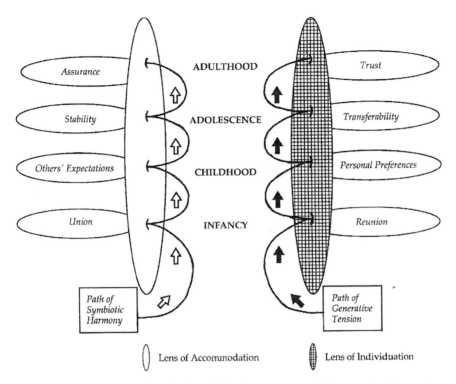

Fig. 2 Eastern developmental path of symbiotic harmony versus Western path of generative tension through lifespan (*Source:* Rothbaum et al., 2000)

from caregivers and others for "early independence" and "individuality". At the same time, there are strong cultural norms concerning "togetherness", "intimacy", "loyalty", and acceptance of "dependence". Rothbaum et al. (2000) point out many intriguing implications of this developmental tension for people in our culture, including the fact that "ego-drive", "self-determination", "individual intentionality", "taking life into your own hands", etc. become prominent aspects of self-perception, albeit always in competition with social considerations. Too much "I" and "Me", as expressed in insufficient self-regulation and social responsibility, may cause loss of intimacy, if one violates social and cultural ground rules, e.g. "tolerance" and "respect for others". Thus, this inherent conflict between individual and others becomes an almost "natural" and unquestioned part of childrearing in Western cultures. Parental beliefs supporting a path of generative tension has in fact been documented in Scandinavia: A representational, selected group of Danish parents with $3\frac{1}{2}$-year-old children picked "independence" as the most important quality in children. Number two on their list of priorities was "regard for others" (Sommer, 2005).

The vital point here is that classical universal developmental theories have incorporated this specific cultural tension into their basic concepts presenting their theories; not realizing that they in fact represent a local view with limited cross-cultural applicability. For example, the classical developmentalist Erik Erikson

(1950) – although open to cultural differences – includes an early psychosocial phase for *independence* versus shame/doubt in his well-known developmental model. The positive outcome of this phase is *willpower* as well as *self-restraint*, a clear example of the culturally specific generative tension mentioned above. Erikson (1950) also has a phase for individual *initiative* versus guilt. The positive outcome of this phase is for the individual to develop *intentionality*. Here, we see the clear positive emphasis on the Western ideal of an autonomous, wilful, and goal-oriented individual – who is also required to master self-restraint and impulse control. This is an example of theories within developmental psychology that are inadvertently ethnocentric. Now, it may be claimed that Erikson (1950) actually believes that culture has a key impact on development. Indeed, he describes how approaches to childrearing in various Indian tribes foster distinctly different personality features. But in introducing his epigenetic theory, he presents it as a general stage theory. It posits eight critical universal stages that people go through in their lifespan. This is an example from what in the definitions part early in this book is called a top-down non-child perspective theory.

This brings us to the other cultural lens and the special way it refracts the basic panhuman universals. According to Rothbaum et al. (2000) the Eastern cultural lens filters the biological basis towards social accommodation. Studies have shown that Japanese culture has a much stronger emphasis on so-called *symbiotic harmony* than, say, Scandinavian culture. This means that both a cultural ideal and childcare and parenting practices place a high priority on the child's dependence and adjustment. A prototype of symbiotic harmony is the way Japanese mothers "spoil" and "dote on" their children (as filtered by Western norms of self-independence!) and the children's *amae* – i.e. complete dependency on the mother. Self-articulation and volition would meet with no encouragement and little approval. On the other hand, the mother offers the child a guarantee against the frustration of needs. Often, the mother knows what the child wants, before the child has even become aware of it. Thus, children do not have to suffer frustrations and express unfilled needs to mothers. This bolsters the children's dependency and dampens their individuation (Rothbaum et al., 2000). In time, this becomes what Markus and Kitayama have called the culturally specific development of an interdependent self. The strong norm for children to learn *omoiyari* (empathy) helps promote the formation of this interdependent self. *Omoiyari* takes top priority in the morals hierarchy in Japanese culture (Lebra, 1994). An adequate culturally meaningful embedded understanding and analysis of a child perspective and children's perspectives has to some extent to integrate such culturally defined developmental pathways in order to be ecologically valid.

This does not mean, however, that children in collectivistic cultures do not perceive themselves as entities distinct from others, with their own mind and feelings. There may be an awareness sense that actions spring from "me", at the same time, as the child feels closely linked with others. However, the individual's autonomous influence does not receive nearly as much appraisal in collectivistic cultures as they do in the West. Ergo, children' early sense of themselves as separated from others, seems to be less profound in collectively oriented cultures than in individually oriented cultures. What we can say here is that the *emphasis and the accent* on individual independence/dependence and autonomy (=the balance between inter-dependence and independence) are culturally channelled. However, seen in the perspective of the contextual, developmental psychology, that was presented in Part I, the basic and initial constitution of the self per se is probably characterized by interdependence in any culture, in other words a panhuman similarity.

A voice of caution should be raised about the over-interpretation of Results from cross-cultural studies of differences between the Major World (not the Third World) and the West. Statements as "the Indian Self . . ., the Japanese Mother. . ., the Latin American simpatia" are just a few examples of that tendency, in order to keep a sober balance study after study finds *similar* human characteristics and behaviour patterns among countries as diverse as India, Korea, Mexico, Greece, and Japan that remain implicit (Kagitcibasi, 2007).

In her seminal work Kagitcibasi (2007) does not subscribe to an "either-or" stance in the debate that universalism (e.g. humans are similar) is contradicting a culture-contextual approach (e.g. humans are different) and visa versa. On a solid basis in solid empirical research, she argues convincingly for a complementary posi-tion that makes clear that universal patterns in principle are possible to detect in human development across cultures:

> . . . when studies that take content into considerations are repeated in different cultural con-texts, and similar Results are obtained, this provides grounds for possible universal patterns. (p. 9)

As argued in this book, some of the universals are founded in the shared phy-logenetic history of human beings, but other global similarities across cultures and countries may be "due to analogous functional links among behaviours in different cultures, rather than to biological commonalities" (Kagitcibasi, 2007, p. 15). This "both-and" approach opens for a global usability of child perspectives and children's perspectives approach in theory and practice. Not imported as a package or imple-mented as a "top-down" set of rules, but sensitively adapted to and used in specific contexts.

Conclusion

There are three aspects we want to lighten in our concluding remarks. These are the *global* aspect of child perspectives or children's perspectives, the *everyday life* of children and the caring process from a child perspective and children's perspectives, and child perspectives and children's perspectives in *young children's education*.

On the global level we will relate to the *UN Convention of the Right of the Child* (1989), signed by several hundred countries representing a great variety of cultures all over the world. Many articles could be related to, indeed, and has been during the work and research by, for example, UNICEF (2008). There's a present awareness that the statement about the "protection of the child" has been and still is highly important. But this focus has, to certain degree, put the global implementation of other important articles somewhat behind. Addressing this we will highlight article 3 about "the best for the child", articles 12 and 13 "the right to express oneself, and freedom to information". In all situations where children are involved, in official societal institutions and in the privacy of the family, what is best for the child should always be in the mind of the carer or educator. This mean that article 3 clearly indicates and opens for a child perspective as defined and elaborated in detail in this book. If we look at articles 12 and 13, it is stated that children are obliged to speak freely, concur or give information, and express their thoughts, verbally or in writing, as well as in artistic forms or other means. In order to make this possible this necessitates not only an orientation towards, but also a deep understanding and ability to take in and promote children's perspectives, thus letting their thoughts, feelings, and perceptions to be articulated.

Summarizing the global perspective, there is a strong base both for child perspectives and for children's perspectives as put forward in this book in the most important document of today about children's rights. But as we have pointed to as well in Part IV, despite the globalization and late modernity effects that homogenize living conditions for children, there still exist a great variety in customs, ways of living, and fundamental beliefs in cultures of today. Fundamental beliefs about "child", "family", "mother", "father", "care", "upbringing", "self-other", and the like seem not to be the same in Asia, Africa, Europe, and the USA. In fact, growing research has shown very distinct cultural differences, for example, the degree of how Eastern and Western "lenses" of inter- and interdependence shape developmental pathways from early infancy to adulthood. This opens a variety in the cultural interpretations of the *UN Conventions of the Right of the Child*. This perspective shows how children become "different". On the other hand, we have, for example in Parts II and IV, presented and discussed groundbreaking research with infants and in the nature and developmental function of the intimate caregiver–child relationship that points very convincingly to panhuman similarities as well. Such a perspective shows how children are "similar" all over the world and have common needs for care and learning guidance. Examples of panhuman similarity is what Rothbaum et al. (2000) in their outstanding paper call the *biological substrate of relationships*, which includes a child's tendency to "proximity seeking", "contact maintaining", as well as "separation protest", and the caregiver as a "safe haven". As argued in this book, there seems to be some fundamental panhuman stepping stones from which a globally usable child perspective paradigm can be elaborated.

On the level of *children's everyday life* and the practice of caring, we can also see in article 19 about "protection", 7 and 8 about "belonging, culture, and identity". The Part II observations and discussion of "when emphatic care is obstructed", for example by negative definitions, stigmatization, and dehumanization of children in very difficult circumstances, are examples of how children are treated illegal in relation to the *UN Conventions of the Right of the Child*. To be cared for as a human person by the adults most close to the child is necessary for basic survival as well as for healthy development. Protection of the child is a fundamental right of the child, but relationships that develop a sense of identity and feeling of belonging to a culture and group is an obligation for society and the individual caregiver as well.

This means in a global perspective that if not adults live in a relatively safe society and out of poverty their reserve of strengths will be jeopardized with negative consequences for the relationship with the child. Interpreting the convention, from a societal to a personal level, the "best for each child" has to be a guiding principle, which means that a child perspective orientation and the understanding and implementation of children's own perspectives will be a necessity.

In the field of young children's education, child perspectives (for example called child-centredness) have always been strong. Knowledge of child development has helped the professionals to put realistic expectations and demands on children in early childhood education. This means that teachers working with young children most often are sensitive both to their need of care and to what interests them, which could be built on for extending children's understanding of the world around them. The idea of the *UN Convention of the Right of the Child* has very much been driven by professionals from early childhood education, who held and practised a child perspective. At the same time another movement, which we have dealt with in this book has taken place, that is, theories in childhood sociology and child development have shown a great interest in questions about child perspectives or children's perspectives during the last decade. ECE globally shares today an idea of directing the attention with children towards key notions like communication, interaction, and participation. At the same time a goal orientation in ECE is becoming visible in most curricula. In the crossroad between children's worlds and the intentions of the teachers, the question about children's perspectives and not only child perspectives for education of young children becomes central. The reason for this is at least twofold: educational and democratic. Educational means that children always build their understanding on the meaning they have gained, which will come through in their expression of meaning – that is their perspectives. Democratic means that children are respected and accepted as equal human beings in early childhood education and by this have to be active partners in their daily life – their perspective must be listened to.

References

Åberg, A., & Lenz Taguchi, H. (2005). *Lyssnandets pedagogik* [The pedagogy of listening, in Swedish]. Stockholm: Liber.

Ackesjö, H. (2006). "Det är ju ingenting vi bett om." En studie av en integrationsprocess mellan förskoleklass och skola, med fokus på personal i förändring (No. 2006:3). ["This is nothing we have asked for." A study on an integration process between preschool class and school, with focus on staff in change, in Swedish.] Högskolan i Kalmar: Institutionen för Hälso- och Beteendevetenskap.

Ainsworth, M., Blehar, M., Waters, E., & Wall, S. (1978). *Patterns of Attachment*. Hillsdale, NJ: Erlbaum.

Aitken, K. J., & Trevarthen, C. (1997). Self/other organization in human psychological development. *Development and Psychopathology, 9*(4), 653–677.

Alanen, L. (1988). Rethinking childhood. *Acta Sociologica, 31*(1), 56–67.

Alanen, L., & Mayall, B. (2001). *Conceptualising child–adult relations*. London: Falmer Press.

Allardt, E. (1975). *Att ha, att vara. Om velfärd i Norden*. Lund: Argos.

Allardt, E. (1998). Det goda samhället: Välfärd, livsstil og medborgerdygder. *Tidsskrift for velferdsforskning, 1*(3), 123–133.

Alvestad, M., & Pramling Samuelsson, I. (2001). A comparison of the national preschool curricula in Norway and Sweden. *Early Childhood Research & Practice, 1*(2), 1–12.

Alvestad, T. (2001). *Hvis jeg fikk bestemme. En video om barns innflytelse på eget liv.* [If I was allowed to decide. A video on children's influence on their own life, in Norwegian.] Oslo: Pedagogisk Forum (www.pedagogiskforum.no).

Andersen, D., & Højlund, O. (2007). *Interview med 11-årige børn*. København: SFI.

Andersen, D., & Kjærulff, A. (2003). *Hvad kan børn svare på?* København: Socialforskningsinstituttet, Nr. 07.

Andersen, D., & Ottesen, M.H. (2002). *Børn som respondenter.* København: Socialforskningsinstituttet, Nr. 23.

Andersen, J. (2001). *Med barnets øjne – barneperspektivet i pædagogikken*. Århus: Dansk Pædagogisk Forum, Forlaget.

Andersen, M. B. (2005). Kronik. *Politiken*, 13 March and *Replik*, 3 April.

Andersen, R. (1995). *Kjøn och kultur. En studie av voksnes deltagelse i barns kjønnssosialisering på grunnlag av observasjonsmateriale fra norske barnehager*. Doktorgradsavhandling. Institutt for samfundsvitenskap, Universitetet i Tromsø.

Aries, P. (1979). *Centuries of childhood*. London: Penguin Books.

Askland, L., & Sataøen, S. O. (2003). *Utvecklingspsykologiska perspektiv på barns uppväxt*. [Developmental psychological perspectives on children's childhood, in Swedish.] Stockholm: Liber.

Asplund Carlsson, M., Kärrby, G., & Pramling Samuelsson, I. (2001). *Strukturella faktorer och pedagogisk kvalitet i barnomsorg och skola – En kunskapsöversikt.* [Structural factors and pedagogic quality in childcare and school – An Overview, in Swedish.] Skolverkets monografiserie. Stockholm: Liber.

Astington, J. W. (1998). Theory of mind goes to school. *Educational Leadership, 56*(3), 46–48.

Athey, C. (1990). *Extending thought in young children.* London: Paul Chapman Publishing Ltd.

Aukrust Grøver, V. (1992). *Fortellinger fra stellerommet. To-åringer i barnehage: En studie av språkbruk – innehåll och struktur.* Doktorsavhadnling. Pedagogisk forskningsinstitutt, Universitet i Oslo.

Aukrust Grøvre, V., & Snow, C. (1998). Narratives and explanations in Norwegian and American mealtime conversations. *Language in Society, 27*(2), 221–246.

Bae, B. (2004). *Dialoger mellom førskolelærer og barn – en beskrivende og fortolkende studie.* Høgskolen i Oslo: Avdelningen for lærerutdanning, (HiO-rapport nr 25). www.hio.no

Baillargeon, R. (1994). How do infants learn about the physical world? *Current Directions in Psychological Science, 3,* 133–140.

Baron-Cohen, S., Tager-Flusberg, H., & Cohen, D. J. (Eds.) (1993). *Understanding other minds.* Oxford: Oxford University Press.

Bauman, Z. (1996). *Modernity and the holocaust.* London: Polity Press.

Bauman, Z. (1999). Postmodernitet, identitet og moral. In A. J. Vetlesen (Ed.), *Nærhetsetikk* (pp. 90–121). Oslo: Ad Notam Gyldendal.

Bauman, Z. (1989). *Modernity and the holocaust.* London: Policy Press.

Baumrind, D. (1993). The average expectable environment is not good enough: A response to Scarr. *Child Development, 64,* 1299–1317.

Beck, U. (1997). *Risikosamfundet – på vej mod en ny modernitet.* København: Hans Reitzels Forlag.

Berger, P., & Luckman, T. (1966). *The social construction of reality.* London: Penguin Books.

Berk, L. (2006a). *Child development* (6th ed.). Boston: Allyn and Bacon.

Berk, L. (2006b). *Development through the lifespan* (4th ed.). Boston: Allyn and Bacon.

Berk, L. E. (2006). *Child development* (7th ed.). Boston: Pearson.

Bertram, H. (2006). *Overview of child well being in Germany: Policy towards a supportive environment for children.* Florence: UNICEF, Innocenti Research Center.

Bewan, W. (1991). Contemporary psychology. A tour inside the onion. *American Psychologist, 46*(5), 475–483.

BIN. Konferenceindkaldelse. April, 2005.

Bjørgo, T. (1997). *Racist and right-wing violence in Scandinavia: Patterns, perpetrators and responses.* Oslo: Tano Aschoug.

Björklund, C. (2007). *Hållpunkter för lärande. Småbarns möten med matematik.* [Some fixed points for learning. Young children encountering mathematics, in Swedish.] Åbo: Åbo Akademi förlag.

Björklund, E. (2008). Den mångskiftande literaciteten. Litteracitetshändelser och litteracitetspraktik bland de yngsta barnen i förskolan.

Björnberg, U. (2002). Ideology and choice between work and care: Swedish family policy for working parents. *Critical Social Policy, 22*(1), 33–52.

Björneloo, I. (2007). *Innebörder av hållbar utveckling. En studie av lärares utsagor om undervisning.* Göteborg: Acta Universitatis Gothoburgensis.

Boyd, D., & Bee, H. (2006). *Lifespan development* (4th int. ed.). Boston: Pearson.

Bracken, P., & Petty, C. (1998). *Rethinking the trauma of war.* London: Free Ass. Books, Ltd., (Save the Children).

Bråten, S. (1998). *Intersubjective communication and emotion in early ontogeny.* Cambridge, MA: Cambridge University Press.

Bråten, S. (1999). *Modellmakt og altersentriske spedbarn.* Bergen: Sigma Forlag.

Bråten, S. (2003). Participant perception of others' acts: Virtual otherness in infants and adults. *Cultural and Psychology, 9*(3). 261–276.

Bråten, S. (2007). *On being moved – From mirror neurons to empathy.* New York: John Benjamin's Publishing Company.

Bredekamp, S., & Copple, C. (1997). *Developmentally appropriate practice in early childhood programs*. Washington, DC: National Association for the Education of Young Children.

Bronfenbrenner, U. (1979). *The ecology of human development*. Cambridge, MA: Harvard University Press.

Bruce, T. (1987, 2005 3rd ed.) *Early childhood education*. London: Hodder Arnold.

Bruner, J., & Haste, H. (1987). *Making sense. The child's construction of the world*. New York: Methuen.

Bruner, J. (1990). *Acts of meaning*. Cambridge, MA: Cambridge University Press.

Bruner, J. (1996). *The culture of education*. Cambridge, MA: Harvard University Press.

Carlson, H. L. (1993). "Impact of Societal Orientations on Early Childhood Programmes and Parents and Professionals views of those Programmes: Sweden, England, United States". *International Journal of Early Childhood*, 25(1), 20–26.

Carlsson, M.A. (2003). Om barnperspektivet i barndomslitteraturen. *Pedagogisk Forskning i Sverige*, 8(1–2). Tema: "Barns perspektiv och Barnperspektiv".

Carstensen, T. (2005). *Kvarteret I børnehøjde: Om steder og strækninger I moderne børns hverdagsliv*. Ph.D. dissertation, Aarhus Arkitektskole, Denmark.

Children's Welfare in an Ageing Europe. www.svt.ntnu.no/noseb/costa19/nytt/ welfare/book.php

Clarke-Stewart, A., & Allhusen, V. D. (2005). *What we know about childcare*. Cambridge, MA: Harvard University Press.

Cole, M. (1996). *Cultural psychology: A once and future discipline*. Cambridge, MA: Harvard University Press.

Corsaro, W. (1992). Interpretative reproduction in children's peer-cultures. *Social Psychology Quarterly*, 55, 160–177.

Corsaro, W. (1996). Transitions in early childhood: The promise of comparative, longitudinal ethnography. In R. Jessor, A. Colby, & R. Shweder (Eds.), *Ethnography and human development* (pp. 419–457). Chicago: University of Chicago Press.

Corsaro, W. (2002). *Barndommens sociologi*. København: Gyldendal Socialpædagogisk Bibliotek.

Corsaro, W. A., & Miller, P. (1992). Interpretative approaches to children's socialisation. *New directions for child development*. No. 58. San Francisco: Jossey-Bass Publishers.

Corsaro, W. A. (2005). *The sociology of childhood* (2nd ed.). Thousand Oaks, CA: Pine Forge Press.

Cunningham, C., & Davis, H. (1985). *Working with parents: Frameworks for collaboration*. Milton Keynes, England: Open University Press.

Cunningham, H. (1995). *Children and childhood in western society since 1500*. London: Addison Wesley Longman Limited.

Csikszentmihayli, M. (1992) *Flow: They psychology of happiness*. London: Rider.

Dagtilbudsloven (2007). (Law of daycare offer) www.minff/1/familieomradet/

Dahlberg, G., & Lenz Taguchi, H. (1994). *Förskola och skola – om två skilda traditioner och om visionen om en mötesplats*. Stockholm: HLS Förlag.

Dahlberg, G., & P. Moss, et al. (1999). Beyond Quality in Early Childhood Education and Care – Postmodern Perspectives, Falmer Press, Taylor & Francis Inc., USA.

Dahlberg, G. (2006). A pedagogy of welcoming and hospitality built on listening: An ethical and political perspective on early childhood education. *International Journal of Early Childhood Education, The Korean Society for Early Childhood Education*, 12(2), 5–28.

Dahlgren, G., & Olsson, L. E. (1985). *Läsning i barnperspektiv*. [Reading from children's perspective, in Swedish.] Göteborg: Acta Universitatis Gothoburgensis.

Dahlgren, G., Gustafsson, K., Mellgren, E., & Olsson, L.-E. (2006). *Barn upptäcker skriftspråket*. [Children discover the written language, in Swedish.] (3rd ed.). Stockholm: Liber.

Dahlgren, L., & Hultqvist, K. (Eds.) (1995). *Seendet och seendets villkor – en bok om barns och ungas välfärd*. Stockholm: HLS-Förlag.

Danish Ministry of Science. (2007). Technology and Innovation. www.workindenmark.dk/ Welfare. *Danmarks Statistik*.

DeHart, G. B., Sroufe, L. A., & Cooper, R. (2000). *Child development. Its nature and course* (4th ed.). Boston: McGraw-Hill Higher Education

de Jonghe, I. (2001). *International state of the art on children's playing.* Leen Schillermans Research Centre Child & Society. Retrieved from http://www.ndo.be

de Mause, L. B. (1976). *The history of childhood.* London: Souvenir Press.

Dencik, L., & Jørgensen, P. S. (1999). *Børn og familie i det postmoderne samfund.* København: Hans Reitzels Forlag.

Dencik, L. (1989). Growing up in the post-modern age. *Sociologica, 2,* 155–180.

Dencik, L., Jørgensen, P. S., & Sommer, D. (2008). *Familie og børn i en opbrudstid.* København: Hans Reitzels Forlag.

Dockrell, J., Lewis, A., & Lindsay, G. (2000). Researching children's perspectives: A psychological dimension. In A. L. Lewis & G. Lindsay (Eds.), *Researching children's perspectives.* Buckingham, UK: Open University Press.

Doverborg, E., & Anstett, S. (2003). *Barn ritar och berättar – Dokumentationens pedagogiska möjligheter.* [Children draw and tell stories – The pedagogical possibilities of documentation, in Swedish.] In E. Johansson & I. Pramling Samuelsson (Eds.), *Förskolan – Barns första skola* [Preschool – Children's first school, in Swedish.] (pp. 83–104). Lund: Studentlitteratur.

Doverborg, E., & Emanuelsson, G. (2006). *Små barns matematik* [Young children's mathematics, in Swedish.] Göteborg: Göteborgs universitet, NCM.

Doverborg, E., & Pramling Samuelsson, I. (1985/2000). *Att försttå barns tankar. Metodik för barnintervjuer.* [To Understand Children's Thinking – Methods for Interviewing Children]. Stockholm: Liber.

Doverborg, E., & Pramling Samuelsson, I. (1999a). *Förskolebarn i matematikens värld.* [Preschool children in the world of mathematics, in Swedish.] Stockholm: Liber.

Doverborg, E., & Pramling Samuelsson, I. (1999c). Apple cutting and creativity as a mathematical beginning. *Kindergarten Education: Theory, Research and Practice, 4*(2), 87–103.

Doverborg, E., & Pramling Samuelsson, I. (2000a). To develop young children's conception of numbers. *Early Child Development and Care, 162,* 81–107.

Doverborg, E., & Pramling Samuelsson, I. (2000b). *Att förstå barns tankar. Metodik för barnintervjuer* [Understanding children's thoughts: Methodology for interviewing children, in Swedish.] (2nd Rev. ed.). Stockholm: Liber.

Doverborg, E., & Pramling, I. (1995). *Mångfaldens pedagogiska möjligheter. Att arbeta med att utveckla barns förståelse för sin omvärld.* [Pedagogical possibilities of diversity. Working with the development of children's understanding of the world around them, in Swedish.] Stockholm: Utbildningsförlaget.

Doverborg, E., & Pramling, I. (1988). *Temaarbete. Lärarens metodik och barns förståelse.* [Working with themes. Teacher's methods and children's understanding, in Swedish.] Stockholm: Utbildningsförlaget.

Dunn, J. (1978). *The beginnings of social understanding.* Oxford: Basic Blackwell, UK Social.

Dunn, J. (1993). *Young children's relationships. Beyond attachment.* London: Sage Publications.

Edwards, C. (1999). The company children keep. In S. Bråten (Ed.), *Intersubjective communication and emotion in early ontogeny.* Cambridge, MA: Cambridge University Press.

Edwards, C., & Mercer, N. (1987). *Common knowledge.* London: Routledge.

Edwards, D., & Mercer, N. (1988). *Common knowledge: Development of Understanding in the Classroom.* Barnes and Nobles.

Eide, J. B., & Winge, N. (2003). *Fra barnets synsvinkel.* Oslo: Cappelen, Akademisk Forlag.

Eisenberg, N. (1992). *The caring child.* Cambridge: Harvard University Press.

Ekman, P., & Friesen, W. (1975). *Unmasking the face.* Englewood Cliffs, NJ: Prentice-Hall.

Elkind, D. (1988). The resistance to developmentally appropriate education practice with young children: The real issue. In C. Wanger (Ed.), *Public school early childhood programs.* Alexandria: Association for Supervision and Curriculum Development.

Elkind, D. (2003). Thanks for the memory: The lasting value of true play. *Young Children, 58*(3), 46–51.

Elkind, D. (2007). *The power of play*. Cambridge: Da Capo Books.
Emanuelsson, G., & Doverborg, E. (Eds.) (2006). *Matematik i förskolan (Nämnaren TEMA)*. Göteborg: Göteborgs universitet, NCM.
Emilson, A. (2007). Young children's influence in preschool. *International Journal of Early Childhood Education, 39*(1), 11–38.
Erikson, E. H. (1950). *Childhood and society*. New York: Norton.
Eriksen Odegaard, E. (2007). *Meningsskaping i barnehagen. Innhold og bruk av barn og voksnes samtalefortellinger* (Göteborg Studies in Educational Sciences, 255). Göteborg, Sweden: Acta Universitatis Gothoburgensis.
Espersen, L. D., Langsted, O., & Uggerhøj, L. (2006). Se & Hør børnene. *Tidsskriftet Vera*. No. 34.
Esping-Andersen, G. (1990). *The three worlds of welfare capitalism*. Cambridge: Polity Press.
EUROCORES Programme (2005). *Consciousness in a natural and cultural context (CNCC)*. Retrieved from http://www.esf.org/eurocores
Feldman, R. S. (2001). *Child development* (2nd ed.). New Jersey: Prentice Hall.
Field, T. (1990). *Infancy*. Cambridge: Harvard University Press.
Fleer, M. (1995). The importance of conceptually focused teacher–child interaction in early childhood science learning. *International Journal of Science Education, 17*(3), 325–342.
Fogel, A. (1993). *Developing through relationship. Origins of communication, self and culture*. New York: Harwester Wheatsheaf.
Fonagy, P., Steele, H., Moran, G., & Higgit, A. (1991). The capacity for understanding mental states: The reflective self in parent and child and its significance for security of attachment. *Infant Mental Health, 13*, 200–217.
Fotel, T. (2007). *Mobilitet i børnehøjde*. Ph.D. dissertation, Roskilde University Center, Denmark.
Foucault, M. (1980): *Power/Knowledge: Selected interviews and other writings*. UK: Harvester.
France, A., Bendlow, G., & Williams, S. (2000). A 'risky' business: Researching the health beliefs of children and young people. In A. L. Lewis & G. Lindsay (Eds.), *Researching children's perspectives*. Buckingham, UK: Open University Press.
Fröbel, F. (1863/1995). *Människan fostran*. Lund: Studentlitteratur. [The fostering of mankind].
Frønes, I. (1995). *Among peers. On the meaning of peers in process of socialisation*. Oslo: Scandinavian University Press.
Gardner, H. (1993). *Multiple intelligences: The theory in practice*. New York: Basic Books.
Gerrbo, I. (2008). Från d till g. [From d to g, in Swedish.] In N. Pramling & I. Pramling Samuelsson (Eds.), *Lärstudier i arbetet med barn i yngre åldrar*. [Learning studies in the work with young children, in Swedish.] Stockholm: Gleerup.
Gesell, A., & Ilg, F. (1961). *Barnens värld och vår*. [The children's world and our's, in Swedish.] Stockholm: Natur och Kultur.
Giddens, A. (1990). *The consequences of modernity*. Cambridge: Polity.
Giddens, A. (1994). *Modernitetens konsekvenser*. København: Hans Reitzels Forlag.
Gilbrandsen, L., Johansson, J.-E., & Dyblie Nilsen, R. (2002). *Forskning om barnehager. En kunnskapsstatus*. Oslo: Norges forskningsråd.
Giota, J. (2000). *Adolecents' perceptions of school and reasons for learning*. Göteborg: Acta Universitatis Gohenburgensis.
Ginsburg, H. (1972). *The myth of the deprived child: Poor children's intellectual development and education*. Englewood Cliffs, NJ: Prentice-Hall.
Gjems, L. (2006). *Hva lærer barn når de forteller? En studie av barns læringsprosesser gjennom narrativ praksis*. Oslo: Pedagogisk forskningsinstitutt, Det utdanningsvitenskapelige fakultet, Universitetet i Oslo.
Goffman, E. (1974). *Frame analysis*. New York: Harper & Row.
Gonzalez-Mena, J. (1986, November). Toddlers: What to expect? *Young Children, 42*(1), 47–51.
Gopnik, A., Meltzoff, A. N., & Kuhl, P. A. (2001). *The scientist in the crib: Minds, brains, and how children learn*. Farfield, NJ: William Morrow & Col., Inc.

228

References

Greenfield, P. M., Suzuki, L. K., & Rothstein-Fisch, C. (2006). Cultural pathways through human development. In K. A. Renninger & I. E. Sigel (Eds.), *Handbook of child psychology* (6th ed., Vol. 1, Chap. 17). New York: John Wiley & Sons.

Gulløv, E., & Højlund, S. (2003). *Feltarbejde blandt børn. Metodologi og etik i Etnografisk børneforskning.* København: Gyldendal.

Gustafsson, K., & Mellgren, E. (2005). *Barns skriftspråkande – att bli en skrivande och läsande person.* [Children's written language – becoming a writing and reading person, in Swedish.] Göteborg: Acta Universitatis Gothoburgensis.

Gustavsson, J. E., & Myhrberg, E. (2002). *Ekonomiska resursers betydelse för pedagogiska resultat: en kunskapsöversikt.* [The importance of financial resources for the pedagogical result: an Overview, in Swedish.] Skolverkets monografiserie.. Stockholm: Liber.

Hadley, E. (2002). Playful disruptions. *Early Years, 22*(1), 9–17.

Hagtvet-Eriksen, B. (1997). *Skriftsprogsudvikling gennem leg – stimulering til opdagende læsning i førskolealderen.* [Developing the written language through play – stimulating initial reading in preschool, in Danish.] Danmark: Gyldendal.

Hagtvet-Eriksen, B. (2004). *Språkstimulering 1: Tal och skrift i förskoleåldern.* [Language stimulation 1 – Oral and written language in preschool, in Swedish.] Stockholm: Natur och Kultur.

Hagtvet-Eriksen, B. (2006). *Språkstimulering 2: Aktiviteter och åtgärder i förskoleåldern.* [Language stimulation 2 – Activities and proceedings in preschool, in Swedish.] Stockholm: Natur och Kultur.

Halldén, G. (2003). Barnperspektiv som ideologisk och/eller metodologiskt begrepp. *Pedagogisk Forskning i Sverige, 8*(1–2). Tema: "Barns perspektiv och Barnperspektiv".

Halldén, G. (2007). *Den moderna barndomen och barns vardagsliv.* Stockholm: Carlssons.

Harold Garfinkel (1967). *Studies in Ethnomethodology* Englewood Cliffs.

Harre, R., & van Langenhove, L. (1999). *Positioning theory.* London: Basil Blackwell.

Harris, P. L. (2006). Social cognition. In R. M. Lerner (Ed.), *Handbook of child psychology* (Vol. 2, Chap. 19). New York: John Wiley & Sons.

Hart, S. (2006). *Betydningen af samhørighed – Om neutoaffektiv udviklingspsykologi.* København: Hans Reitzels Forlag.

Harwood, R., Miller, S. A., & Vasta, R. (2007). *Child psychology – Development in a changing society.* New York: John Wiley & Sons.

Haug, P. (2003). *Om kvalitet I förskolan. Forskning om och utvärdering av förskolan 1998–2001.* Stockholm: Skolverket.

Haugen, S., Løkken, G., & Röthle, M. (Eds.) (2005). *Ny rammeplan – ny barnehagepedagogik?* Oslo: Universitetsforlaget.

Hetherington, M. E., & Parke, R. D. (1999). *Child psychology. A contemporary viewpoint* (5th ed.). Boston: McGraw-Hill College.

Hoffman, M. (2000). *Empathy and moral development.* Cambridge, MA: Cambridge University Press.

Holt, J. (1975). *What do we do on Monday?* London: Pelican Paperback.

Hundeide, K. (1981). Contractual congruence and logical consistency. *Quarterly Newsletter of Laboratory of Comparative Human Cognition, 3,* 77–79.

Hundeide, K. (1985). *Piaget i skolen.* Oslo: Cappelen.

Hundeide, K. (1991). *Helping disadvantaged children. Psycho-social intervention in a third world context.* London: Jessica Kingsley.

Hundeide, K. (2000). *Ledet Samspill fra Spedbarn til Skolealder. (Guided interaction from infancy to school age).* Asker: Vett og Viten.

Hundeide, K. (2001). Reactivation of cultural mediational practices. *Psychology and Developing Societies, 13,* 1.

Hundeide, K. (2002). The mind between us. *Nordisk Psykologi, 54*(1), 69–90.

Hundeide, K. (2003a). A new identity, a new lifestyle. In A. N. Perret-Clermont, C. Pontecorvo, & L. B. Resnick (Eds.), *Youth, learning and society.* Cambridge, MA: Cambridge University Press.

Hundeide, K. (2003b). Becoming a committed insider. *Cultural Psychology*, 9(2), 107–127.

Hundeide, K (2003c). *Barns livsverden: Kulturelle rammer for barns utvikling*. [Cultural frames for the child's development.] Oslo: Cappelen Forlag.

Hundeide, K. (2003d). From early interaction to class-room communication. In A. Arnesen (Ed.), *The resilient child*. Oslo: The Norwegian Therapost Association.

Hundeide, K., & Egebjerg, I. (2003). *ICDP project in Angola*. Oslo: Upublisert fra ICDP stiftelsen.

Hundeide, K. (2006). *Sociokulturella ramar för barns utveckling – barns livsvärldar*. Lund: Studentlitteratur.

Hundeide, K. (2007). When emphatic care is obstructed: Excluding the child from the zone of intimacy. In S. Bråten (Ed.), *On being moved – From mirror neurons to emphaty*. New York: John Benjamins Publishing Company.

Hunt, M. (1982). Towards solutions of early education. In Nir-Jav, Spodek, Steg (Eds.), *Early childhood education* (pp. 30–40). New York: Plenum Press.

Hwang, P., Lundberg, I., Rönnberg, J., & Smedler, A.-C. (Eds.) (2005). *Vår tids psykologi*. [Today's psychology, in Swedish.] Stockholm: Natur och kultur.

James, A., & Prout, A. (1990). *Constructing and reconstructing childhood*. London: Falmer Press.

James, A., Jenks, C., & Prout, A. (1998). *Theorizing childhood*. Cambridge, UK: Polity.

Johansen, E., & Pramling Samuelsson, I. (Eds.) (2003). *Pedagogisk Forskning i Sverige*. Tema: Barns perspektiv och barnperspektiv, 1–2).

Johansson, B. (2000). *"Kom och ät! Jag ska bara dö först."* Datorn i barns vardag. ["Come and eat now! I just have to die first, mum..."]. The computer in children's everyday life, in Swedish.] Göteborgs universitet: Etnologiska institutionen.

Johansson, E., & Pramling-Samuelsson, I. (Eds.) (2003). *Förskolan. Barns första skola!* Lund: Studentlitteratur.

Johansson, E. (1999). *Etik i små barns värld. Om värden och normer bland de yngsta barnen i förskolan*. [Ethics in young children's world. About values and norms among the youngest children in preschool, in Swedish.] Göteborg: Acta Universitatis Gothoburgensis.

Johansson, E. (2003). *Möten för lärande. Pedagogisk verksamhet för de yngsta barnen i förskolan*. [Encounters for learning. Pedagogical activities for the youngest children in preschool, in Swedish.]. Stockholm: Fritzes.

Johansson, E. (2005). Children's integrity – A marginalised right. *International Journal of Early Childhood. Special Theme: Children's Rights*, 37(3), 109–124.

Johansson, E:, & Pramling Samuelsson, I. (2006). *Lek och läroplan. Möten mellan barn och lärare i förskola och skola*. [Play and curriculum. Encounters between children and teachers in preschool and school, in Swedish.] Göteborg: Acta Universitatis Gothoburgensis.

Johansson, J-E. (2007). Familj, natur och fabrik, verkstad eller laboratorium – vart går barne-hagepedagogiken idag? [Family, nature and factory, workshop or laboratory – where is early childhood pedagogy heading today?] In T. Maser & M. Röthle (Eds.), *Ny rammeplan – nu barnehagepedagogik*. Oslo: Universitetsforlaget.

Johnson, J. E., Christie, J. F., & Yawkey, T. D. (1999). *Play and early childhood development*. Harlow, England: Longman.

Jørgensen, C. R. (2002). *Psykologien i senmoderniteten*. Copenhagen: Hans Reitzels Forlag.

Jørgensen, P. S., Dencik, L., & Sommer, D. (2008). Familien – kontinuitet og forandring. In P. S. Jørgensen, L. Dencik, & D. Sommer (Eds.), *Familie og børn i en opbrudstid*. Kapitel 1: København Hans Reitzels Forlag.

Juncker, B. (2006). *Om processen. Det æstetiskes betydning i børns kultur*. København: Tiderne skifter.

Kagitcibasi, C. (2007). *Family, self, and human development across cultures* (2nd ed.). New Jersey: Lawrence Aelbaum Associates, Publishers.

Kampmann, J. (2000). Børn som informanter og børneperspektiv. In P. Schultz Jørgensen & J. Kampmann (Eds.), *Børn som informanter*. Copenhagen: Børnerådet/The Danish Ministry of Social Affairs.

Kampmann, J. (2003). Barndomssociologi – fra marginaliseret provokation til mainstream leverandør. *Dansk Sociologi*, 14(2), 79–94.

Karlsson, M., Melander, H., Perez Prieto, H., & Sahlström, F. (2006). *Förskoleklassen – ett tionde skolår?* [The preschool class – a 10th school year? in Swedish.] Stockholm: Liber.

Karlsson-Lohmander, M. L., & Pramling Samuelsson, I. (Eds.) (2003). *Researching early childhood: Care, play and learning. Curricula for early childhood education, Vol. 5.* Göteborg University: Department of Education.

Karmiloff-Smith, A. (1995). Annotation: The extraordinary cognitive journey from foetus through infancy. *Journal of Child Psychology and Psychiatry, 36*(8), 1293–1313.

Keen, E. (1975). *A primer in phenomenological psychology.* New York: Holt, Rinehart and Winston Inc.

Kelly, G. (1955). *Theory of personal constructs.* New York: Norton Publishers.

Kitayama, S., & Markus, H. R. (1994). Culture and self: How cultures influence the way we see ourselves. In D. Matusomo (Ed.), *People. Psychology from a cultural perspective.* Pacific Grove, CA: Brooks/Cole Publishing Company.

Kjørholt, A. T. (1991). Børneperspektivet: Romantiske frihetslengsler og nostalgisk søken etter en tapt barndom, eller nye erkjennelsesdimensjoner? *Barn. Nytt fra Forskning om Barnet i Norge, 1,* 66–70.

Kjørholt, A. T. (2001). 'The participating child'. A vital pillar in this century? *Nordisk Pedagogik, 21,* 65–81.

Klein, P., & Hundeide, K. (1995). *Early intervention: A mediational approach on the cross cultural application of the MISC program.* New York: Garland Publishing.

Klein, P. (1989). *Formiddlet learning.* [Mediated learning, in Norwegian.] Oslo: Universitetsforlaget.

Klerfelt, A. (2002). *Var ligger forskningsfronten? – 67 avhandlingar i barnpedagogik under två decennier, 1980–1999* [Where lies the research frontline? – 67 theses in child pedagogy during two decades, 1980–1999, in Swedish]. (Skolverksrapport). Stockholm: Liber Distribution.

Klugman, E., & Smilansky, S. (Eds.) (1990). *Children's play and learning: Perspectives and policy implications.* New York: Teachers College Press.

Knutsdotter-Olofsson, B. (1993). *Varför leker inte barnen?* [Why are the children not playing? in Swedish.] Stockholm: HLS.

Korczak, J. (1998). *Barnets rätt till respect* (The child's right to respect). Translated by R-M Hartman. Stockholm: Natur & Kultur.

Korpi, B. M. (2006). *Förskolan i politiken – om intentioner och beslut bakom den svenska förskolans framväxt.* [Preschool in politics – on intentions and decisions behind the Swedish preschool's development, in Swedish.] Stockholm: Regeringskansliet.

Kousholt, D. (2006). *Familieliv fra et børneperspektiv.* Ph.D. dissertation, Roskilde Universitetscenter, DK-Roskilde.

Krarup, S. (2001). Hvad er det at være dansk? Skræp. *Nomos.* (www.nomos-dk)

Kress, G. (1996). Writing and learning to write. In D. R. Olson & N. Torrance (Eds.), *Handbook of education and human development: New models of learning, teaching and schooling* (pp. 225–256). Oxford: Basin Blackwell.

Kress, G. (2003). Perspectives on making meaning: The differential principles and means of adults and children. In I. Nigel Hall, J. Larson, & J. Marsh (Eds.), *Handbook of early childhood literacy.* London:Sage.

Kristjansson, B. (2002). På spaning efter det 'nordiska' och 'nordbarnet'. *Barn, 3,* 47–71. [Searching for the Nordic and the Nordchild'].

Kristjansson, B. (2006). The making of Nordic childhoods. In J. Einarsdotter & J. Wagner (Eds.), *Nordic childhoods and early education.* Greenwich, CT: IAP.

Krøjgaard, P. (2001). Økologisk Validitet og Eksperimentel Spædbarnsforskning. *Psyke & Logos, 22,* 635–661.

Krøjgaard, P. (2002). "Jeg ved, hvad du vil!" Om udviklingen af børns forståelse af sig selv og andre mennesker som intentionelle væsener". In M. Hermansen & A. Poulsen (Eds.), *Samfundets børn.* Gylling: Klim Forlag.

Kunnskapsdepartementet (2006). Rammeplan for barnehagens innehold og oppgaver. www.academica.no

Kunskapsdepartementet (2006:227). St.meld. nr. 16. . . .*og ingen sto igjen.*

Kvale, S. (Ed.) (1992). *Psychology and postmodernism.* London: Sage Publications.

Kvale, S. (1996). *Interviews. An introduction to qualitative research interviewing.* Thousand Oaks, Sage Publications.

Kvistad, K., & Søbstad, F. (2005). *Kvalitetsarbeid i barnehagen.* [Quality work in preschool, in Norwegian.] Oslo: Cappelen Akademisk Forlag.

Kärrby, G. (1985). *22.000 minuter i förskolan* [22.000 minutes in preschool, in Swedish.] (Vol. 9). Göteborgs universitet: Institutionen för pedagogik.

Labov, W. (1972). The language of nonstandard English. In P. P. Giglioli (Ed.), *Language and social conetxt.* London: Penguin Books.

Laevers, F. (1993). Deep level learning – An exemplary application on the area of physical knowledge. *European Early Childhood Education Research Journal, 1*(1), 53–68.

Lamb, M. E., & Ahnert, L. (2006). Nonparental child care: Context, concepts, correlates and consequences. In R. M. Learner (Ed.), *Handbook of child psychology* (Vol. 4, Chap. 23). New York: John Wiley & Sons.

Langer, E. (1997). *The power of mindful learning.* Harlow: Addison/Wesley Publishing Company.

Lasch (1984). *The Minimal Self: Psychic Survival in Troubled Times* Basic Books.

Lave, J., & Wenger, E. (1991). *Situated learning: Legitimate peripheral participation.* Cambridge, MA: Cambridge University Press.

Lebra, T. S. (1994). Mother and child in Japanese socialization. A Japan-U.S. Comparison. In P. Greenfield & R. Cocking (Eds.), *Cross-cultural roots of minority child development.* Hillsdale, NJ: Erlbaum.

Legerstee, M. (1992). A review of the animate-inanimate distinction in infancy: Implications for models of social and cognitive knowing. *Early Development and Learning, 1*(2), 59–67.

Lerner, R. M. (Ed.) (2006). *Handbook of child psychology* (Vol. 1–4.). New York: John Wiley & Sons.

LeVine, R. R. (1988). Human Parental Care: Universal Goals, Cultural Strategies, Individual Behavior. I. W. Damon (Red.), *Parental Behavior in Diverse Societies* (Vol. 40). San Francisco: Jossey-Bass Inc.

Lewis, A. L., & Lindsay, G. (2000). *Researching children's perspectives.* Buckingham: Open University Press.

Lindahl, M. (1996). *Inlärning och erfarande. Ettåringars möte med förskolans värld* [Learning and experience. One year old children encountering the world of preschool, in Swedish]. Göteborg: Acta Universitatis Gothoburgensis.

Lindahl, M. (2002). *Vårda – Vägleda – Lära. Effektstudie av ett kompetensutvecklings-program för pedagoger i förskolemiljön* [Care – Direct – Learn. A study of the effects of an in-service development programme for pedagogues in preschool settings, in Swedish]. Göteborg: Acta Universitatis Gothoburgensis.

Lindahl, M. (2005). Children's right to democratic upbringings. *International Journal of Early Childhood. Special Theme: Children's Rights, 37*(3), 33–47.

Lindahl, M., & Pramling Samuelsson, I. (2002). Imitation and variation. Toddlers' strategies for learning. *Scandinavian Journal of Educational Research, 46*(1), 25–45.

Lindner, E. G. (2000). *The Psychology of Humiliation.* Doctoral Dissertation. Department of Psychology, University of Oslo.

Lloyd-Smith, M., & Tarr, J. (2000). Researching children's perspectives: A sociological dimension. In A. L. Lewis & G. Lindsay (Eds.), *Researching children's perspectives.* Buckingham: Open University Press.

Løkken, G. (2004). *Toddlerkultur. Om ett- og toåringers sosiale omgang i barnehagen* [Toddler culture. About one and two years old children's social relations in preschool, in Norwegian]. Oslo: Cappelen Akademisk Forlag.

Mahler, M. (1998). *Barnets Psykiske Fødsel.* København: Hans Reitzels Forlag.

Mannheim, K. (1936). *Ideology and utopia: An Introduction to the sociology of knowledge.* New York: Harcourt Brace.

Marcon, R. (2002). Moving up the grades: Relationships between preschool model and later school success. *Early Childhood Research & Practice, 4*(2), 1–23 Spring.

Markus, H. R., & Kitayama, S. (1991). Culture and the self: Implications for cognition, emotion and motivation. *Psychological Review, 98*(2), 224–253.

Marton, F., & Booth, S. (1997). *Learning and awareness.* Mahwah, NJ: Lawrence Erlbaum.

Marton, F. (1981a). Phenomenography – Describing conceptions of the world around us. *Instructional Science, 10,* 177–200.

Marton, F. (1981b). Studying conceptions of reality – A meta theoretical note. *Scandinavian Journal of Educational Research, 25,* 159–169.

Marton, F. (1992). Phenomenography and "the art of teaching all things to all men". *Qualitative Studies in Education, 5*(3), 253–267.

Marton, F., Tsui, A., et al. (2004). *Classroom discourse and the space of learning.* Mahwah, NJ: Lawrence Earlbaum.

Marzano, R. J. (1998). *A theory-based meta-analysis of research on instruction.* Aurora, CO: Midcontinent regional Educational Laboratory. Retrieved from http://www.mcrel.org/products/learning/meta.pdf

Maturana, H., & Rwezepka, E. (1998). *Humana e Capacitacao,* Sima Nisis D Busca Pe.

Mehan, H., et al. (1996). *Constructing school success.* Cambridge, MA: Cambridge University Press.

Meltzoff, A. N., & Moore, M. K. (1998). Infant intersubjectivity. Broadening the dialogue to include imitation, identity and intention. In S. Bråten (Ed.), *Intersubjective communication and emotion in early ontogeny.* Cambridge, MA: Cambridge University Press.

Michélsen, E. (2005). *Samspel på småbarnsavdelningen* [Interplay in toddler group, in Swedish]. Stockholm: Liber.

Mills, R., & Duck, S. (2000). *The developmental psychology of personal relationships.* New York: Wiley & Sons.

Ministry for Family- and Consumer Affairs (2007). Retrieved from www.minff.dk

Monrad. (1936). *Moderens dagbog.* København: Gyldendal.

Morelli, G. A., & Rogoff, B. (1992). Cultural variation in infant's sleeping arrangements: Questions of independence. *Developmental Psychology, 28*(4), 604–613.

Murphy, B. (2004). *Irish Infant Classroom Practice – A case of imaginary play.* Paper presented at the OMEP European Meeting, Dublin, April 15.

Murray, L., & Trevarthen, C. (1985). Emotional regulation of interactions between two-month-olds and their mothers. In T. M. Field & N. A. Fox (Eds.), *Social perception in infants* (pp. 137–187). Norwood, NJ: Ablex.

Myrdal, A., & Myrdal, G. (1934). *Kris i befolkningsfrågan.* Stockholm: Bonnier. (Crises in population development in Sweden).

National Research Council. (2001). *Eager to learn. Educating our preschoolers.* Washington: National Academy Press.

Nelson, K. (1996). *Language in cognitive development. The emergence of the mediated mind.* Cambridge: University Press.

Newnes, N., & Radcliffe, N. (2005). *Making and breaking children's lives.* Ross-on-Wyn: PCCS Books.

Next Generation Forum. (2000). *Next generation annual report 2000. First draft.* Billund: Next Generation Forum. Retrieved from http://www.nextgenerationforum.org

Nilsen, R. D. (2000). *Livet i barnehagen. En etnografisk studie av sosialiseringsprosessen* (Diss.). Trondheim, Norway: NTNU, Pedagogisk institutt/NOSEB.

Norwegian Centre for Child Research. (2003). Children's Perspectives in Childhood Research – Prospects and Challenges. *Seminar,* April 23, Trondheim, Norway.

NSIN Research Matters. (2001). Learning about Learning Enhances Performance. *NSIN Research Matters, 13.*

Nutbrown, C. (1994). *Threads of thinking. Young children's learning and the role of early education.* London: Paul Chapman Publishing Ltd.

Nyt fra Danmarks Statistik (2006).

Oberheumer, P. (2005). international perspectives on early childhood curricula. *International Journal of Early Childhood, 37*(1), 27–37.

Olfman, S. (Ed.) (2003). *All work and no play...: How educational reforms are harming our preschoolers.* Westport: Praeger Publishers.

Oppenheim, D., Koren-Karie, N., & Sagi, A. (2003). Mother's Empathic Understanding of their preschoolers' internal experience: Relations with early attachment. *From internet: Oppenheim's homepage.*

Ottesen, M. H. (2002). Forskning og erfaringer på feltet. In D. Andersen & M. H. Ottesen (Eds.), *Børn som respondenter.* Copenhagen: Socialforskningsinstituttet. Nr. 23.

Ottesen, M. H. (2002). Forskning og erfaringer på feltet. In D. Andersen & M. H. Ottesen (Eds.), *Børn som respondenter.* Copenhagen: Socialforskningsinstituttet. Nr. 23.

Pædagogisk-Psykologisk Opslagsbog. (2006). Copenhagen: Hans Reitzels Forlag.

Palludan, C. (2005). *Børnehaven gør forskel* [Preschool makes a difference, in Danish]. København: Danmarks Pedagogiske Universitets.

Palmérus, K., Pramling, I., & Lindahl, M. (1991). *Daghem för småbarn. En utvecklingsstudie av personalens pedagogiska och psykologiska kunnande* [Preschool for young children. A development study of the staff's pedagogical and psychological knowledge, in Swedish]. Göteborg: Göteborgs universitet Institutionen för metodik i lärarutbildningen.

Palmer, R. E. (1969). *Hermeneutics.* Evanston: Northwestern University Press.

Papousek, H., & Papousek, M. (1991). Innate and cultural guidance of infants' integrative competencies: China, United States and Germany. In M. Bornstein (Ed.), *Cultural approaches to parenting.* Hillsdale, NJ: Erlbaum Ass.

Parke, R. D. (1989). Social development in infancy: A 25-year perspective. *Advances in Child Development and Behavior, 21,* 1-48.

Pedagogisk Forskning i Sverige. (2003). Vol. 8. No. 1–2. Theme issue: "Barns perspektiv och Barnperspektiv". Guest editors: E. Johansson & I. Pramling Samuelsson.

Pelzer, D. (1995). *A child called "it".* London: Orion Paperback.

Peters, K., & Richards, P. (1998). Fighting with open eyes: Youth combatants talking about war in Sierra Leone. In P. Bracken & C. Petty (Eds.), *Rethinking the trauma of war.* London: Free Ass. Books, Ltd. (Save the Children).

Piaget, J. (1970[1929]). *Structuralism.* Cranbury, NJ: Litterfield, Adams & Co.

Piaget, J. (1976[1929]). *The child's conception of the world.* Cranbury, NJ: Littlefied Adams.

Piaget, J. (1972): *To understand is to invent.* Viking Press.

Pramling Samuelsson, I., & Asplund Carlsson, M. (2003). *Det lekande lärande barnet – I en utvecklingspedagogisk teori* [The playing learning child – In a developmental pedagogic theory, in Swedish]. Stockholm: Liber.

Pramling Samuelsson, I., & Doverborg, E. (2007). *Numeracy among 1 to 3 years old children in preschool.* Paper presented at the EECERA conference, Prague, 29 August – 1 September.

Pramling Samuelsson, I., & Fleer, M. (2008). *Play and learning in early childhood, 1–3 years. A study from 7 countries.* New York: Springer Verlag.

Pramling Samuelsson, I., & Kaga, Y. (Eds.). (2008). *The contribution of early childhood education to a sustainable society.* Paris: UNESCO.

Pramling Samuelsson, I., & Lindahl, M. (1999). *Att förstå det lilla barnets värld – Med videons hjälp* [To understand the young child's world – With the help of a video camera, in Swedish]. Stockholm: Liber.

Pramling Samuelsson, I., & Mårdsjö Olsson, A.-C. (2007). *Grundläggande färdigheter och färdigheters grundläggande* [Basic abilities and the foundation of abilities, in Swedish] (2nd ed). Lund: Studentlitteratur.

Pramling Samuelsson, I., & Pramling, N. (2009). Children's perspectives as 'touch downs' in time: assessing and developing children's understanding simultaneously. *Early Child Development and Care. 179*(2), 205–216.

Pramling Samuelsson, I., & Sheridan, S. (2003). Delaktighet som värdering och pedagogik [Participation as valuation and pedagogy, in Swedish]. *Pedagogisk Forskning i Sverige. Tema: Barns perspektiv och barnperspektiv, 1-2*, 70–84.

Pramling Samuelsson, I. (2000). Kreativitet och lärande – en utmaning för pedagogen [Creativity and learning – A challenge for the pedagogue]. In I. Johansson & I. Holmbäck-Rholander (Eds.), *Vägar till pedagogiken i förskola och fritidshem* [Ways to pedagogy in preschool and after school centres, in Swedish]. Stockholm: Liber.

Pramling Samuelsson, I. (2006). Teaching and learning in preschool and the first years of elementary school in Sweden. In J. Einarsdóttír & T. J. Wagner (Eds.), *Nordic early childhood education*. International Perspectives on Educational Policy, Research and Practice, K. M. Borman (Series Editor). Charlotte, NC: Information Age Publishing.

Pramling Samuelsson, I., et al. (2006). *Learning to discern*. Ansökan till Riksbankens Jubileumsfond [Research application] Göteborg University: Department of Education.

Pramling Samuelsson, I., Asplund-Carlsson, M., Olsson, B., Pramling, N., & Wallerstedt, C. (2008). *Konsten att lära barn estetik – med fokus på rörelse, poesi och musik* [The art of teaching children aesthetics – Focusing on movement, poetry and music, in Swedish]. Stockholm: Nordstedts.

Pramling Samuelsson, I., & Asplund Carlsson, M. (2008). The playing learning child. Towards a pedagogy of early childhood. *Accepted for publishing in Scandinavian Journal of Education, 52*(6), 623–641.

Pramling Samuelsson, I., Sheridan, S., & Williams, P. (2006). Five preschool curricula. Comparative perspective. *International Journal of Early Childhood, 38*(1), 11–30.

Pramling, I. (1983). *The child's conception of learning*. Göteborg: Acta Universitatis Gothoburgensis.

Pramling, I. (1990). *Learning to learn. A study of Swedish Preschool Children*. New York: Springer Verlag.

Pramling, I. (1994). *Kunnandet grunder. Prövning av en fenomenografisk ansats till att utveckla barns sätt att uppfatta sin omvärld* [The foundations of knowing. Test of a phenomenographic effort to develop children's ways of understanding their surrounding world, in Swedish] . Göteborg: Acta Universitatis Gothoburgensis.

Pramling, I. (1995). A mediational approach to early intervention: Upgrading quality of education in Swedish toddler groups. In P. Klein & K. Hundeide (Eds.), *Early intervention: A mediational approach on the cross cultural application of the MISC program*. New York: Garland Publishing.

Pramling, I. (1996). Understanding and empowering the child as a learner. In D. Olson & N. Torrance (Eds.), *Handbook of education and human development: New models of learning, teaching and schooling*. Oxford: Basil Blackwell.

Pramling, I., Asplund Carlsson, M., & Klerfelt, A. (1993). *Lära av sagan* [Learning from a fairy tale, in Swedish]. Lund: Studentlitteratur.

Pramling Samuelsson, I., & Pramling, N. (Eds.). (2008). *Didaktiska studier från förskola och skola* [Didactical studies from preschool and school, in Swedish]. Lund: Gleerup.

Pramling, N. (2006). *Minding metaphors. Using figurative language in learning to represent*. (Göteborg Studies in Educational Sciences, 238.). Göteborg: Acta Universitatis Gothoburgensis.

Pramling, N., & Pramling Samuelsson, I. (2001). It is floating 'cause there is a hole'. A young child experience of natural science. *Early Years, 21*(2), 139–149.

Qvarsell, B. (2003). Barns perspektiv och mänskliga rättigheder: Godhetsmaximering eller kunskapsbildning? *Pedagogisk forskning i Sverige*. Årg. 8, Nr 1–2. Temanummer: "Barns perspektiv och barnperspektiv".

Qvortrup, J. (1994a). *Børn til halv pris – nordisk barndom i samfundsperspektiv*. Esbjerg: Sydjysk Universitetsforlag.

Qvortrup, J., et al. (1994b). *Childhood matters: Social theory, practice and politics*. Averybury: Aldershot.

Qvortrup, J. (1999). Barndom og samfund. In L. Dencik & P. S. Jørgensen (Eds.), *Børn og familie i det postmoderne samfund*. Copenhagen: Hans Reitzels Forlag.

Qvortrup, J. (2002). Sociology of childhood: Conceptual liberation. In F. Mouritsen & J. Qvortrup (Eds.), *Childhood and children's culture*. Denmark: University Press of Southern Denmark.

Rasmussen, G. L. (2002). Barneperspektiv – i forskning og praksis. In P. Ø. Andersen & H. H. Knoop (Ed.), *Forskning i børns liv og læreprocesser i det moderne samfund*. Værløse: Billesø & Baltzer.

Reddy, V., Hay, D., Murray, L., & Trevarthen, C. (1997). Communication in infancy: Mutual regulation of affect and attention. In G. Bremner, A. Slater, & G. Butterworth (Eds.), *Infant development. Recent advances*. Hillsdale, NJ: Erlbaum.

Reed, S. E. (1993). The intention to use a specific affordance: A conceptual framework for psychology. In R. Wazniak & K. Fisher (Eds.), *Development in context: Acting and thinking in specific environments* (pp. 133–176). Hillsdale, NJ: L. Erlbaum Ass.

Reimer, L., Schousboe, I., & Thorborg, P. (2000). *I nærheden – en antologi om børneperspektiver*. København: Hans Reitzels Forlag.

Resnick, L., & Nelson-LeGall, S. (1997). Socializing intelligence. In L. Smith, J. Dockrell, & P. Tomlinson (Eds.), *Piaget, vygotsky and beyond*. London: Routledge.

Rinaldi, C. (2001). Documentation and assessment: What is the relationship? In C. Giudici, C. Rinaldi & M. Krechevsky (Eds.), *Making learning visible. Children as individual and group learners* (pp. 78–93). Reggio Emilia: Reggio Children and Project Zero.

Rogers, C. (1995). *On becoming a person*. Boston: Houghton Mufflin.

Rogoff, B. (1990). *Apprenticeship in thinking – Cognitive development in social context*. Oxford: Oxford University Press.

Rogoff, B. (2003). *The cultural nature of human development*. Oxford: Oxford University Press.

Rommetveit, R. (1998). Intersubjective attunement and linguistically mediated meaning in discourse. In S. Bråten (Ed.), *Intersubjective communication and emotion en early ontogeny* (pp. 354–372). Cambridge, MA: Cambridge University Press.

Rommetveit, R. (1992). Outline of a dialogically based social-cognitive approach to human cognition and communication. In A. H. Wold (Ed.), *The dialogue alternative*. Chichester: Wiley & Sons.

Rommetveit, R. (1974). *On message structure*. New York: Wiley & Sons.

Roos, C. (2004). *Skriftspråkande döva barn. En studie om skriftspråkligt lärande i förskola och skola* [Deaf children's written language. A study about learning written language in preschool and school, in Swedish]. Göteborg: Acta Universitatis Gothoburgensis.

Rothbaum, F., Pott, M., Azuma, H., Miyake, K., & Weiss, J. (2000). The development of close relationships in Japan and the United States: Paths of symbiotic harmony and generative tension. *Child Development, 71*(5), 1121–1142.

Rudberg, M. (1983). *Dydige, sterke, lykkelige barn*. Oslo: Universitetsforlaget.

Runesson, U. (1999). *Variationens pedagogik* [The pedagogy of variation, in Swedish]. Göteborg: Acta Universitatis Gothoburgensis.

Ryan, J., & Tomas, F. (1976). *The Politics of mental handicap*. London: Vintage Press.

Rye, H. (2003). *Tidelig hjelp til bedre samspill*. (Early assistance for better interaction) Revised in 2003. Oslo: Universitetsforlaget.

Sameroff, A. J., & Fiese, B. H. (1990). Transactional regulation and early intervention. In S. Meisels & J. Shonkoff, *Handbook of early childhood intervention*. Cambridge, MA: Cambridge University Press.

Sandberg, A., & Pramling Samuelsson, I. (2003). Preschool teacher's play experience – Then and now. *Early Childhood Research & Practice, 5*(1). Retrieved from http://ecrp.uiuc.edu/v5n1/index.html, online

Sawyer, R. K. (1997). *Pretend play as improvisation. Conversation in the preschool classroom*. Mahwak, NJ: Earlbaum.

Scarr, S. (1992). Developmental theories for the 1990s: Development and individual differences. *Child Development, 63*, 1–19 (target article).

Scarr, S. (1993). Biological and cultural diversity: The legacy of Darwin for development. *Child Development*, 64, 1333–1353.

Scheper-Hughes, N. (1992). *Death without weeping*. Berkeley, CA: University of California Press.

Schjøtt Rohweder, M. (2006). *Leg og Lær. En guide om pædagogiske læreplaner til alle dagtilbud of forældre med børn i dagtilbud*. Ministeriet for Familie- og Forbrugeranliggender. Retrieved from www.minff.dk

Schwartz, S. L. (2005). *Teaching young children mathematics*. Westport: Praeger.

Schyl-Bjurman, G., & Strömstedt-Lind, K. (1976). *Dialogpedagogik* [Dialogue Pedagogy, in Swedish]. Lund: Studentlitteratur.

Sheridan, S., & Williams, P. (2007). *Konstruktiv konkurrens* [Constructive concurrence, in Swedish]. Göteborg: Acta Universitatis Gothoburgensis.

Sheridan, S. (2007). Dimensions of pedagogical quality in preschool. *International Journal of Early Years Education*, 15(2), 198-217 June.

Sheridan, S., & Pramling Samuelsson, I. (2001). Children's conceptions of participation and influence in preschool. *A Perspective on Pedagogical Quality. Contemporary Issues in Early Childhood*, 2(2), 169–194. Retrieved from http://www. triangle.co.uk/ciec/.

Shweder, R. A., Goodnow, J. J., Hatano, G., LeVine, R., Markus, H. R., & Miller, P. J. (2006). The cultural psychology of development: One mind, many mentalities. In R. M. Learner (Ed.), *Handbook of child psychology* (Vol. 1, Chap. 13). New York: John Wiley & Sons.

Siraj-Blatchford, I. (1999). Early childhood pedagogy: Practice, principles and research. In P. Mortimor (Ed.), *Understanding pedagogy and its impact on learning* (pp. 20–45). London: Paul Chapman.

Siraj-Blatchford, I., et al. (2002). *Researching effective pedagogy in the early years*. Oxford: University of Oxford: Department of Educational Studies.

Siraj-Blatchford, I., & Manni, L. (2008). "Would you like to tidy up now? An analysis of adult questioning in the English Foundation Stage", *Early Years: An International Journal of Research and Development*, 28(1), 5–22.

Skolverket. (2004). *Förskola i brytningstid. Nationell utvärdering av förskolan* [Preschool during changes in time. National evaluation of preschool, in Swedish] (No. 239). Stockholm: Fritzes.

Skolverket. (2005). *Kvalitet i förskolan. Allmänna råd och kommentarer* [Quality in preschool. General guidelines and comments, in Swedish]. Skolverkets allmänna råd. Stockholm: Fritzes.

Skolverket. (2006a). *Curriculum for the pre-school Lpfö98*. Stockholm: Fritzes. Retrieved from www.skolverket.se

Skolverket. (2006b). *Curriculum for the compulsory school system, the preschool class and the leisure-time centre Lpo 94*. Stockholm: Fritzes. Retrieved from www.skolverket.se

Skolöverstyrelsen. (1980). *Läroplan för grundskolan. Allmän del* [Curriculum for compulsory school, in Swedish]. Stockholm: Liber Utbildningsförlaget.

Smedslund, J. (1997). *The structure of psychological common sense*. Mahwah, NJ: Earlbaum Publishers.

Smedslund, J. (1983). *Praktisk psykologi*. Oslo: Universitetsforlaget.

Socialstyrelsen. (1987:3). *Pedagogiskt program för förskolan* [Pedagogic programme for preschool, in Swedish]. Stockholm: Allmänna förlaget.

Sommer, D. (2001). *At blive en person – forældreskab og børns tidlige følelser*. København: Hans Reitzels Forlag.

Sommer, D. (2005). Values at stake in late modernity. *International Journal of Early Childhood*, 37(1), 95–116.

Sommer, D. (2005a). *Barndomspsykologi. Utveckling i en förändrad värld* [Childhood psychology. Development in a changing world, in Danish] (2nd ed.). Stockholm: Runa.

Sommer, D. (2005b). *Barndomspsykologiska fasetter* [Childhood psychological facets, in Danish]. Stockholm: Liber.

Sommer, D. (2005c). Situation og relation – et barndomspsykologisk perspektiv.In T. Ritchie (Ed.), *Relationer i psykologien*. Værløse: Billesø & Baltzer. Kapitel 8.

Sommer, D. (2007). Barndomspsykologiens læringssyn. In T. Ritchie (Ed.), *Teorier om læring*. Værløse:: Billesø & Baltzer. Kapitel 9.

Sommer, D. (2008a). Børnefamilien – dynamik og relationer. Kapitel 4 [The child family – Dynamics and relationships. Chapter 4]. In L. Dencik, P. S. Jørgensen, & D. Sommer (Eds.), *Familie og børn i en opbrudstid* [Family and Children in a Time of Breaking Up]. København: Hans Reitzels Forlag.

Sommer, D. (2008b). Familie og børn – tal og tendenser. In L. Dencik, P. S. Jørgensen, & D. Sommer (Eds.), *Familie og børn i en opbrudstid*. København: Hans Reitzels Forlag. Kapitel 2.

Sommer, D. (2010). *Childhood psychology. A shift in Paradigm*. London: Palgrave-McMillan Publishers.

SOU. (2000:3). *Välfärd vid vägskäl*. Utveckling under 1900-talet. Delbetänkande/kommittén Välfärdsbokslut. Stockholm: Fritzes.

SOU. (2006:75). *Jämställd förskola – om betydelsen av jämställdhet och genus i förskolans pedagogiska arbete. Slutbetänkande från delegationen för jämställdhet i förskolan* [An equal preschool – About the importance of equality and gender in the pedagogical work in preschool, in Swedish]. Stockholm: Fritzes.

SOU. (1992:72). *Det kommunala medlemsskapet. Delbetänkande av Lokaldemokratikommittén* [The membership of the local government, in Swedish]. Stockholm: Allmänna förlaget.

Statistisk Årbog. (2007). *Arbejdsmarked og løn*. København: Danmarks Statistik.

Statistical Yearbook. (2008). Copenhagen: Denmark's Statistics.

Stern, D. (1985). *The interpersonal world of the infant*. New York: Basic Books. Inc. Publishers.

Stern, D. (1991). *Ett litet barns dagbok* [A young child's diary, in Swedish]. Stockholm: Natur & Kultur.

Stern, D. (1995). *The motherhood constellation*. New York: Basic Books. Inc. Publishers.

Stern, D. (1998). *Barnets interpersonelle verden*. København: Hans Reitzels Forlag.

Stern, D. (2000). Introduction to the paperback edition. In D. Stern (Ed.), *The interpersonal world of the infant* (pp. xi–xxxix). New York: Basic Books.

Stern, D. (2004). *The present moment*. New York: W.W. Norton & Company.

Sutton Smith, B. (1997). *The ambiguity of play*. London: Harvard University Press.

Sylva, K., Melhuish, E., Sammons, P., Siraj-Blatchford, I., & Taggart, B. (2004). *The effective pre-school education (EPPE) project: Final report. A longitudinal study funded by the DfES 1997–2004*. Nottingham: DfES Publications.

Säljö, R. (1982). *Learning and understanding*. Göteborg: Acta Universitatis Gothoburgensis.

Søbstad, F. (1990). *Føskolebarn of humor*. Trondheim: Doktorsavhandling. Pedagogisk institutt, Samfunnsvitenskaplig fakultet, Universitet i Trondheim.

Telhaug, A. O. (1991). Barneperspektivet i historisk lys. *Barn. Nytt fra Forskning om Barnet i Norge, 1*.

The Danish Ministry of Science Technology and Innovation. Retrieved from www.workinden mark.dk/Welfare

The NICHD Early Child Care Research Group. (2005). *Child care and child development*. New York: The Guildford Press.

Therborn, G. (1993). The politics of childhood: The rights of children in modern times. In F. G. Castles (Ed.), *Families of nations: Patterns of public policy in western democracies* (pp. 241–291). Aldershof: Dartmouth.

Thomas, W. I., & Thomas, D. S. (1928). *The child in America*. New York: Alfred P. Knopf.

Thomsen, Y., & Berntsen, D. (2002). "Rørte han ved dig?" Børns pålidelighed som vidner belyst ud fra vidnepsykologiske eksperimenter og studier af erindringsevnens udvikling. In M. Hermansen & A. Poulsen (Eds.), *Samfundets børn*. Gylling: Klim Forlag.

Thulin, S. (2006). *Vad händer med lärandets objekt? En studie av hur lärare och barn i förskolan kommunicerar naturvetenskapliga fenomen* [What happens with the object of learning? A study about how teachers and children in school communicate natural science phenomena, in Swedish]. Växjö: Växjö University Press.

Tiller, P. O. (1984). Barns ytringsfrihed og bruk av barn som informanter. Barn. Nytt fra Forskning om Barnet i Norge, 4.

Tiller, P. O. (1989). Hverandre. En bok om barneforskning. Oslo: Gyldendal Norsk Forlag.

Tiller, P. O. (1991). Barneperspektivet: Om å se og bli sett. Vårt perspektiv på barn – eller omvendt? Barn. Nytt fra Forskning om Barnet i Norge, 1.

Tolshinsky-Landsman, L., & Levin, J. (1985). Writing in pre-schoolers: An age-related analysis. Applied Psycholinguistics, 6, 319–339.

Trageton, A. (2005). Att skriva sig till läsning. IKT i förskola och skola. Stockholm: Liber. (To write to become a reader).

Trevarthen, C., & Aitken, K. J. (2001). Infant intersubjectivity: Research, theory, an clinical applications. Journal of Child Psychology, Psychiatry, 42, 1.

Trevarthen, C. (1988). The concept and foundation of infant intersubjectivity. In S. Bråten (Ed.), Intersubjective communication and emotion in early ontogeny. Cambridge, MA: Cambridge University Press.

Trevarthen, C. (1989). Infants trying to talk: How a child invites communication from the human world. In R. Søderberg (Ed.), Children's creative communication (pp. 46–79). Lund: Lund University Press.

Trevarthen, C. (1998). Children's need to learn a culture. In M. Woodhead, D. Faulkner, & K. Littleton (Eds.), Cultural worlds of early childhood. London: Routledge.

Tufte, B., Kampmann, J., & Juncker, B. (2001). Børnekultur. Hvilke børn? Og hvis kultur? Copenhagen: Akademisk Forlag.

Tullgren, C. (2004). Den välreglerade friheten. Att konstruera det lekande barnet [The well-regulated freedom. To construct the playing child, in Swedish] (Malmö Studies in Educational Sciences, 10). Malmö Högskola: Lärarutbildningen.

UNICEF. (2007a). An Overview of child well being in rich countries. Florence: UNICEF Innocenti Research Center.

UNICEF. (2007b, February). Educations statistics. Denmark. Retrieved from http://childinfo.org

UNICEF. (2008). The state of the world's children 2008 – Child survival. New York: United Nations Plaza.

Vaihinger, H. (2001[1924]). The philosophy of "as if": A system of the theoretical, practical, and religious fictions of mankind (6th Rev. ed., C. K. Ogden, Trans.). London: Routledge.

Vallberg Roth, A.-C. (2002). De yngre barnens läroplanshistoria [The history of young children's curricula, in Swedish]. Lund: Studentlitteratur.

Vallberg Roth, A.-C. (2006). Early childhood curricula in Sweden – From the 1850s to the present. International Journal of Early Childhood, 38(1), 77–98.

Valsiner, J. (1989). Human development and culture. Boston: Lexington Books.

Vanderberg, B. (1999). Levinas and the ethical context of human development. Human Development, 43, 3144.

Vygotsky, L. S. (1972[1934]). Taenking og språg I og II [Thought and Language I and II, in Danish]. Köpenhamn: Mezhdunarodnaja Kinga og Hans Reitzels Forlag A/S.

Wagner, J. (2006). An outsider perspective. In J. Einarsdottir & J. Wagner (Eds.), Nordic childhoods and early education. Greenwich: Information Age Publishing.

Warming, H. (2005a). Har andre plejebørn det som mig? København: Frydenlund.

Warming, H. (2005b). Erkendelse gennem oplevelse; Når indlevelse ikke er mulig. I. In M. Järvinen & N. Mik-Meyer (Eds.), Kvalitative metoder i interaktionistisk perspektiv. København: Hans Reitzels Forlag.

Warming, H. (2007). Diskussioner om børneperspektiv og inddragelse af børn – er barnet på vej ud med badevandet? Dansk Pædagogisk Tidsskrift (pp. 4–13). Tema: Barndom og barndomsforskning.

Wason, P. C., & Johnson-Laird, P. N. (1972). Psychology of reasoning. Cambridge: Harvard University Press.

Weissner, T. S., & Gallimore, R. (1977). My brother's keeper: Child and sibling caretaking. Current Anthropology, 18, 169–190.

Westcott, H. L., Davies, G. M., & Bull, R. H. (2002). *Children's testimony – A handbook of psychological research and forensic practice.* New York: John Wiley & Sons.

Whiting, B., & Edwards, C. (1988). *Children of different world: The formation of social behavior* Cambridge, Mass.: Harvard University Press, 1988.

Williams, P. (2001). *Barn lär av varandra. Samlärande i förskola och skola* [Children learn from each other – In preschool and school, in Swedish] (Göteborg Studies in educational Sciences 163.). Göteborg: Acta Universitatis Gothoburgensis.

Williams, P., Sheridan, S., & Pramling Samuelsson, I. (2000). *Barns samlärande – en forskningsöversikt* [Children working together – A research Overview, in Swedish]. Stockholm: Liber.

Witherington, D. C. (2007). The dynamic-systems approach as metatheory for developmental psychology. *Human Development, 50,* 127–153.

Wittgenstein, L. (1971). *Tractatus logico-philosophicus.* London: Routledge & Kegan.

Woodhead, M. (1999). Reconstructing developmental psychology: Some first steps. *Children and Society, 13,* 3–19.

Wrosch, C., & Freund, A. M. (2001). Self-regulation of normative and non-normative developmental challenges. *Human Development, 44,* 264–283.

www.SourceOECD.org

Wyndhamn, J. (1993). *Problem solving revised. On school mathematics as a situated practice* (p. 98). Linköping: Linköping Studies in Arts and Sciences.

Zimbardo, P. G. (2004). A situationist perspective on the psychology of evil: Understanding how good people are transformed into perpetrators. In A. Miller (Ed.), *The social psychology of good and evil: Understanding our capacity for kindness and cruelty.* New York: Guildford Press.

Author Index

Subject Index

A

Act of learning, 144–145, 174, 176, 185, 195, 201
Adult-centrist, 43
Agency, 30, 66, 211
Altero-centric participation, 88
Anthropological approach, 48
Anti-humanist values, 14
"As-if" assumptions, 36–39, 53

B

Becoming literate, 141, 188, 201
Both-and approach to the constructivist approach, 209, 219

C

Caregiver's definition of the child, 92
Challenging activities, 153
Child as being, 41
Child-centredness, 8, 11, 13–14, 145–149, 199, 206–207, 209–210, 221
Child concept, 74, 215
Childhood in the Nordic countries, 203
The child as a person, 84, 87, 89, 107–108, 111, 117, 120
Children as objects, 107–108, 117
Children's ethics, 154
Children's influence, 154, 158
Children's interpretive reproduction, 35–40, 45, 49, 53
Children's participation, 1, 16–17, 19, 149, 158–160, 196
The child's rationality is taken for granted, 120
Child as a subject, 42, 44, 77, 198
Citizenship, 13
Collective improvisations, 169
Competent, 33, 37–38, 40, 53, 60, 66, 78, 130, 134, 141, 146, 153–154, 160, 200, 213, 215
Consensual frame, 79

Contextualism, 60–61, 68
Creativity, 17, 34, 52, 136, 155, 168, 172, 184, 193
Cultural lenses, 216, 218
Cultures, 14, 21, 36, 46, 197, 200, 206, 211–219
Curricula ECE guidelines, 15

D

Daycare for preschoolers, 4
Declaration of the Rights of the Child, 12–13
De-contextualized child, 41, 70
Deficient intersubjectivity, 129
Democracy, 13–17, 159, 176, 196, 205–207
Descartes, 78
Descartesian dichotomy, 213
Developmentally appropriate, 144
Developmental pedagogy, 74, 139, 163–178, 185, 193, 201, 206
Dialogical self, 79
Dialogicity, 87–88
Discern, 154, 191–195
Distributed self, 79
Dual socialization, 6

E

Early childhood education, 1, 4, 6, 9, 15–19, 139–149, 159, 163, 166–168, 173, 176, 184, 187–196, 198, 200–201, 206–207, 221
Ecological validity, 61
EFA (Education For All), 205
Emotional, 20, 35, 65, 92, 94, 102–103, 109–111, 113–117, 136, 153, 155, 167–168, 176, 213
Emotional accessibility, 101
Emotional inclusion, 136
Empathic care and identification, 200
Empathic identification, 83, 95, 99, 101, 104, 107–111, 114–115, 117, 119, 200

Breinigsville, PA USA
16 April 2010
236196BV00009B/15/P